POPULAR ART

PAST & PRESENT

ANCIENT SHEPHERDS. A.U.
This is to Certify that
was duly admitted a Member of the
No. of as Witness
our hands
W.M.
Secy.

POPULAR ART

PAST & PRESENT

A. J. LEWERY

David & Charles

British Library Cataloguing in Publication Data

Lewery, A.J.
Popular art.
I. Title
745.0941

ISBN 0-7153-9495-9

Typeset by ACE FILMSETTING LTD, Frome, Somerset
Designed by PETER BRIDGEWATER,
and printed in The Netherlands by ROTOSMEETS OFFSET
for David & Charles plc
Brunel House Newton Abbot Devon

"THEN SHE RODE FORTH LIKE AN ANGEL OF LIGHT ON A MISSION OF MERCY."

CONTENTS

ACKNOWLEDGEMENTS

MANY PEOPLE have helped me with this book, by allowing me to see and photograph their collections or by freely giving me their time and information, or technical assistance and encouragement. I am grateful to all the following people and to many more who, I fear, have escaped my memory. Please accept my thanks Harry Arnold, James Ayres, Mike Blaker, Alan Brindle, Malcolm Bristow, Percy Brooks, Nigel and Diane Carter, Fred Darrington, Hazel and Ben Davis, Andy Durr, Paul Eathorne, Jill Edmonds, Lawrence Ferguson, John Gorman, Peter Gould, Hector Handiside, Alex Hastie, Emily and Arthur Hayes, Will Hudson, Andreas Kalman, Hugh Malet, Andy and Lynette Millward, Pamela and Edward Paget-Tomlinson, Joe Pattison, Rachel Reckitt, Ivor and Sue Roberts, Saz Saunders, A. Shindler of Watergate Antiques in Chester, Eric Smith, Brian Talbot, Jack Taylor, Ross Williams, and Paul Wilson and Marilyn Tucker of the Wren Trust.

Thanks, too, are due to several groups who patiently allowed me to follow and photograph them whilst they were getting on with their traditional business; the Soulcakers of Antrobus and Comberbach in Cheshire, the Minehead Hobby Horse team, and Ray Veale and the Knutsford Sanders. I am increasingly a museum fan, and the majority are helpful and welcoming when faced with extra questions and requests, but I would like to offer extra thanks to the following for help well beyond the call of duty: the Museum of English Naive Art in Bath; the Grosvenor Museum, Chester; Angela Bowyer at Gwent Rural Life Museum, Usk; Nicholas Mansfield and staff at the National Museum of Labour History, Manchester; Mike Stammers and staff at Liverpool Maritime Museum; Peter Ingram at the Romany Folklore Museum in Selborne; and Stephen Penney and staff at the Salt Museum, Northwich.

Finally I should like to thank my wife Mary for all her work in transmuting my tangled manuscript into neat typescript, and for her rock-solid support throughout the research and writing of this book.

TONY LEWERY, *Preston Brook, January 1991*

INTRODUCTION

MEET THE FAMILY: POPULAR, NAIVE AND FOLK ART

WELCOME TO an attempt to tread a fresh path through the confusingly broad subject known as Popular Art. 'Popular' and 'Art' are the best words available, but each has such a wide range of meanings that it might be useful to have some narrow definitions at the outset. 'Popular' means to be liked or admired by a lot of people, and the 'people' in the present context are the general populace, defined rather rudely in my old dictionary as 'the common people, the rabble'. The same word could, until quite recently, equally have meant the illiterate or the academically uneducated. An extra level of meaning is added to the word popular when it is used in this book: that of time. For inclusion here a popular art form needs to have been popular for long enough to be more than a fashion, for posterity to have had a hand, and this means probably three or more generations. If the art form is liked and respected by both young and old simultaneously there must surely be some special value in it which is worthy of respect, or at least consideration, whether one likes it or not.

This is a nettle to be grasped: the acceptance that much that falls within the field may not be to the taste of the inhibited eye of the more formally educated. Some judgements of taste have to be made to keep the subject manageable, but they need to be made gently, with a consciousness that education and acquired tastes may be trying to censor some of the elements that helped popular art survive despite the disapproval of critics and pundits. Some of the filtering has already been done for us by the use of the word 'art', for in its broadest sense it describes the results of a human activity that touches our sensibilities in some positive way, and creates an intentional emotional response. If there was no response, or the effect was negative and unpleasant, then the art form probably would not have achieved sustained popularity anyway.

However, that broad meaning of art also encompasses music and conversation as well as painting and cake decoration, and it too needs to be narrowed down in order to be useful in our context. Here it means the result of handcrafted creative work which shows evidence of the individuality of the artist. In most cases, therefore, the individual pieces of work cannot be duplicated exactly, but the paradox is that they all need to fit into a recognisable and familiar convention of technique or subject-matter to qualify for inclusion.

If an artwork is not within a convention it must be the expression of one artist's creativity. If the artist is exploring new subjects in new ways the work is individual in intent, and regardless of how naive or primitive the results are, they are not the mutual message of popular art, the exchange of a familiar artistic currency. It may be art of a high order – fine art or folk art – but it will not be popular art as defined here, the reflection of the people's taste over a period of time.

It may be an unfortunate connection to have to make, but a good gauge of popularity in popular art is sometimes pure commercialism. If the public like it they will pay money for it, and if they pay enough the artist can afford to make more. For the poorest and widest section of society to be able to afford it the art has to be relatively cheap, and as time is always equated with money somewhere, the art has to be created quite quickly. Thinking, inventing new images or trying new techniques take time, so there is another obvious pressure on the popular artist – in whatever field – to use a practised technique to a set formula. Innovations, if any, are only introduced slowly, although any short cuts, any savings of time and materials, are gratefully accepted.

Is the result good or bad? Is it pandering to the lowest common denominator of taste, or is it a true reflection of the customer's innermost needs and nature expressed through the intuitive response of the popular artist, the self-expression of the people by proxy? This book is an attempt to offer some evidence and some answers.

The term 'popular art' has been given a fairly precise meaning by a number of books that have looked at the subject in the past. Two produced during the Second World War started the ball rolling, the attractively illustrated *Popular Art in Britain* by Noel Carrington and *English Popular and Traditional Art* by Enid Marx and Margaret Lambert. The seeds were sown, but the upsurge of interest really only flowered when a positive-thinking government pressed ahead with the 1951 Festival of Britain, a morale-boosting celebration of Britishness past, present, and Space Age future. The time was ripe for a thoughtful re-evaluation of our culture and where it was going.

The backlash was a reawakened interest in folk life and popular art as it had existed in the past, before mass production and the war had swept so much of it away. There was nostalgia for what had gone, but there was renewed interest in the survivors too. Rural blacksmiths and thatchers could apply for government grants to help them carry on, and colourful characters like gypsies and canal boatmen were looked upon with a new, nostalgic respect. *English Popular and Traditional Art* was republished in a greatly enlarged form and a major exhibition about the traditional arts, called 'Black Eyes and Lemonade', was mounted at the Whitechapel Art Gallery by Barbara Jones and Tom Ingram as an outrider to the Festival of Britain proper.

Barbara Jones was a painter and illustrator with a special interest in architecture. She had been contributing articles on various aspects of popular and folk art to *The Architectural Review* for a number of years and, also in 1951, these articles were republished as a collection called *The Unsophisticated Arts*. It was that book which caught my interest and led me towards an enthusiasm for popular art, and ultimately to these pages.

Popular Art in England by Geoffrey Fletcher was published in 1962 and completes the list of popular art titles. All have much of great interest and value to a modern reader but all the authors, with the exception of Barbara Jones, write with a heavy consciousness that they are recording the past and leave one, perhaps unwittingly, with the impression that popular art could only flourish amongst a more rural and less sophisticated population than the present one. Perhaps they all felt that universal education would have a greater levelling-up effect than it now appears to have done, or that officially promoted academic teaching would leave no room for popular taste to continue to develop any visual language of its own. Here I think they underestimated the power of popular culture.There are still some healthy, surviving popular arts from the past, as well as a few new ones, and these pages record some present as well as past trends.

Popular art has a considerable overlap into areas that are usually called naive or folk art, and at times the boundaries between one and another are very hazy to say the least. Naive art usually refers to paintings, and although many of them clearly belong within a recognisable convention, like the ship portraits of the pierhead painters discussed in this book, this is not a prerequisite. Naive artists are not concerned in the first instance with reflecting anyone's taste but their own. All that is required is the production of art, usually pictures, by artists without, or despite the influence of, classical or academic art teaching. The best work from these natural artists has a childlike simplicity that refreshes the spirit, a confident unconcern for fashion or pedantry that is as direct as a sunny morning.

The core of formal art teaching for the past few centuries has been illusionism, the attempt to copy or create exactly the visual appearance of an object or a space, to trick the eye into reading three dimensions where only a two-dimensional picture plane exists. This is a good trick and very difficult, but one extra problem is that everyone with eyes, art trained or not, can judge the success of the attempt. Because the visual decision is an easy and instant one to make, it is tempting to equate good art with good illusionism, and not to work any harder to understand the importance of all the abstract or symbolic qualities of a painting when the visual naturalism is removed, as in modern abstract painting, or when it never existed, as in the picture work of the primitive painter, the naive artist, or the folk artist.

The first formal years of art training used to consist of learning the techniques of measured perspective, and 'drawing from life', which in Victorian academies meant drawing for years from plaster casts of famous classical statues. Only when the students could draw statues could they draw the nude model, usually ending up with drawings that made the model look like an ancient statue. This sort of drawing discipline may have disadvantages but it is good for training the eye to recognise relative proportions, the size of the hand compared to the size of the head, and the size of the head to body height.

It is a lack of this ability that characterises much of the work of the naive but professional portrait painters of the eighteenth and early nineteenth century, before photography destroyed the trade. Dickens noted it as a characteristic of Miss La Creevy's work in *Nicholas Nickleby*, when he describes a 'charming whole length of a large-headed little boy, sitting on a stool with his legs foreshortened to the size of salt spoons'. James Ayres in his *English Naive Painting 1750–1900* (1980) – essential reading for all interested in this field – says succinctly that much of it was 'made by professionals whose craft often exceeded their formal artistic training'. Practice makes perfect, but the manual techniques generally improve faster than the critical judgement of the eye; if that judgement was not initially awakened and moulded by conventional academic training, it was unlikely to find the polite society style by accident. These painters did, however, develop a style that can now be recognised as a separate subdivision of naive art, and in America particularly their clear, direct portraits are regarded as a very important part of folk art.

There were also a number of itinerant artists, in America and in Britain, who travelled country districts soliciting for work. Once engaged they could produce an attractive likeness at considerable

Pavement artist creating a very reverential picture of Christ on the paving slabs of Bury shopping precinct, Lancashire. Missionary work, or a good money-spinner?

speed and consequently, we can presume, at a relatively cheap price. They painted for the farmers or the local gentry and followed set formulas that both painter and patron knew would work, simplified versions of the standards set by society portraitists in the cities. Portraits of children were especially important in an age of high infant mortality, but paintings of favourite dogs or prize farm animals, or of the house or farm, were also part of the painter's job, documenting everyday life in craftsmanlike detail.

But it was a job that was very hard hit by photography. Although the broad field of naive art, including the pastimes and hobbies of more leisured classes, and the individualistic work of untrained artists, continues to the present day, the production of paintings with a purpose beyond being a coloured pattern to hang on the wall ceased for most of the population after photography entered the field. Whatever other need people felt for pictures on the wall had already been met by cheap engravings, followed by ever more colourful colour printing by chromolithography, and all of these were educating the public eye to accept only work by the accepted masters of art, pictures that achieved a convincing sense of space by an accurate use of perspective and tonal gradations of colour. Perspective has always been a major problem for untrained picture painters. They can see and understand the problem but the visual solution is beyond them, and it only needs a couple of mistakes in the relative size of objects in perspective to destroy any illusion of three dimensions. Either there is an error, or the painting actually records a farm that had a horse as big as the farmhouse.

A double portrait painted in the mid-nineteenth century by a travelling painter for a farmer in Cheshire. Technically very proficient, the odd proportions and invention of shadow and perspective betray a lack of artistic training. Intensely wise eyes are typical of the naive painter, a reflection of his care and worry as he struggles with these most important features of any portrait.

Much of the work in this book could just as easily be called folk art, but that expression tends towards a narrower, more precise meaning for folklorists and scholars, and could exclude much that seems to me important and relevant today. Purists would argue that folk art is the creative work of a settled traditional society without any influence from the world of the educated élite, whereas much that interests and excites me is a direct development of highbrow ideas taken and shaken, as a dog shakes a blanket, into something rougher but more comfortable.

The influence of high art seems all-pervasive. Most of that influence has come to the people through printing – engravings and crude woodcuts until the nineteenth century, and then masses of wood engravings, lithography and the photography that made a badly faded fresco in Milan, Leonardo's 'Last Supper', the most reproduced picture in the world. Then came the advent of mass advertising, creating images that became famous by their association with certain products, and the sly attempt to associate certain products with famous art, as in the celebrated case of the Pears Soap advertisement in the 1880s which featured the painting 'Bubbles' by Sir John Millais. In public he was extremely annoyed by this use of his elevated artwork for a commercial advertising campaign, but thereafter he and many other artists just happened to paint a number of pictures which were eminently suitable for advertising purposes.

The influence of printing on the popular arts and the subject of printing as a popular art in itself are both immense. Although I make a number of references to this relationship throughout this book, there is much work to be done in this field. My approach has been rather faint-hearted, taking refuge in my earlier definition of that subject as the result of handcrafted individual creative work. This should also exclude anything made in large numbers by mass production, but Staffordshire pottery figures do seem to take on a vitality and individuality from the spirited, not to say slap-dash, painting of the pottery decorators. The figures have been included in previous books and are included here.

The Staffordshire figures often began life as a printed image, an interesting parallel with the work of many modern pavement artists. Armed only with chalks and a squared-up picture postcard, they are now providing a most interesting gallery of popular art, or at least the images that make the most money from the passing public. Recent visits to the tourist-trap pavements outside York cathedral found several religious paintings reproduced, which perhaps was not too surprising. A huge Van Gogh self-portrait was more unexpected, but it is a very famous image and his expressive directional brushstrokes translate to coloured chalk and pastel very well. What was quite unexpected was 'The Last of England' by Ford Madox Brown, a mid-Victorian painting, which in this setting seemed quite surreal.

A number of areas have been skimmed over here which could have been given more detailed attention in a larger book. Needlework, for example, is one such subject, but as all the components were listed each part seemed too narrow for a separate titled section, even though the list was long enough to make a book of its own. Shepherd's smock embroidery and the gansey knitting of fishermen's wives would be important, as would the arts of patchwork, smocking and quilting, and the modern tradition of needlepoint kneeler embroidery that enlivens many churches today. With some regret I decided that the subject was beyond the scope and experience of this author.

Two separate approaches run concurrently through this book. Each is a description of some of the constituent parts of popular art, but whilst the first describes techniques and history in a series of separate entries throughout the book, the second approach is by the subject-matter of the imagery, and forms the main material of the chapters. Gravestones, for example, are given their own separate entry on page 88, but gravestone angels and Old Father Time form part of chapter 4, whilst carved hearts and scrollwork reappear as part of the imagery and designs discussed in chapter 5. Each subject that has its own separate entry is set in bold type where it occurs within the text (ie **FIGUREHEADS**, **PUB SIGNS**, **FAIRGROUNDS**) and the relevant page number for that entry will be found on the contents page as well as in the general index.

The 'crinoline lady' design emerged in the 1930s but still has its adherents today. This one is built up with coloured ribbons and white lace over a cardboard former, mounted on black paper. The problem of making a pretty face to suit has been bypassed by using a cut-out magazine illustration, resulting in this slightly surrealistic delight. 11in × 9in (279 × 228mm), about 1950?

Fred Darrington at work on one of his huge sand sculptures on the beach at Weymouth, Dorset. Fred has been modelling for the holidaymakers' pleasure, and their money, since he was a child in the 1920s. Every year he creates a wide gallery of popular imagery – ships, mermaids, royal portraits or, as in this case in 1990, an animal piece copied from a magazine cover.

This dual approach seemed sensible for two reasons. It was clear that each of the commonly used and expected subdivisions of popular art should be covered and easily found (and I wanted to add a few of my own to that list), but because I started out as a painter I have a fascination with the recurrence of certain patterns and images in widely dissimilar fields. The actual visual response to these popular designs did not seem to have been considered very much in the past, and as a map reference needs two co-ordinates to fix an accurate position, so perhaps this two-way approach could help to plan out the subject and find a way within it. The usefulness of this idea is now for the reader to judge.

Having been offered some guidelines for the subject, the reader may be annoyed or relieved to discover that the ground-rules have been bent several times. The inclusion or exclusion of some of the subject matter has ultimately been decided by the author's personal hunch that certain subjects are interesting or relevant parts of a modern popular culture. The hope is that this presentation of an enthusiast's opinion will be a useful spring-board for further research and an interesting introduction for the reader who is not a specialist in any particular field.

I have skirted round many arts and crafts that could be and have been the subject-matter of complete books, and I may disappoint some scholars by not giving their own speciality more value. I apologise, but one main concern is to draw connections across boundaries and strengthen an awareness of the continuing existence of a popular culture separate from the commercially promoted and academically sanctioned art of the gallery world. In some cases this culture is made up of historic survivors from an older, slower society, but in others it is a quite modern flowering of a communal creative impulse. Its continued existence, despite the pressures of commercial supply, is a cause for optimism in this author. Because of my own interests and experience the book is primarily concerned with visual art, with a bias towards the pictorial and the painter, but I hope the connections of ideas are more widely relevant. I will be satisfied if the book awakens interest in some of these popular arts in just a few readers, or gives encouragement to a few more to make such art themselves. Bon voyage.

SHOP SIGNS AND TRADING SYMBOLS

SHOP SIGNS share their early history with that of PUB SIGNS, being the result of a need to recognise an individual building in a town, particularly the fast-growing towns of the seventeenth and eighteenth centuries. Owners marked their houses by hanging out a symbol of some sort, which then became their 'address'; thus Mr Smith might live at the 'Sun in Splendour' in Mill Street, whilst Mr Jones was to be found at the sign of 'The Moon'. If the symbol bore some relationship to the owner's trade it was even better, and many wool merchants took the 'Golden Fleece' for their sign, whilst the 'Hand and Shears' was often adopted by tailors.

Heraldry played a major part in supplying symbols, not only from the personal arms of the owner but from the corporate arms of the city guilds: compasses from the carpenters, for example, or a swan from the Musicians' Company. Complexities were compounded as tradesmen moved house, taking with them the sign that had become associated with their own business and combining it with their new address, rather as heraldry 'quarters' or 'dimidiates' arms together to create a new shield. Many of our odder pub names originate in this seventeenth-century practice, like the 'Black Lion' and 'Seven Stars' or 'Lamb and Dolphin'. Competition and variety increased the number, size and complexity of signboards to a ridiculous extent, with elaborate confections of wrought ironwork, carved wood framing and involved painted designs. A specialist signmaker's trade soon evolved to supply the demand, and in London was concentrated around Harp Alley.

Between 1765 and 1770 most of the London parishes implemented powers granted by an Act of George III to have all projecting or hanging signs removed, or fixed back against the front of the building. It was the official end of an era which had seen humble signboards expand and proliferate to become an impediment to light and air in the narrow streets, and a positive danger to the public in some cases – four people were killed in 1718 when a signboard pulled down the front of a building in Bride Lane. However, it was increased literacy and the acceptance of street numbering as an alternative which finally brought about the change.

A century later, in their still-excellent *The History of Signboards* (1866), Jacob Larwood and John Hotten regret that the book '. . . was not undertaken many years ago . . . London is so rapidly changing its aspect that ten years hence many of the particulars here gathered could no longer be collected.' He was a mite pessimistic there, for over another century later pub signs are generally still surviving successfully. Shop signs, however, have not fared quite so well. Larwood suggested '. . . not a few shops simply suspended at their doors some prominent article of their trade, which custom has outlived the more elegant signboards, and may be daily witnessed in our streets . . .' and quoted ironmongers' frying pans, hardware dealers' teapots and grocers' tea canisters as everyday examples.

These are now quite rare, but a number of trade symbols do remain in use, sometimes as mementoes of the old times, but often in disguise as traditional emblems on modern packaging. Some are directly symbolic, unequivocal signs that describe what goes on within, like carved gloves or gilded hats for glovers or hatters. Survivors in this group include large boots or clogs for shoe repairers, a huge pair of spectacles for the optician, scissors for a cutler and great padlocks and keys for the locksmith, now embraced by the general hardware shop. Legend has it that barbers' poles originated by displaying the blood-stained pole gripped by patients experiencing blood-letting in medieval times, with a bandage wrapped round it. It is a good story, even if untrue. By 1700 the pole was simply a symbol, a blue and white striped one for a barber, with a bit of red rag attached for a surgeon.

The meaning of other signs, which was obvious in the past, has become obscure to later generations due to changes in packaging. Few would now recognise three tall white or gilded cones as loaves of sugar, the lump form in which it was previously sold, and the old-accepted sign for a grocery shop. In 1866 Larwood and Hotten already say the sugar-loaf was common 'in former times' but these had still been in regular use in the mid-eighteenth century, when signmakers' trade cards mention them as standard items available 'off the shelf', along with gilded bunches of grapes for taverns. In 1762 Hogarth and some friends arranged an exhibition of signboards to lampoon an academic art exhibition just down the road. Amongst the pictorial signs were '. . . several tobacco rolls, sugar loaves, hats, wigs, stockings, gloves &c &c hung round the room' – all the standard street signs of the time, in fact.

Few people today would recognise a roll of tobacco for what it was either, but more might recognise the carved figures that have come to be associated with tobacconists' shops right through to the present day. The history of the industry can be read in the imagery of the older ones. The

A well-executed and unambiguous signboard alongside the A49, outside Tarporley, Cheshire. This old one had to give way to a road improvement scheme, but a good and similar replacement now continues the tradition.

native American Indian of tobacco's country of origin, dressed in nothing but a few feathers according to travellers' tales, was soon confused or combined with the black African slave imported to work on the plantations to produce a generic 'Black Boy' or 'Blackamoor'. Dressed in little but a turban and some feathery tobacco leaves, he became one of the standard signs of the tobacco industry in the seventeenth century. The sailor who imported tobacco, chewed it and smoked it soon became a symbolic partner as well, and the rollicking association of cigarettes and the sea is still fostered by the advertisers of Navy Cut tobacco.

Smoking has always been friends with drinking and, whilst hard-smoking sailors drank rum, so hard-whisky-drinking Scotsmen took snuff and the kilted Highlander became another favourite sign for tobacconists. The common feature is that they are all free-standing figures carved in wood, the minimal remains of a whole class of three-dimensional signs in the past. In the London of Dickens' *Dombey and Son* '. . . little timber midshipmen in obsolete naval uniforms (were) eternally employed outside the shop doors of nautical instrument makers'. The detailed description of Solomon Gills' shop sign suggests it was a spirited piece of carving in the proper **SHIPS' FIGUREHEAD** tradition. Architectural details of shopfronts in shipbuilding towns still show signs of the local wood-carving trade, but carving was commoner in the past and wooden figures advertised boys' schools and chimney sweeps far inland as well.

The three brass balls of the pawnbroker are a sign that is now becoming mercifully rare. Several explanations are offered for the symbolism and most of them relate it to the charges on the shield of the Medici family, a set of merchants from Lombardy who were the first to lend money against assets in London. But although we now know them as 'golden' balls, Larwood and Hotten's book describes them as usually being painted blue. Chambers' *The Book of Days* of 1864 relates both signs and heraldic symbol to the fourth-century legend of St Nicholas, who saved a poor man's three daughters from poverty and prostitution by giving them each a bag of gold for a dowry. However, the common saying was that the sign meant that the odds were two to one against the objects pledged ever being redeemed.

BUTCHERY, CATTLE AND DOGS

MANY FARMS have a pictorial sign hanging by the gate which features an animal typical of the herd or flock that is bred there, and the farm gate is a good basic place to start looking for modern popular art. Some of these signs are commercially produced as advertisements for particular brands of cattle food, but they are popular, and are part of a pictorial tradition.

The most interesting ones are individual creations by a local artist or blacksmith, or a member of the family, and are simple statements of personal pride and a gift to the passing traveller. They are not advertisements in the usual sense of the word, any more than is the signpost that points the way to the village, for the commercial business of the farm is done at the market. They are decorations, created for the self-satisfaction of the farmer and his pride in his animals and his job.

Most follow the simple formula of a side-view portrait of a beast, a standard layout that has been common for a couple of hundred years. As society becomes more divorced and protected from the realities of breeding animals for food, the idea that an animal can be reared and loved, appreciated for its form and gentle temperament, and then butchered and eaten with untroubled enjoyment becomes more difficult for everyone to accept. To commission a portrait of the animal first seems even more morbid, but it was common, and the animal signs by the farm gate are a logical continuation of that tradition.

In the mid-eighteenth century a series of animal breeding experiments took place which changed the quality of British livestock, particularly cattle, quite dramatically. Experiments by Robert Bakewell in Leicestershire led to the realisation that animals could be bred for specific qualities – weight, fat content, or even colour – and that significant changes could be made within a few animal generations. By selecting the best possible beasts for parents and then breeding and interbreeding the progeny, whilst ruthlessly excluding any offspring that did not show the particular characteristic that was being sought, the breed could be changed quite radically and quite quickly and would continue to breed true to type thereafter. An old farming saying is, 'The bull is half the herd' because of the number of offspring he can sire in a lifetime. His importance was reflected in the way proud owners began to name their individual bulls and even commission painted portraits of them. Horses, particularly racehorses, had long been accorded this honour but individual cattle were new to it.

So too were some of the farmers. Although some of these improving animal breeders were of aristocratic stock, men of educated taste in the arts, others were of much humbler origins and made less exalted demands of their paintings. So the quality of these animal paintings varies accordingly, from the refined excellence of George Stubbs to the crude simplicities of many unnamed provincial painters. However, they nearly all fall into one easily defined category of picture painting. Each is a portrait, an image of one particular beast viewed from the side to show off all the finer points of the animal, with perhaps a person standing at the animal's head to give the picture a sense of scale. This may be the owner, the stockman who reared the

(Right) *The present sign of the Bull Inn, Broughton, in Yorkshire. It is modern, but painted from an old 1840s engraving which recorded a prize-winning beast from the local estate of Sir Charles Tempest.*

(Previous page) *This glass-eyed bull's head is built up entirely of butterflies collected on one particular farm in South Wales by Harry Scott, a 'naturalist'. After many years in the farmhouse, it was hung in a butcher's shop in Usk to serve as a very unusual version of the common butcher's trade sign.*

beast or the butcher who slaughtered it, but the main item is the animal, correctly delineated and coloured. After that comes the background skyscape and landscape, and perhaps buildings, which may be quite precise pictorial references to the animal's home farm. Coming a poor last was any idea of an original or unusual composition. This set pattern still continues today on numerous signs, as well as in magazine photographs of winners at local agricultural shows. It works well and has little need for improvement.

In the eighteenth century the qualities most desired in livestock were size and weight, whether fat or lean, and by the end of the century there were some truly massive beasts in existence, causing a considerable stir in agricultural circles. One of the most celebrated was bred by the brothers Robert and Charles Colling and became known simply as 'The Durham Ox'. It was 11ft (3.3m) long and 3ft (0.9m) wide across its back, and turned the scales at over 1¼ tons (1.27 tonnes) by the time it was five years old. It was such a prodigy for its time that it was sold to a showman who toured it as a side-show for another six years, bringing it to the attention of a huge public. J. Whessell made an etching in 1802 from a portrait of this wonder animal, painted by J. Boultbee, and from the text on one version of the print it is known that at least 2,000 copies were published.

As well as promoting the fashion for hugely fat animals, this print encouraged the custom of drawing and painting these prizewinners in a way that tried to exaggerate even further their monstrous proportions. After all, there was little left but the picture when the butcher had finished his work, and plenty of artists would happily cater to the self-esteem of the owner by painting the animal to look even bigger than reality, for the sake of the commission. Thomas Berwick's autobiography describes an occasion when his accurately observed drawings of prize sheep were rejected because he had refused to add rolls of fat in his pictures, where none existed in life. He observed very accurately that 'Many of these paintings will mark the times and, by the exaggerated productions of the artists, serve to be laughed at when the folly and self-interested motives which gave birth to them are done away with.' But the paintings continued to be produced until the quality of the meat or milk began to be valued above the size of the animal, and when photography made this sort of pictorial lying more difficult to get away with.

Not all the animal portraits were created so dishonestly and there are many neat and attractive paintings and prints that record notable animals, both locally and nationally. Some live on as **PUBLIC HOUSE SIGNS**, and names like 'The Craven Heifer', 'The Airedale Heifer' or 'The Blackwell Ox' celebrate some of the most renowned beasts, especially in the areas where they were reared. Several of the many 'Bulls' and 'Cows', whether red, white, black or pied, probably refer to local prizewinners of the past, and some pub signs actually follow the old tradition and feature a portrait of a locally famous animal.

The butcher shared this local pride as well, and some pictures feature the meat retailer who slaughtered the beast instead of the breeder. It is still common for butchers' shops to display a picture or a symbol of the trade, and although it may now only be a large pair of horns on the wall, it was only a generation ago that paintings of sheep, pigs, and cattle featured very strongly. Paintings of bulls' or pigs' heads very often flank the proprietor's name on the fascia board of the most modern shopfront. These are emblems that, quite apart from their obvious descriptive purpose, also have a history rooted in heraldry. The official arms of the Butchers' Company, granted in 1605 by King James I, have a pig's head at the top of the shield, with three bulls' heads between two axes below it. The instant dignity bestowed by such honour may be part of the reason for the healthy survival of these symbols of dead animals. The company claimed St Luke as its patron saint and his emblem, the winged bull, appears as the crest and supporter of the arms (see chapter 2).

Inside the shop the need for cleanliness and easily washed surfaces led to the use of tiles and mosaics, and this ceramic work opened up a

A pair of contrasting farm gate signs in Staffordshire. They are both friendly, but the direct simplicity of the top one highlights the uninspired dullness of the lower, cast-metal sign, produced by a specialist sign company.

Fine mosaic work in the doorway of a butcher's shop in Barnton, Cheshire. Built around 1882, it remained a butcher's shop until converted to a hardware store in 1981. Luckily the proprietor appreciates these things and did not destroy the mosaic in the name of modernisation.

This delightful wood-engraved pig and its accompanying catalogue of Victorian letter styles is from a paper bag recently discovered in an attic in Winsford, Cheshire. It provides a wonderful link between the exaggerated animal portraits of pre-photographic days and the modern advertising pictures of contented animals which still appear on the paper bags and bill heads of many traditional butchers.

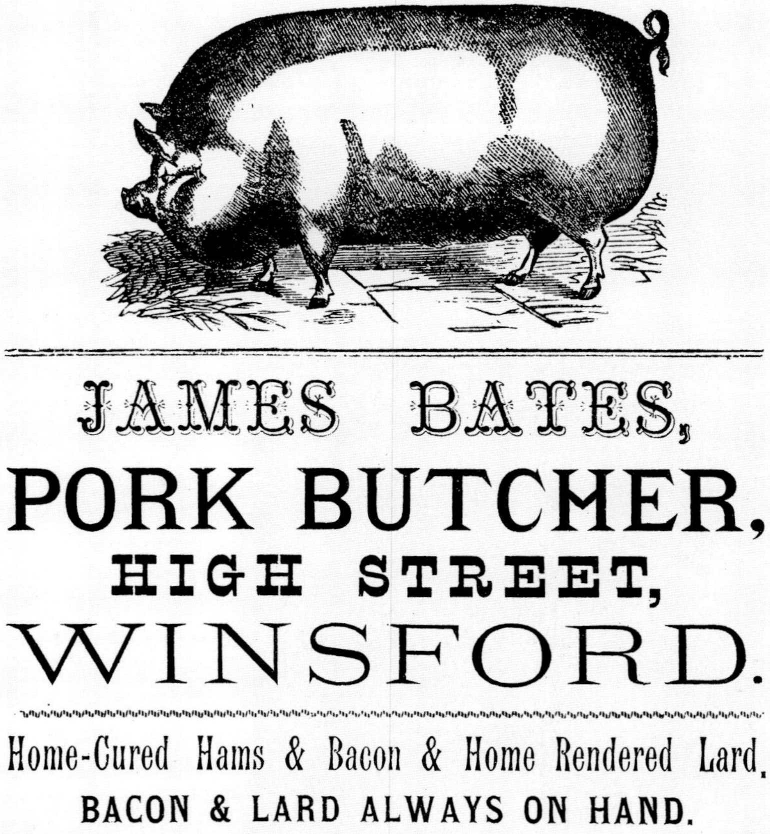
JAMES BATES,
PORK BUTCHER,
HIGH STREET,
WINSFORD.
Home-Cured Hams & Bacon & Home Rendered Lard.
BACON & LARD ALWAYS ON HAND.

whole new field for public art. In the nineteenth and early twentieth centuries shops dealing with fresh food – grocers, dairies and fishmongers as well as butchers – featured tilework pictures quite extensively, and because of the extraordinary permanence of the medium we still have a splendid legacy of these paintings despite changing fashions. Some may be small, simple side views of single animals, but many are far more adventurous, depicting complete scenes of several animals in a landscape and painted over twenty or thirty tiles.

The romance of the Scottish Highlands made them a favourite theme, with shaggy longhorn cattle browsing in the heather, whilst sheep usually stand contentedly in sunny buttercupped meadows. The most accomplished work is in exactly the same fanciful vein as the mass of academic landscape paintings that were in vogue in Queen Victoria's time, with the animals brought a little more to the forefront, an imagined rural tranquillity brought into the middle of the town. Something of this old-fashioned romanticism can still be found on the bill heads and paper bags of some modern butchers, where a group of animals stand peacefully awaiting their fate. Whether they will survive transference to plastic bags and computerised tills remains to be seen.

Another link in the chain between the field and the dinner table is the truck which transports the livestock from field to market. A large farm may have a lorry of its own, but most of the vehicles belong to specialist companies and some carry very attractive paintings mounted on the front of the box body where it extends over the lorry cab. A blank space above the driver cries out for an emblem of some sort, like a figurehead on a ship or a banner leading a procession, and this minor tradition will probably continue until truck design changes radically.

The same sort of vehicles transport horses and, although custom-built horse-boxes rarely have more than a horse's head transfer on the cab door, humbler boxes often carry paintings on the front of the body. These are purely for pride and are less constrained by a tradition. Many have adventurous compositions, including riders and jumps. As in all these fields the standard varies enormously, from high-class academic art through the delightfully simple and naive to the truly appalling, but the tradition is alive and well and makes the local gymkhana and horse show an interesting hunting ground for popular art.

There is no doubt about what cattle are for, at least since draught oxen stopped working. They are bred to be eaten, or to supply the dairy produce that is to be eaten. But, illogically, we are rather repelled by the idea of eating horseflesh, and if we should find a sculpted horse's head jutting out over a shop or doorway it will certainly not be advertising horsemeat, as it would be in France, but will be the traditional sign of a saddler's shop or a stableyard.

Before the internal combustion engine took over, the majority of horses were draught animals, pulling carts and wagons in the streets and the plough or haywain in the fields. Most working people's experience was with horses in harness, but the image of the animal in popular art is generally that of the elegant riding horse or the hunter. There seems to have been a universal appreciation of a graceful horse, even though the ownership of such a beast was beyond the means of the great majority. There is even a general appreciation of the horseriding sports of the gentry, a mixture perhaps of envy and good-natured loyalty to one's betters, for pictures of foxhunting have always been popular and seem set fair to remain so. The beauty of the animals is only part of the attraction, for the pageantry of red coats galloping over the rolling countryside or drinking a stirrup cup outside old pubs paints a very seductive picture of the security of the good old days – if you are not a fox, or have not had your fields and hedges trampled. To those in town the PUB SIGN outside the 'Fox and Hounds' may be a classic expression of imagined Englishness with little reality, but in the countryside hunting is still a first-hand experience for many.

Attitudes toward the sport are confused to say the least, a many-sided conflict between tradition, class, money, conservation, dead chickens and dead foxes. Despite the confusion, or perhaps because of it, the imagery is still very popular on the PUB SIGN outside, the bar wall inside, and on calendars everywhere. A fox is probably the most common weather-vane shape after cockerels, and appears all over the country on garden sheds and stable blocks alike, proclaiming allegiance to this most traditional English sport and a peculiar love–hate relationship with the wily enemy, Reynard. (*To p. 23*)

One of a set of six tile pictures painted by S. Bagshaw in 1928 for Sidney Fitton's custom-built butcher's shop in Middlewich, Cheshire. It closed in 1988, and the pictures are now hidden behind the shelves of a video library.

A Somerset livestock lorry, with paintings and lettering on a board painted by Mr Magor of Wellington in about 1970. The additional date is when the owner, Mr Maltravers, took over from his father and went independent in 1985.

THE GYPSY CARAVAN

Modern horse-drawn travellers on the way south after visiting the annual horse fair at Appleby-in-Westmorland, Cumbria. Light bow-top wagons on easy-running, rubber-tyred wheels are now the commonest vehicles, but each still needs two horses for today's slippery road surfaces, designed for tyres instead of horseshoes. Scrolls and horses' heads are still the traditional decoration, however.

THE MOST seductive image of a romantic travelling life is the horse-drawn gypsy caravan. There are often mixed feelings about the modern population of motorised 'travellers', as they prefer to call themselves, parked in the layby, but the sight of piebald horses and colourful wagons on the grass verge has become a welcome symbol of slower times, part of the warm self-delusion of the good old days. There is never any doubt that these are the *real* gypsies, unlike the scrap dealers and tarmac layers with their lorries and trailer caravans just down the road, so it might surprise many to learn that gypsies neither invented, built nor painted their living wagons themselves (with a few outstanding exceptions) any more than they make the lorries or caravans in which most modern gypsy families now live. Specialist firms have always supplied their particular needs, and it was these firms which really developed the visual gypsy style by proxy, by responding to the tastes and fashions of their customers. Nevertheless the living wagon was likely to be a Romany family's biggest investment and it became a potent symbol of the family's success and separate culture, both for the family and for outsiders.

The wagons divide into two easily distinguished groups: the wooden house on wheels, replete with windows, shutters and carved porch brackets; and the lighter ones with a rounded canvas roof. These 'bow-tops' are probably the closest to a gypsy original for they follow the principle, common to many old carriers' carts and wagons, of simply stretching canvas over hoops of wood or iron to make a roof. It is the same system that has been used for centuries to make the bender tents of the Romanies and tinkers, where rods of hazel or willow are stuck into the ground and twisted together to make a hooped frame to support a roof. Whether or not the bow-tops were the first, they are likely to be the last in regular use because, as horses have become less common and roads more slippery, the more lightweight the living wagon can be the better it is.

Heavy ornate wagons only became practical as the roads improved during the nineteenth century, and it was the travelling showmen who seem to have developed the idea initially. Dickens provides an early description in *The Old Curiosity Shop*, published in 1841, of a 'smart little house upon wheels, with white dimity curtains festooning the windows' but he can only differentiate it from a gypsy caravan by the sight of Mrs Jarley dressed in a 'large bonnet trembling with bows' taking a lady-like cup of tea. Both showmen and gypsies try to distance themselves from each other, but in fact they shared the same fairground fields and practical problems of a travelling life, and there was considerable intermarriage of both lovers and ideas. In the early days there was probably little difference between their living wagons, but a separate recognisable gypsy style soon developed, even though the gypsies often employed the same wagon builders as the showmen.

Fairground paintwork and gypsy wagon decoration also share something of the same ancestry, but a major part of the intricacy of caravan decoration is derived directly from one of the practical arts of the farm wagon builders: the graceful chamfering of the corners of nearly every piece of wood. This was not enough for the gypsies, however, who wanted their main public asset to express their ability to pay for ostentatious display. The chamfering is taken to extreme lengths, with curves cutting alternately inwards and outwards along the corners to create a more intricate and attractive pattern. Some living wagons seem to have been constructed inside out expressly to offer more chances for a display of chamfering on the ribs and corner posts, and mid-rails and weatherboards below the eaves of the roof are added, with sweeping butterfly chamfers.

But the actual shaping of the wood is only the beginning, for after the bodywork is finished and painted in its base colour each individual facet of the chamfering is picked out in a series of contrasting colours, or in gold leaf. Then another part of the old wainwright's or coachbuilder's trade is brought into exaggerated play, for each shaped facet of the framework and undercarriage is outlined with fine lines of yet another colour to create yet another level of sparkle.

At the turn of this century, when the industry was at its peak, many wagons were heavily encrusted with carved woodwork, picked out in gold leaf, outlined and shaded with colour. Carved brackets supported the roof where it extended beyond the body at front and back, and low-relief carvings were fitted in any available corner of the structural framework, or attached to the centre of every possible panel, depending on the construction. The crownboard over the front doorway was a prime location, along with the separate panels of the door itself. Bunches of grapes, leaves and flowers, horses' heads and lion-head

A 'ledge' wagon, built in Yorkshire by William Wright in 1906, in Peter Ingram's repair yard at his museum in Selborne, Hampshire, after major restoration work in 1990.

From a little extra chrome streamlining on their lorries in the 1950s, modern motorised travellers and gypsies have developed a new, brash tradition of ostentation, with chrome plate and cut glass in superabundance to show off their standing in their own society. This crystal palace of a trailer caravan cost £32,000 when new.

gargoyles at the roof corners all found a place, and were all intermeshed with the rolling acanthus scrollwork described more fully in chapter 5.

But this carving was heavy as well as expensive, and it was gradually superseded by painted decorations on the panels, mainly based around freehand brushstroke scrollwork. The travellers themselves were now able to tackle the paintwork, instead of using the professional woodcarvers previously employed by the wagon builders, and the painting became part of their own folk culture, with a few men becoming the accepted and respected masters of the art. The skill of the late Jim Berry, who died in 1989, is already the stuff of legend, and many stories already circulate of his ability to line a wheel with three brushes simultaneously, holding them in one hand whilst spinning the wheel with the other. This was, of course, after drinking legendary quantities of beer. But his work certainly is outstanding and his freehand scrollwork flows so naturally along the shafts and down the wagon steps that it looks easy. He has now gone, but his legacy remains. He set the standard, and much of his work stays with us on numerous wagons and small spring carts, in museums and on the road.

Realistically, the day of the horse-drawn wagon is over, for only a score or so are now lived in and travelled in continuously by born-to-the-road travellers, with a few more used by newcomers trying to find an alternative to our modern motorised lifestyle. A considerable number come out from retirement each year as gypsy families take to the road again for a summer holiday, but the really vital part of the gypsy decorative tradition has now been transferred to modern trailer caravans.

Today's travellers have cultivated a new twentieth-century image and have created a style of trailer home that shouts 'traveller' very proudly from half a mile away, glittering with extra chrome trimmings and cut-glass windows. The interiors are richly carpeted, lined with engraved mirrors and china ornaments, with white lace curtains with bobble fringing at the windows. It is a rather surreal experience to discover these gleaming monsters of ostentation parked haphazardly in untidy areas of industrial wasteland on the fringes of the city, where they stand washed and polished but surrounded by litter and the smoke of burning motor tyres.

Times have changed, but the gypsies' ability to sidestep regulations designed to curtail their lifestyle or assimilate them into wider society seems to be as strong now as it ever has been during their previous five hundred years of British existence. They always come up with a surprising survival tactic: taking something from the settled society, exaggerating it and making it their own. In the nineteenth century it was the Victorian version of Renaissance scrollwork, whilst the twentieth century has provided the chrome-plated streamlining of the motor age. Now for the twenty-first century . . .

Horses appear in many roles on PUB SIGNS, both in groups – as in the 'Coach and Horses' – or singly. Individual horses are often heraldic in origin, like the Saxon white horse of Kent or the galloping white horse of the House of Hanover, which was a heraldic charge introduced into the royal arms on the accession of George I to the throne. A few are famous named horses of history, like 'Eclipse' who was the fastest racehorse of his time in the late 1770s and made his owner an enormous amount of money, but most are simply an anonymous 'Black Horse' or 'Bay Mare'. They may have been local prizewinners in their day, like the prize bulls that spawned so many paintings and engravings, but the details have usually been lost.

Before photography it fell to the painter to take a likeness of a favourite horse and there are many run-of-the-mill horse portraits in existence, the side view of a standing animal in a stable, perhaps with the groom or owner posing woodenly by his head. Many of these darkening oil paintings owe much to the compositions of George Stubbs and George Morland, but repetition and a lower standard of artistic skill generally left them pretty uninspired, if practical. It seems likely that specialists in this field travelled from farm to farm seeking work, much as itinerant portrait painters did, and they would be the perfect men to produce a quick pub sign in return for bed and board. A lucky publican might get Morland himself to paint a sign to settle his drinking bill, and a number of famous artists are known to have painted PUB SIGNS to earn a living or settle a debt.

It is not surprising that horses are a key image in the decoration of some GYPSY CARAVANS, as the whole gypsy way of life is so bound up

(Far left) *Dignified lettering with some slightly less serious animals painted by Mr Biles, a large-scale gable sign facing along the main street in Bridport, Dorset.*

(Left) *The lower door of the 1906 Bill Wright wagon shown on page 21, bearing a version of the carved horse that became something of a trademark for this firm. The carving was probably supplied to order by the local firm of Collier's of Leeds. Painting, gilding and lining is by Peter Ingram.*

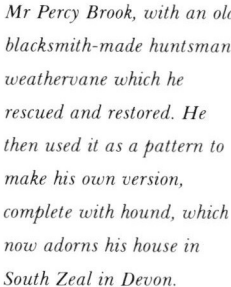

Mr Percy Brook, with an old blacksmith-made huntsman weathervane which he rescued and restored. He then used it as a pattern to make his own version, complete with hound, which now adorns his house in South Zeal in Devon.

with horses. The well-known wagon builder William Wright of Leeds used a low-relief carved horse as his decorative trademark on his living wagons, stretched out at a gallop above the door, or standing proudly as the central motif on the lower door panel. Other Yorkshire builders used the same wood carvers and similar subject-matter. The famous Reading firm of Dunton and Sons featured a carved horse's head as a central image on the back and front crownboards, and inside on the archway over the bed. The head is in profile, but deeply carved to jut through a horseshoe as if looking out of a stable door.

The production of these heavily carved wagons petered out between the wars, but the carved horses seem to have provided the inspiration for painted versions that became the trademark of subsequent wagon painters, like the late Jim Berry. A spirited painting of a horse's head surrounded by scrollwork appears on the kettleboxes of wagons painted by him, and as the central motif in the backboard design of the light Yorkshire spring carts used by horse-drawn general dealers. With arched necks, dished noses and flared nostrils, they are reminiscent of horses of the FAIRGROUND roundabout. (*To p. 28*)

THE FABULOUS FAIRGROUND

IT IS difficult to overstate the influence that the travelling fairground has had on the popular arts, and it is impossible to do proper justice to the complexity of the subject in a few hundred words. A big fair is a total wrap-around experience of sight, sound and sensation, a crazy mixture of simple old-time amusements and up-to-the-minute high technology thrills that defies easy categorisation. Even without the smell of hot dogs and candyfloss, or the sound of fairground organs vying with the latest pop music laced with sirens, the visual experience alone is extraordinary. Art Deco streamlining is tangled with Renaissance scrollwork, and space-age astronauts do battle with the wild beasts of a nineteenth-century jungle. Luckily the fairground world is becoming well documented, and fairs continue to adapt, travel and do business, providing live illustrations of this mixed-media tradition everywhere in the country at some time during the year.

The fairs have a long history as important local occasions for trade and finding employment, but it was only in the mid-nineteenth century that their importance as pleasuregrounds began to exceed that as employment agencies or shopping opportunities. They came into existence originally as annual horse sales or livestock markets, or as hiring fairs where unemployed servants and farmhands offered themselves for work during the following year, but they all gathered together an unusual number of people in one place, with money to spend. The jugglers, acrobats and magicians of the medieval fairs developed into more formal side-shows, with travelling exhibitions of wild animals or extraordinary human beings. Booths and stages were set up with large painted banners hung over the top to advertise the attractions, the precursors of today's painted fronts to the 'side stuff' and also related to the processional painted **BANNERS** of the Sunday schools and trade unions.

Banners, flags and show cloths were a wonderful investment for horse-drawn showmen travelling on poor roads, for they were large and impressive, but light in weight and easily demountable. The hand-turned 'dobby-horse' roundabouts and swingboats were also small and light until steam engines were developed to both rotate the roundabout and move it about. Steam traction engines allowed much more machinery, carved decoration and elaborate imagination to travel the roads, and the period from the 1880s to the First World War became the golden age for the fair in more ways than one. Huge roundabouts were built with gondolas, carriages and peacocks travelling round the track as well as the still-familiar horses, all carved and painted with an excess of late Victorian baroque decoration, and all glittering with gold leaf, inset mirrors and cut glass.

The fairs made money, too, and many of the modern fairground family dynasties were founded during this expansive time of innovation and imperial British prosperity. Many of the design ingredients which still form part of the funfair mixture were also introduced then, the elaborate Louis XIV scrollwork for example, and the very complex painted lettering. Paintings of romantic landscapes, classical-style sculpture, and portraits of national heroes all reflected the Edwardian confidence of showman and punter

Fairground decorator Alan Brindle working on a set of miniature gallopers, probably made by Mellors of Manchester just before the First World War.

All the fun of the fair has to include being scared half to death in a ghost train, a haunted house or, in this case, Pat Collins' Frankenstein's Castle at Nottingham.

alike, but the ghastly First World War was soon to change everything.

Austerity, the Depression, Picasso and the Futurists all had an impact on popular taste after the war, and the development of motor cars and aeroplanes as fairground rides all required a new style of imagery to express the speed of the twentieth century. Looking back with the hindsight of posterity, we can see that the sharp-angled Art Deco designs which grew out of Cubism and Vorticism were just that image, although it must have seemed like poverty to the older generation. But it was lighter and cheaper, and helped the travelling fair to adapt and survive. It also added another strand to the web of decoration upon which it is possible for the fairground decorator to call.

The cinema had grown up too, and portraits of film stars replaced the generals, and famous scenes from blockbuster films like *Ben Hur* appeared on the fronts of the speedway roundabouts. Wild animals in jungle scenes remained popular, exercising a fascination unbroken since the days of the travelling menageries of Wombwell and Bostock in the 1820s, but Tarzan brought the real thing much closer, at least on film.

The carved scrollwork of the earlier fairground was still popular but now it had to be translated into a painter's language. A new painted, popular art form came of age in the 1930s although the old carved gallopers and gondolas still survived alongside. Few new ones were built, however, because now the concentration was on the dodgems and the speedier 'waltzers' and 'dive bombers'. Things were looking quite good again when yet another World War intervened.

As Britain recovered from the Second World War the travelling fairs went through another difficult period. Television took its toll for a while, but a fair cannot be compared to an armchair in front of a small screen. They inhabit different worlds, and just as fairs survived the onset of the cinema and the radio, so television's threat soon receded into the living-room. What seemed to have been the technological enemy actually helped the rescue, transistorising sound systems and switching on the lights to more spectacular effect.

The post-war 'discovery' of teenagers, and the development of a pop music industry aimed directly at them helped too, because the entrance steps of the waltzer became a natural home for Rock and Roll, an unofficial discotheque. The painters picked up the influences, and pop singers and disco dancers soon appeared as part of the decoration, although still surrounded by rococo scrolls and marbled pillars. Speedway motorbikes stretched out to become *Easy Rider* Harley Davidsons, and the painted dollybirds wore flowered, flared trousers. Space travel also left its mark, first in comic-book style with characters sitting astride rockets like a firework advertisement or in streamlined spaceships that owed much to Dan Dare, but since the 1960s reality and engineering technology have arrived, with silver-suited spacemen floating alongside communication satellites painted on the showfronts.

The big problem with trying to be fashionable is the speed with which images go out of date, for the paintwork may last thirty years whilst the fashion only lasts three. The paintwork is only really successful because it appears as part of the complete

web of colour, design, sound and light that makes up the fair, a mixture that can as easily include an 1890 roundabout as a 1990 astronaut, or a coconut shy as a slot machine arcade.

And yet there is a cohesion, a definite fairground style which binds all these disparate ideas together, and which is saying something very distinct about popular taste. There is the intensity with which patterns are applied, the overall texture and richness achieved by painting every available space with an active design, whether depicting Walt Disney figures or abstract repeats of a lightning flash. There is the impact of the colours, using every shade and tone possible, with translucent tints laid over silver leaf for the greatest luminous intensity, all edged with a black line for the sharpest clarity. There is also the rhythm of the repeat pattern, the batwing-cum-sunburst design from the corner of a panel that is repeated in reverse in the next like a kaleidoscope or a butterfly, or the explosive knot of painted ribbons and scrolls that fills every lower shutter of the round stalls and the rounding boards of the juvenile rides.

These colours and abstract borders, the mainstream of modern fairground painting, unify the images and blend with the incredibly inventive lettering to set the pulse racing even before the fair opens, offering a magic mixture of excitement and nostalgia. If the fairground can keep alive this mad mixture of past and present it will surely have a secure future, and the finest popular art form will be safe for the twenty-first century.

(Left) *A modern painted version of the old language of fairground decoration on the Barrels of Fun sideshow at Nottingham Goose Fair in 1989. Flamboyant lettering and exuberant scrollwork grow closer together as the chunky, old-fashioned lettering throws out curved arms and flourishes, and the scrollwork becomes more abstract and expressive. It is indeed exciting and fantastic. Decoration by Tate Decor, 1983.*

(Above) *Waltzer cars on Anthony Harris' 1977 machine, with coloured plastics and a multitude of lights competing with the traditional paintwork for attention and customers. Chester Fair, 1989.*

Many of the well-known builders made living wagons for both gypsies and showmen, and some produced fairground equipment as well, employing the same team of carvers. As the prime time for both wagon and fairground carving was the end of the nineteenth century, much of the output shares the same contemporary decorative fashions of carving and gilding, with rolling baroque scrollwork as the most obvious ingredient. The ornate gallopers of the big roundabouts at last offered the humble shopworker and his girlfriend the chance to join temporarily the riding classes. The golden beauty of the carving made the gallopers almost better than the real thing, and they were certainly safer.

The roundabout horses were carved and painted to an extraordinary state of fantasy, but for the primary commercial reason of tempting all the world and his wife to spend money and have a good time. In contrast the decoration of the GYPSY CARAVAN is an entirely personal matter, one of pride and self-esteem. As one might expect from people dealing daily in the horse trade, their painted horses remained more like portraits of an ideal, portraits that transferred quite readily to the cab door of the gypsy lorry as most travellers became mechanised after the Second World War. From there it is a short drive back to the lorry park at the horse sale, with the grained and coach-painted horse-boxes and cattle trucks of the livestock transporters, although the truck drivers might not wish to acknowledge any similarity of taste to that of the gypsies.

Pigs make an occasional appearance on the front of livestock lorries too, and are regular partners to bulls on the butcher's shopfront, but they do suffer from a serious disadvantage. However accurate the portrait or serious the intent, pigs always appear rather comical. With tiny eyes, big ears, a flat twitchy nose, and pink colouring, it is difficult to envisage a pig as the embodiment of anything deep and meaningful or graceful, and a closer acquaintance with the real thing does not improve the impression much. Even their name resembles an expletive, leaving the mouth like an insult, so their cause is almost lost from the outset. Humble domestic swine do have devotees, of course, and the fat friendly silhouette of a pig, cut out of sheet metal, forms the background design for very satisfactory farm signs all over the country.

Weathercock of Wybunbury church tower, Cheshire.

But a boar is a different matter and even the word demands more respect. The wild boar was formidable, and although he was hunted out of existence in Britain centuries ago his image remains quite common in heraldry. He became a supporter to the arms of the Brushmakers' Company because the very best paintbrush bristles came from Russian and Chinese hogs, and was appropriated from there to become part of the insignia of the brushmakers' union in the nineteenth century. An old brush factory in Kendal, Cumbria, still displays a fine wooden carving of a bristly black boar as its street sign. This is a good replica of a very old original, which is now in retirement in the local museum.

After a thousand years of weathervane duty on top of the local church, the farmyard cockerel is probably the most instantly recognisable animal silhouette. He is the almost perfect blend of beauty with symbolic attributes, a memorable image with a good storyline. Aesthetically the cockerel looks splendid, and knows it.

With strutting walk, beautiful tailfeathers and arrogant cockscomb, he is the perfect archetype of pride, which it is difficult to deny him. His main attributes are bravery and watchfulness, particularly watching for the break of day. This probably means little to a modern town-dweller, but anyone who has kept chickens will have experienced the mixed blessing of being woken by the cock crowing; mixed because this may well be three o'clock in the morning in the summer. But the cockerel is linked to light and sun, and folklore tells stories of the devil being scared away by a cock crowing, because he thought that daylight was imminent.

The cockerel's most public place is on top of the church tower or steeple, a constant reminder to the Christian to 'Watch and wait' as instructed in Mark's gospel (Mark chapter XIII, verses 33–5), and of Jesus' prophesy that Peter would refuse to acknowledge him three times before the cock crowed on the morning of the crucifixion. Some of these church weathercocks are very old, and are folk art of the highest order forged out of sheet iron or hammered out of sheet copper before being covered in the best gold leaf. But, regardless of skill of craftsmanship or humility of religious spirit, they all start with the advantage of a flamboyant bird which can be stylised decoratively without losing its instant recognisability. When you also consider that the real bird's tail, sticking up and out at the back, makes it the perfect practical shape for a windvane, it is not surprising that the weathercock remains very common and popular.

As the cockerel by its early morning watchfulness became a symbol of vigilance, so the dog by its obedience and faithfulness became the symbol of fidelity. Considering the high moral value we accord this virtue, we treat our dogs with an extraordinarily wide range of attitudes, from pure love to bestial cruelty. Like cockerels, dogs have suffered from the peculiarity of man's sporting instinct in the past, bred and reared with care for the sole purpose of being pitted against a killer opponent, either one of its own kind or against bears, bulls or even a lion. We hunt other animals to death with packs of dogs, herd sheep with them, chain them up as guard dogs, teach them circus tricks, shampoo them in pets' parlours and parade them along the road as a fashion or character accessory. Perhaps this ambivalent attitude towards dogs is the reason why they are not such a common

This is the Cock that crowed in the morn, that waked the Priest all shaven and shorn, that married the Man all tattered and torn, that kissed the Maiden all forlorn, that milked the Cow with the crumpled horn, that tossed the Dog, that worried the Cat, that killed the Rat, that ate the Malt that lay in the House that Jack built.

Farmyard cockerel illustrating the traditional rhyme in an early nineteenth-century chap-book printed in Alnwick, Northumberland.

Two longcase clock dials painted, probably in the Birmingham area, with hunting scenes featuring gun dogs and hare-coursing greyhounds. The corner pictures of the right-hand one also follow another favourite dial painter's theme, the four seasons, although they are more usually represented by emblematic ladies than sporting gentlemen.

image in popular art as their huge numbers suggest they ought to be.

In the eighteenth century dogs appear in many fashionable portraits as a useful compositional ingredient, animating a dead part of the picture – if you will excuse the pun – and adding colour and texture, or a gentle comment about the taste or nature of the sitter. Gainsborough and Stubbs include them in this way, whilst Hogarth uses dogs in his moralising pictures to parallel the point of his story or to make a clearer comment on it. A picture of a sportsman shooting game, whether on canvas or clock dial, was not complete without a gun dog or two but it was not until the first quarter of the nineteenth century that the dog became the subject of the picture instead of an adjective.

This was due almost entirely to the work of Edwin Landseer, already well known by the 1820s although only born in 1802. He certainly started his career with a number of advantages. He was born into an artistic family that mixed quite freely in aristocratic circles and both his father and elder brother were highly skilled engravers, which helped bring his work to a wider public as print reproduction expanded with the century. He was also born with a precocious artistic talent, for he was making etchings by the time he was seven and had paintings exhibited by the Royal Academy at the age of thirteen. He attended the RA schools and progressed steadily up a ladder of wealth and prestige. A commission to paint a portrait of Sir Walter Scott in 1824 introduced him to Scotland and kindled a lifelong interest in deerhunting and Scottish life. What more could a young successful painter need for complete fame and satisfaction?

It was apparently achieved in 1839 when he painted his first portrait of Queen Victoria. For the rest of his life he was a friend of the court, painting many portraits of the royal children and many more of the royal pets, gaining a knighthood along the way in 1850. His remarkable talent for painting animals was used to record the queen's taste in pets and, the public could assume, her attitude towards them. As the royal family inspired increasing devotion, its values became fashionable and the favourite court painter was accorded enormous respect and honour.

Respect for Sir Edwin's pictures, championed as they were by the queen herself, was almost a token of respect and loyalty to the Crown,

but even this royal patronage was not the final key to his success. The interlocking circle of artistic talent, fashionable society and commercial printmaking was completed by Landseer's ability to touch the emotional sensibilities of his time. He used his animals to tell stories about humans, to express tragedy and comedy, and as allegories for human situations and responses. With incredible skill he gave the eyes and faces of his animals such touching expressions of humanity that they found an immediate response in the sentimental heartstrings of the nineteenth century. He made a great deal of money and his pictures remained very popular throughout the rest of the century. A huge number of prints were made of his work, in all sorts of sizes and to all levels of expense, and he almost single-handedly created the genre of sentimental pictures of animals with appealing limpid eyes that adorn calendars and birthday cards to the present day.

He may have created the painted genre, but he plugged into an existing mood and a set of stories of dog behaviour that were already almost folklore. The abilities of the guide-dogs of the monastery of St Bernard in the Alps were well known early in the century, but British stories of dog bravery seem to centre on the Newfoundland breed. Chambers' 1864 *The Book of Days* tells the story of a Mr Phillips who was saved from drowning at Portsmouth by such a dog. He subsequently bought the animal, rewarded it with good living, and commissioned a portrait of it by Morland and an engraving by Bartolozzi, which must date the event prior to Morland's death in 1804.

Another Newfoundland dog called Hero saved two little boys from drowning in a canal in London in 1834, and it may be this dog which was painted by Landseer lying proudly on a quayside or liferaft as 'A Distinguished Member of the Humane Society', exhibited in 1839. But he had already painted several others of the breed, including 'Bashaw' in 1829. This dog was the beloved pet of the eccentric Earl of Dudley, who commissioned a fabulously expensive marble sculpture of him that was still making news at the Great Exhibition of 1851. The painted portrait was entitled 'Off to the Rescue', in line with the breed's reputation for courage and intelligence, and engravings of it were sold in large numbers after 1858.

One of Landseer's most famous and well-loved paintings is 'The Shepherd's Chief Mourner', which shows a collie dog sitting beside

A swiftly painted horse's head on the backboard of a two-wheel spring cart, the pictorial autograph of the gypsy master decorator Jim Berry.

Detail of the carved decoration on a wagon built by Dunton's of Reading in 1921, with characteristic chamfering on the ribs, carving between them, and griffins on the ends of all projecting timbers. Worcestershire County Folk Museum, Hartlebury.

the coffin of his dead master. Here too is a storyline that appeals across the generations. A contemporary chap-book from the north of England quotes a story of a spaniel in London that, when his master died in 1827, refused to leave the grave until he died himself two years later. Eric Delderfield gives a very similar story in *British Inn Signs* to explain the name 'Greyfriars Bobby Inn' in Edinburgh. In this one the shepherd's terrier Bobby refused to leave his master's grave for fourteen years, and was finally buried nearby in the same graveyard in 1872. If neither story were true they ought to be, for they offer a sort of simplistic but valuable emotional lifebelt to cling to when faced with the real confusion of human deceit. We all need some simplicities, and part of the job of popular art is to supply the visual version of some common poetic truths. A pair of Staffordshire pottery dogs on the mantelpiece gives a sense of security as they gaze at us with unblinking faithfulness from the past. It is a great pity that so many people feel the need for a real dog chained up in the yard as well.

'The twa dogs', a wood-engraved version of an expensive steel engraving done from the even more expensive original picture by Sir Edwin Landseer. The illustration is from Cassell's 1854 Works of Eminent Masters *and is typical of the way these images reached a wider public, and of the anthropomorphic quality of much of Landseer's animal painting.*

A pair of nineteenth-century Staffordshire china dogs.

PUB SIGNS

THE MOST common popular art in modern Britain is the pub sign, and if importance is judged on quantity alone a well-balanced book of popular arts would need to devote at least half its pages to pub signs. Luckily the subject has always had its devotees, even back in the eighteenth century, and it has been well and lovingly documented ever since. The derivations of many signs have been unravelled and there would be little point in explaining a few in this short section, for so many more would have to be left unexplained due to lack of space. Several names and subjects are mentioned in the main text and most others can be found by referring to the specialist books listed in the bibliography. These introductory paragraphs can only discuss the most common general categories of pub sign and act as stepping-stones into deeper research.

The tavern sign has an honourable and continuous history from the ancient world to its modern popularity, and there seems little reason to doubt that it has a healthy future too. The Romans seem to have introduced tavern signs, and it is to the Romans that we owe many of the 'trade' signs of pubs, visual emblems of the business carried on within. The vine or the grapes are the most obvious, and many sign brackets from the eighteenth century onwards have a little hooked extension to carry a carved and gilded bunch of grapes, quite regardless of the official name of the house. The bush appears to be a continuation of the ancient Roman idea of hanging a bunch of ivy or vine leaves outside, for garlands of evergreens were dedicated to Bacchus, the god of wine, women and song.

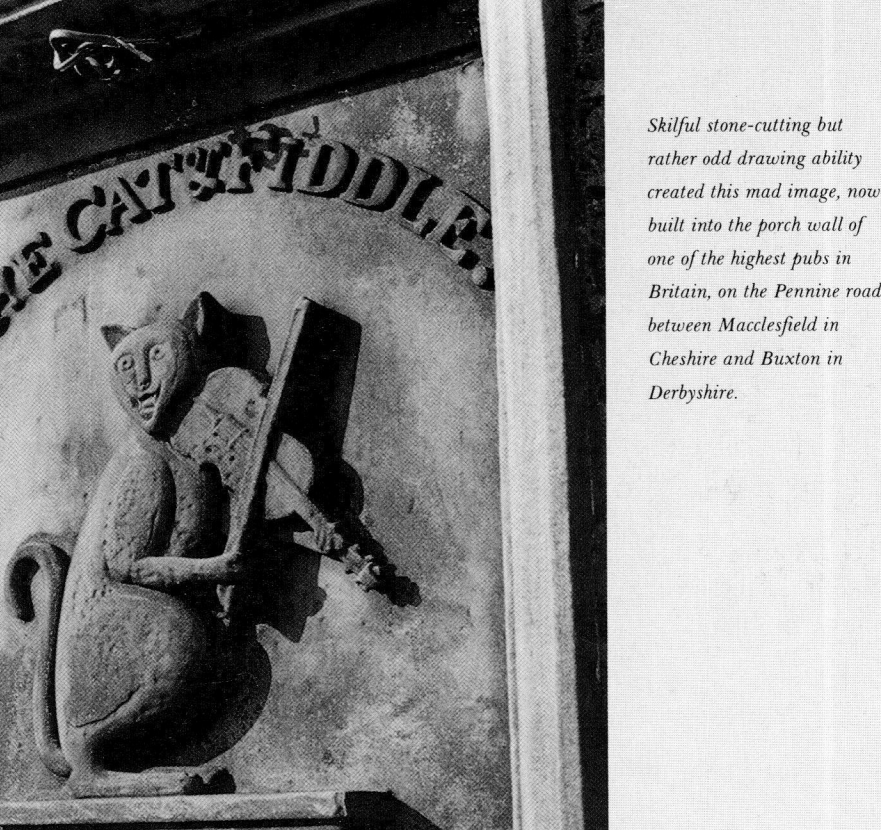

Skilful stone-cutting but rather odd drawing ability created this mad image, now built into the porch wall of one of the highest pubs in Britain, on the Pennine road between Macclesfield in Cheshire and Buxton in Derbyshire.

An attractive conjunction of pub sign, supporting ironwork and public house architecture at Woodseaves, Staffordshire. The cockerel on the other side is trimmed and spurred for fighting, and is subtitled 'War'.

Medieval references to the 'alestake' of the public house may reveal a direct unbroken connection with the Roman occupation, for the bush was hung upon the stake. Fourteenth- and fifteenth-century legislation makes it clear that anybody selling ale had to hang out a public sign, and threats to landlords to 'have their alestakes removed' seem to indicate that the sign was synonymous with a licence to operate.

By the eighteenth century another symbol had become common, the chequers, and many of Hogarth's prints clearly show a chequerboard pattern painted on the doorpost, regardless of the house name. Various origins are ascribed to this symbol – moneylending, the arms of the Warrennes who at one time granted the licences, or the red painted latticework over windows, but these explanations seem rather unsatisfactory when we know how common chequers once was, and how unworthy of remark at the time—it was such common knowledge that it has now been totally forgotten. Jolly brewers, jugs and barrels are self-explanatory but three barrels are often a reference to the three tuns of the arms of the Vintner's Company, granted in 1447. They, like the grapes, often appear as an added symbol regardless of the name of the pub.

The flag-waving and gallantry of the Boer War remembered on a dramatic signboard in Okehampton, Devon.

Heraldry provides the ingredients for a wide range of signs, the familiar 'Golden Lions' and 'Blue Boars' for example, but even such an innocuous name as 'The Dog' may refer to the heraldic crest of the local landowner. In the country, heraldic signs are usually connected with a local family or the history of the estate, but in the town they may be far less logical.

Signs as addresses, as ways of distinguishing particular buildings, proliferated as the urban population increased during the seventeenth and eighteenth centuries and gave us what became the golden age of signboards. They were not confined just to public drinking houses or coffee shops, for most businesses and many private houses took signs to advertise themselves (see SHOP SIGNS AND TRADING SYMBOLS). They increased in number and in size as they vied with their neighbours for attention, and also increased in complexity of carving, gilding and elaborate ironwork.

The painted designs became more complicated too, partly in order to be unlike any others, but partly as a consequence of tradesmen moving premises. They took the symbol that had become associated with their business to their new address and marked up their own emblem with that of the

A clear self-explanatory pub sign at Addingham in Yorkshire, celebrating a famous local animal. It is lifted out of the ordinary by the lyrical atmosphere of the background, a cross between a nursery book illustration and a Samuel Palmer.

This 1864 illustration of a contemporary inn sign in London, from Chambers' The Book of Days, *is a reminder of a class of livery servant which was already extinct when the book was published. These servants were employed to run before the carriages of the gentry to open gates and pay tollkeepers, but their real job was to provide a visible sign of the wealth and worth of he who followed in the coach. Note the traditional grapes and vine leaves framing the figure.*

previous occupier, creating some very odd partnerships. More widespread literacy and street numbering in the nineteenth century reduced the practical necessity for such signs. It has been left largely to pubs and hotels to carry on the tradition of pictorial emblematic signboards, which they have done with spectacular success.

The largest single group of pub names is probably connected with royalty and national loyalty, even excluding the obviously heraldic ones like 'The King's (or Queen's) Arms' and 'The Royal Standard'. Some are in disguise, like 'The White Hart', the badge of Richard II, or 'The Dragon', a supporter to the royal arms before the unicorn; most are fairly clear, however, like the Tudor 'Rose and Crown', the 'Royal Oak' of Charles II's escape to France, and the innumerable 'King's Head' and 'Queen's Head' of history.

Portraits have always been favourites, and quite often display the signpainter's version of works by famous easel artists, which before the age of photography were the best-known records of what our monarchs looked like. Versions of Holbein's Henry VIII, Hilliard's Queen Elizabeth, and Van Dyke's Charles I are probably more familiar to most people from pub signs than from art galleries. In earlier times the engravings and woodcuts of the chap-books and broadsides sometimes provided the reference material for the local signpainter, and he was not to know that the printer had used the same block to illustrate the face of several different kings. Neither were his customers, so all were satisfied.

National heroes follow the monarchy closely in popularity, and admirals and generals of patriotic fame feature strongly. Dickens offers us a perfect early nineteenth-century description in *The Pickwick Papers* of a large signboard 'representing the head and shoulders of a gentleman with an apoplectic countenance in a red coat, with deep blue facings, and a touch of the same over his three-cornered hat, for a sky. Over that again, were a pair of flags, and beneath the last button of his coat were a couple of cannon . . . an expressive and undoubted likeness of the Marquis of Granby of glorious memory'.

After heraldry, royalty and loyalty, the categories become less clear. Real heroes verge on the legendary with a character like Robin Hood or the Green Man, and real houses and castles might turn into three castles on 'The Mason's Arms'. This is heraldry again although they really originate as a trade sign, being symbolic examples of the mason's craft, like the grapes of the vintner.

A number of humorous signs continue to tell their centuries-old jokes, like the 'Labour in Vain', which usually features a washerwoman trying to scrub a little negro boy white, or the 'Quiet Woman' which shows a picture of a headless woman, but this 'Nag's Head' humour borders on misogyny. One sign is particularly famous, and appears in all the books, largely because the original is reputed to have been painted by William Hogarth and it was reproduced as an engraving very quickly. This 'Man with a Load of Mischief' staggers through life carrying a magpie, a monkey and his gin-drinking wife, all of which are tormenting him.

Hogarth is particularly important to sign history because, apart from enjoying drinking and painting tavern signs, he included many examples in his numerous engravings and thus provides much contemporary information about, and illustration of, the subject. In 1762 he and his friend Bonnell Thornton organised an exhibition of signs in London, which was seen as a satire of a much more high-minded exhibition of proper art taking place at the time and caused a considerable fuss in the newspapers. These journalistic arguments now provide us with much useful reference material.

A number of famous gallery artists have painted pub signs at some time or other, but the majority are commercial productions by professional signpainters, and none the worse for that. Their standard varies from brilliant to really bad, but their number and variety offer a huge choice in which the discerning traveller can take delight, or to which the local can be loyal. Materials and techniques vary widely too, and although most signs are painted there are examples in tiles and mosaic, stained glass, ironwork, and moulded plasterwork, and lots of full-blown sculptures.

As a final note it is worth remembering that this healthy popular art is thriving without outside subsidy of any sort, appreciated by customers, and paid for by house-proud publicans or profit-seeking breweries. It is traditional, but it is not a revival or an anachronistic survival; it is simply a part of a fully functional, commercial business. Perhaps familiarity leads us to under-value the pub sign as an expression of popular culture.

Two images for one public house name in Todmorden, Yorkshire: a warship and a very capable copy of the coronation portrait of George IV by Sir Thomas Lawrence.

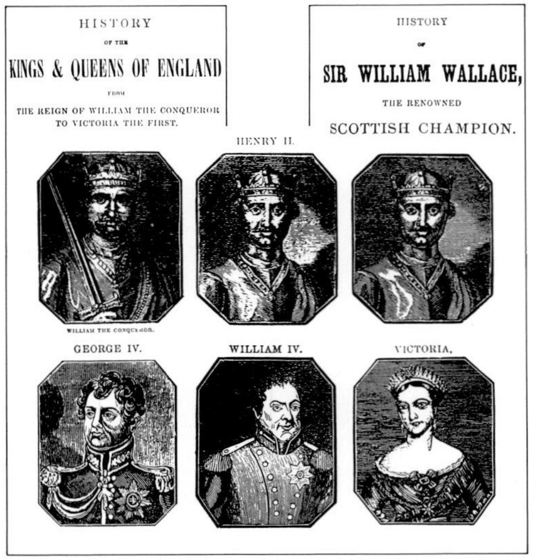

Illustrations from nineteenth-century chap-books, perfect reference material for signpainters, even though the family resemblance in the top row could be regarded as surprising.

BEASTS OF LEGEND AND RULES OF HERALDRY

THE LEGENDARY and fabulous beasts that appear in the popular arts today nearly all owe their survival to use in heraldry in some form. The word fabulous is used here to describe animals which we now know cannot have existed except in art and the imagination, but includes real animals which once were legendary or were believed to have fabulous attributes. Their common popular image still retains those fanciful attributes, even if we now know that they are zoologically incorrect.

The lion is a good example. It has always been a real animal, although the Romans made the European breed extinct by slaughtering the lions wholesale in their barbarous wild animal spectacles in the Colosseum. For the British people of the Middle Ages, therefore, the lion was an almost mythical animal that lived on the furthest edges of the known world. When heraldic designers started using formalised lions on shields in the twelfth century, the beasts were as much an artist's version of a traveller's tale as any attempt to draw the real animal. The lion was already known as the king of beasts, and the paintings were an expressive personification of bravery and pride, a very suitable visual metaphor for the king of a nation.

Richard I had earned the nickname *Coeur de Lion* during a crusade to the Holy Land and took three golden lions as his insignia when he became king. Lions in various numbers and colours were already in haphazard use in the arms of various noble families, but from that date the three golden lions on a red background became the hereditary arms of the monarchy, and the image of the heraldic lion was firmly linked with that of England. In Scotland a single red lion performed a similar duty.

The image of the lion was at least based on fact, if rather embroidered by the imagination, but many long-lived symbols are pure fantasy. At the time they came into use, however, they were thought to be based on real creatures, for many of the beasts were documented in medieval bestiaries, the lists and descriptions of strange animals from faraway places that were in effect the first natural history books. Some of their odd beasts can now be interpreted as poor or exaggerated descriptions of real animals, accompanied by pictures created by an imaginative artist who had never seen them. But the readers were unlikely ever to see them either, so that was fine.

Many of the more fantastic monsters seem like the results of a blind game of animal consequences, starting with the head of one animal at the top of the paper before folding it over and passing it on to someone else to add a body, and to a third for a tail or some feet. Zoologically they are impossible, but symbolically they can be very powerful. If the jaws of a crocodile are grafted onto the wings of a bird, a pretty horrific enemy is immediately invented, the imagined bloodthirstiness of all those teeth attacking with the fast unpredictable mobility of a bird. The combined image is the sum of its visible, symbolic parts. Add horns or claws for more flesh-tearing ability, and a long whiplash snake-like tail, and what we have is a horror that is not far removed from the vile dragons of European folklore.

This 'Valiant Soldier' at Roadwater, Somerset, has fought for existence very successfully, since it was designed and installed around 1930. It was made by Rachel Reckitt in a low-relief technique of wood and tinplate which ensures the survival of the basic design, however rough the subsequent repainting, and a dramatic chiaroscuro. A bold design, with a very satisfying and sympathetic blend of material and image.

The griffin has the head, beak, talons and wings of a huge eagle on the body of a lion, whilst the wyvern has leathery bat-like wings growing from the body of a serpent with two legs. A French version has a female human head, something like the harpies of classical mythology who had the heads and breasts of women with the bodies and talons of ravenous vultures. The list is almost endless and confusing, but once the code is cracked and a different response to each symbolic attribute is isolated, the pattern becomes clearer and the mythical beasts' power to remain meaningful over many centuries, and even millennia in some cases, becomes more understandable.

Bestiaries may also have supplied the models or inspiration for many of the fantastic gargoyles of the medieval church, which provide the human light relief on the soaring spiritual stonework of the finest gothic architecture. Scholars are still undecided whether these are intended as portraits of the outer boundaries of God's creation, or vile spirits that have been captured in essence and stuck up round the church as a warning, much as the gamekeeper nails up his dead vermin to warn off others and show the boss that he is doing his job.

The bestiaries also provided pattern books for the woodcarvers working inside the church. Many misericords, the decorated wooden tip-up seats in the choir stalls of the fourteenth century, feature fabulous beasts amongst the carvings of saints, legends and incidents from ordinary domestic life that now provide us with such a fascinating glimpse of the times, their humour, and their beliefs. They may not be very numerous but both misericords and gargoyles have been staring at the church-going common people for five hundred years or more, and their influence should not be underestimated.

The representation of various bits of animals to describe their abilities is certainly the major part of the story, but any graphic image also works on our sensibilities at another level. It has an effect on the unconscious, creating a response by using certain shapes, patterns, colours or qualities of line – the raw materials of pure abstract art. It could be that the widespread use of the image of certain animals has as much to do with an abstract response as a true knowledge of their real qualities. The teeth of the crocodile or any carnivorous beast can be unmistakably described by two zigzag lines converging together, expressing rigidity, sharpness and a potential for violent movement

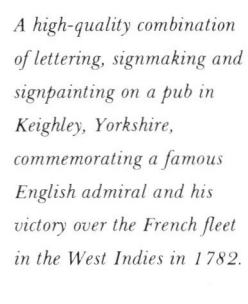

A high-quality combination of lettering, signmaking and signpainting on a pub in Keighley, Yorkshire, commemorating a famous English admiral and his victory over the French fleet in the West Indies in 1782.

by the quality of the mark, much as the sound of an onomatopoeic word describes its meaning. Something of the same inherent pain can be seen in the opposing points of the eagle's beak and talons.

One must not push this idea too far, at least not without more research, but some visual ideas that the reader may care to consider in this light are the smooth watery lines of the fish tail of the mermaid, the feather pattern of formalised wings on angel and eagle, the spiny wings of the bat and the devil, or the comforting curves of the mother's breast. The use of the snake or serpent to represent something evil, or at least unpleasant, is so universal that this abstract interpretation must contribute something towards the snake's perceived or imagined nature, for real snakes are no more offensive in their behaviour in the wild than any other animals. It is true that they do move in a mysterious way, they look as if they would feel slimy to the touch, and of course a number of them are known to be dangerous, but only if attacked or cornered. But it is the fact that movement, feeling, and inherent danger can all be translated into an instantly recognisable image by an active, snaky double line that makes them so useful and common in art and symbolism.

A sighting of the Loch Ness monster was first reported in the 1930s. It could easily have been dismissed as the work of an overactive imagination had it not so closely paralleled other stories of other lakes and cultures, so it was given publicity and more sightings almost inevitably followed. The monster caught the imagination of the public and the press, and caused much excited speculation. Careful scientific surveys were carried out with the most sophisticated equipment, but nothing has been achieved so far beyond some hazy photographs that have simply served to strengthen the enthusiasts in their certainty, and their antagonists in their scepticism. Meanwhile folklorists are fascinated by the apparent need of so many modern people to believe such a story, one that is so similar to other stories of dragons, giant worms or sea monsters which have been current for hundreds of years.

But the popular image of 'Nessie' that has developed in the press cartoon is particularly interesting here, for the dinosaurish head rising from the water is always followed by two or three humps of a long snake-like body and it may be this wriggling, tapering, snake line that is touching the communal soul most profoundly. Coiled up at

Fretwork design for a vase bracket from the Hobbies *handbook, 1947.*

rest this line is a spring or a scroll, static even if full of potential energy, but as it stretches out and begins to undulate it travels with a disturbing creepy rhythm. Look out – it may turn and slither towards you!

In order to stress the visual power of this image no mention has been made so far of Satan as a serpent, although the Adam and Eve story in Genesis III must be the biggest single influence on the British conception of the snake as evil. The first mention is simply that 'the serpent was more subtil than any beast of the field', and although it voices the temptation to eat the forbidden fruit, one feels that the thought would have been lurking in the human minds of Adam and Eve ever since they received the divine command not to eat it. It is only when the appalling and eternal nature of the punishment becomes clear that retribution is heaped retrospectively on the serpent's head. To cause this much misery it must have been commanded by an evil intelligence, therefore it must be the devil incarnate.

The final conjunction is in the last book of Revelations, where the words merge their meanings: 'And the great dragon was cast out, that old serpent called the devil and Satan, which deceiveth the whole world.' From there on the image of the snake in Christian art is definitely a Bad Thing. But it is still a powerful abstract design and symbol, and the combined picture of a naked man, a naked woman, a fruit tree and a wriggly serpent is a potent visual metaphor for life – sex, food and the beauties of nature, laced with a little shiver of horror for piquancy. One wonders whether the picture would have such power if it had been a little bird that had whispered to Eve 'your eyes shall be opened: and ye shall be as gods, knowing good and evil'.

With the words dragon, serpent and Satan so interlinked in that passage in Revelations, the image of the dragon in Christian art is usually the embodiment of evil, being overcome by St Michael in heaven or by a good platoon of saints on earth. Some of these pictures are blending fact and fable, for the conversion of a heathen city by a Christian knight was sometimes represented as the slaying of the dragon of evil ignorance. This allegorical story soon blended in the minds of the credulous with their own local legends of great worms and monsters, stories of much greater age and power that reached into the deepest recesses of their local folk memory. The blend of the two, when local pagan myth is apparently sanctioned by church authority, makes very powerful magic.

St George of England is a good example. The facts of his life are still rather hazy but he probably died a martyr's death around Alexandria in the third century. Nearly a thousand years later he was made the patron saint of England by Edward III and the red cross of St George on a white ground became the starting point for the later British flag. As an archetypal hero he is still popular in both children's fairy stories and on the signboard of many a local pub, and 'God for Harry, England and St George' is one of the few quotations from Shakespeare that most of us can remember (*Henry V*, Act III, Scene 1). (*To p. 44*)

A Book of Days *illustration of 1864 with all the stock characters of the midwinter resurrection plays, although in rather more elaborate costumes and masks than those in use today.*

revelries became increasingly anachronistic, and were in danger of disappearing completely. They were rescued and revived largely by a middle-class movement that sought to preserve these remnants of, as they saw it, the more peaceful and simple world of pre-industrialisation Merrie England. They may have been romantics, but they succeeded, and we owe them a debt of gratitude. Mummers' plays are now performed throughout the British Isles, although very few groups can claim continuous existence from before that romantic movement.

Another decline set in during the 1930s, exacerbated by the war, but the scripts remained in the memory of many, ready to be reclaimed and declaimed again in the present surge of interest. The plays nearly all follow a similar formula, having a fight as the central feature, in which a version of St George slays a Turkish Knight who is

MUMMERS AND MORRIS MEN

GREAT BRITAIN has a legacy of old customs, mummers' plays, morris dances and the annual resurrection of hobby-horses that have roots stretching back several hundred years, and in some cases perhaps thousands. But the country has been through a number of phases that have affected these survivors and make a modern historic interpretation quite difficult.

As a broad generalisation, one can say that many suffered some sort of neglect and decline as the majority of the population shifted its occupations and homes from farm to factory during the nineteenth century. As society settled into this new mould the old midwinter plays and rustic Mayday

The horn dancers of Abbots Bromley in Staffordshire in full swing in the main street during their once-a-year marathon performance. Starting at the church, where the ancient and very heavy horns are kept for the rest of the year, they parade and dance all round the village throughout the day. The traditional ceremony is very popular and the residents have turned the occasion into a full village fête-day in which much money is raised, and much fun is had by all.

then comically and miraculously brought back to life by a doctor. Some have a dragon and a host of subsidiary characters. It is the essential resurrection that is cited as evidence that the plays are the remains of a magical ritual concerning the death of the old year and the birth of the new, particularly as traditionally they took place at Christmas or New Year.

At any summer fête today one of the attractions is likely to be the local team of morris dancers, high-stepping around each other in coloured sashes and bells to the music of a concertina or fiddle. Their history is somewhat similar to the mummers' in that, although undoubtedly a very old tradition, much of their present popularity can be dated back to the work of the Folk Dance Society which was formed in 1911, and in particular to the researches of their founder, Cecil Sharp. There are handkerchief dances, stick dances, clog dances, longsword dances from Yorkshire and shortsword 'rapper' dances from the North East, and most modern teams will perform several of them in addition to their own traditional regional variations. In south Staffordshire an annual horn dance takes place in Abbots Bromley where the team performs a simple dance dozens of times all round the parish, each man carrying a massive set of antlers in front of his face. The dance is old and the antlers are ancient, but the woodland-green costumes with knee-breeches are a Victorian improvement. However, the hypnotic magic of this energetic yet graceful tradition is timeless.

An interesting link between the two activities is provided by the sword dances that culminate in a ritualised beheading of the fool, which may also link them to a seasonal fertility rite of the distant past. Medieval fools in motley and hobby-horse riders have always been regular members of a morris side, but a new convention is developing of having a morris beast in attendance as well, as a mascot or a familiar. This is another dancer covered in an all-encompassing cloak, carrying the animal's head above him on a pole. Often evident too is the odd British reverence for the Robin Hood myth, for he and Maid Marian turn up as extras in the horn dance team and in several mummers' plays. He is also a favourite emblematic figure of Englishness in carnivals and pageants, past and present.

The star performer in the soulcaking plays of Cheshire, standard mummers' plays except that they happen around Hallowe'en, is the 'owd 'oss' who is led in at the end and upstages everyone. This is traditionally a real horse's skull on a pole, painted, with eyes of some sort inserted in the sockets. As he rears and stamps, and clatters his hideous grinning jaws together, one certainly feels that one is on the borders of some very primeval magic. Something similar seems to be at work on Mayday in Padstow and Minehead as their peculiar versions of the hobby-horse take to the streets, with accordians and drums. Each has a painted mask over the face of the operator, which rises from the middle of a frame carried shoulder-high with a long skirt hanging from it down to the ground. In Padstow it is black whilst in Minehead it is painted hessian with a mass of coloured ribbons over the top, like a shaggy multicoloured rug. Skittish at one moment and threatening the next, both have an extraordinary presence and power that is difficult to capture in a photograph. Each has its followers and enthusiasts, and each seems set fair to continue to perform annually for ever.

Street processions were important and popular events in the past, and still are in Northern Ireland; the banners which are a part of that display are discussed separately. Unions, friendly societies and village clubs had a strong theatrical

The 'owd 'oss' and his driver from a Cheshire soul-caking play, a standard mummers' performance apart from the addition of this fearsome beast and the odd quirk of tradition that decrees it should happen around Hallowe'en instead of Christmas. These performers are from the Comberbach team, recently revived after a thirty-year break in continuity.

awareness and supported their image with bands, sashes and glittering regalia. Members carried staves with emblems mounted on the top, images made in polished brass or cut out of tinplate and painted in full colour, each decorated with ribbons and flowers. Tradesmen carried displays of tools specially carved in wood, like a Roman standard, as an image of their trade. In the case of the Bristol shipwrights this was a massive wooden axe with Noah's ark carved on the blade. In the days of the medieval trade guilds, processions on the feast of Corpus Christi and at mid-summer were annual highspots and we have been left intriguing written descriptions of some exciting events. Sixteenth-century Chester had processional images of fish, camels, a dragon and a unicorn as well as four giants. London's Gog and Magog are carved replicas of what were once such processional giants, and Salisbury still has an original one reputed to date from 1496. There is also a Salisbury dragon, quite similar to one in Norwich which dates from 1795, and as they both have a similarity to the Padstow hobby-horse one feels that what remains is just the tip of a large mass of lost public celebration.

We have certainly lost the Jack-in-the-Green. This was a man entirely hidden by a wicker framework covered in greenery, who paraded the streets accompanied by oddly costumed characters clashing brushes and shovels together. He was the chimney sweeps' Mayday centrepiece. This had been the sweeps' special day, for the Jack-in-the-Green had provided the seasonal licence for some very successful begging. Revivalists make Jacks-in-the-Green and parade them in fêtes, but the genuine continuity of folk tradition ceased when legislation finally stopped the trade from using children as climbing boys in the 1870s, and it had virtually died out by 1900.

It is salutary to remember that most of these theatrical traditions owe something of their survival to the poverty of the performers. The collections taken, or the seasonal food and drink offered in return, were of great value to poorly paid workers and if one could earn a shilling and have fun at the same time the human condition was considerably improved. That still applies, so when you have been entertained by such performers please give generously, for most collections now go to a worthwhile charity and the traditions need keeping alive.

(Left) *The 'sailor's horse' of Minehead, Somerset, parading into town on 1 May for the annual mayhem. The performer wears the central mask over his head and carries the hobby horse's body shoulder high. The horse has no head as such, but it has a rope tail that can be lashed with devastating effect on anyone teasing it.*

RAISING OF THE MAY-POLE.

(Below) *Another old tradition recorded attractively, if romantically, in* The Book of Days. *The floral crown atop the pole is particularly interesting, a token of thanks for the Restoration of the monarchy, and of maypoles, in 1660.*

A green dragon on a **PUB SIGN** is usually a reference to St George, but the red dragon is more directly heraldic and is more likely to be a reference to the Tudor kings or to Wales. Henry VII started using one as part of his insignia at the end of the fifteenth century and it remained as a supporter to the royal arms until the end of Elizabeth I's reign. The red dragon had already been in intermittent use for centuries as a device for a general, a pen-dragon, a 'head-leader' in Celtic, and it was strongly associated with the name of Cadwallader, the last Celt to rule Britain. It came by degrees to be associated with Wales alone, and with the recent rise in Welsh nationalism and growth of a Welsh tourist industry the red dragon has an increasing currency as a separate symbol of nationhood. All of this flies in the face of its evil symbolism, but its traditional folkloric reputation as a warlike guardian of hidden treasure suits the new job very well. It would also be far better as a friend than an enemy.

When James VI of Scotland became James I of England in 1603 he deposed the dragon from the royal arms and substituted his Scottish unicorn as a supporter to the shield, where it has remained paired with the English lion ever since. The idea of the unicorn is very ancient. He is mentioned in the Old Testament and by the Greeks and Romans, and may have originated from a description of a rhinoceros or a one-horned wild ox. He is a solitary animal, very rare of course, but very strong and brave. As the descriptions get passed down the centuries and elaborated, he arrives in the Middle Ages with a body like a horse but with a tufted lion's tail and cloven hooves, and a reputation associated with purity. His horn is an infallible antidote to poison and he has only to dip his horn into foul water to make it pure. The only way to beat him in battle is by guile, by tricking him into charging his horn firmly into a tree, an act which is a respectful comment on his immense strength. Most lyrical of all his attributes is his powerlessness when confronted by the purity of a virgin maid, when he will kneel and lay his head in her lap. She could then capture him with her girdle, if she were mean enough after this act of devotional humility.

Like the lion on the other side of the arms, the unicorn's image means much more than a simple description of an animal, for it is symbolic of an inner tension that is almost a poetic concept. The lion's famous courage and ferocity was tempered by his equally well-known magnanimity and wise mercy accorded by legend, whilst the unicorn's strength and violence was balanced by his submission to purity and simplicity. In partnership they make a fine symbol for an ideal monarchy.

From 1762 to the end of his life in 1806, George Stubbs painted and engraved the theme of 'A horse frightened by a lion' many times, a subject believed to have been inspired by an antique marble statue in Rome. The simplest explanation for the theme is that it is a natural dramatic moment which might just have happened, but it is also a clash between two powerful symbols. The horse had become very much an extension of mankind, intelligent and fast but domesticated and tamed to the will of the rider, but under the terror of this situation that veneer has cracked. Stubbs puts all his knowledge of the anatomy and nature of the animals into expressing the latent power and cruelty of an untamed stallion's teeth and hooves, faced with a lion's ferocity and arrogant pride. When all we think we know about horses is faced with all we think we know about lions, in a confrontation that we know has got to end in death, a tension of mythic proportions is created. Both the lion and the horse can represent the power of nature, courage, valour, and grace, or horror, violence, arrogance and power-lust. If only life were simple and one could be on one side or another.

Not surprisingly perhaps, given the warring history of England and Scotland, the heraldic English lion and Scottish unicorn also have something of this symbolic tension in their roles as supporters of the British royal arms. They never look quite like good friends as they face each other on their hind legs supporting the shield, for the unicorn keeps a wary eye on the lion, whilst the lion stares at us to avoid looking at the unicorn. Both appear more relaxed when lying down and facing outwards, a common but totally unofficial arrangement that helps to shape the heraldic group into a longer, landscape format, more suitable for a headpiece to a page of text or for a decorative border. Even then the unicorn is usually 'regardant', with his head turned backwards to keep the lion in view, because, to misquote the old saying, 'The lion may lie down with the lamb, but the lamb won't get much sleep'.

Heraldry has an all-pervasive presence in popular art, which is something of a paradox because it originally belonged very firmly to the high-born nobility, and was strictly hereditary. But just as the royal crown, which can only properly be worn by a king or queen, can become a symbol of loyalty to royalty, or to the country, or even to a hazily understood set of values, so the immense array of symbols and images of heraldry have taken on new roles for the general population, quite separate from that of differentiating particular members of the old ruling classes.

Heraldry provides much of the imagery for possibly the largest block of popular art in existence, the English PUB SIGN, and the standard layout of shield, crest and motto provides the design basis of many certificates and BANNERS, and much advertising and packaging. Flags are an offshoot of heraldry, and heraldic beasts are an important part of carved ship decoration. The royal arms appear in churches, over shops and over Punch and Judy shows; civic coats of arms adorn the town hall and the dustcart; and private arms decorate the graveyard. We are surrounded so constantly by bits of heraldry that it is easy not to notice, or to underestimate, its influence on daily life. It is a complicated and very exact science in its purest form, well documented and well served by specialist books and scholars, but some of the history and basic rules of heraldry do need to be restated before we can appreciate how much it has affected everyday popular art and culture.

The underlying idea is that the medieval hero returned from battle or the tournament, hung his shield on the wall and balanced his helmet with its accoutrements on top. A picture of that group of objects, with the addition of his family's motto or war-cry painted below it, then became his family's trademark or emblem. The shield was painted with the same recognition patterns or devices that appeared on the linen coat that he wore over his chain-mail, his true 'coat of arms', although it is now quite acceptable to use these words to describe just the pattern on the shield or, less correctly, the whole assemblage of heraldic items. This should properly be called the 'achievement of arms'. The distinguishing marks on the shield were at first quite simple: geometric patterns in contrasting colours, some wild beasts – particularly lions – as symbols of fierce bravery, and

A hatchment is a heraldic memorial, and is always painted on a diamond-shaped panel. This one in Adbaston church, Staffordshire, is to Richard Whitworth, a popular though rather eccentric naval admiral who lived locally and died in 1748. He did much to improve conditions for his seamen , and the supporters of these arms are two sailors in early naval uniform. One carries a cross-staff, a navigational instrument, and the other a lead line. When Whitworth retired he dammed the stream on his estate to make a pond where he could continue to fight sea battles with large model warships. The watermill owners downstream had to take him to court several times to get their water back.

When Henry VIII proclaimed himself head of the church he demanded that the royal arms should be prominently displayed in every church to remind the people of this new fact. This law, and the cool shady interiors of most churches, has left us a fine legacy of beautiful heraldic painting stretching back over the centuries. This example, from the country church of Hittisleigh in Devon, is in perfect condition and apparently untouched since it was done in 1819.

visual puns on the name of the soldier, which were particularly popular in the early days. Thus Mr Swinburne might show a pig above water, Mr Shelley some shells and Mr Trumpington trumpets, whilst some devices, or 'charges' as they are called, commemorate particular historic moments or acts of courage or chivalry.

A symbol was also originally marked on the front of the helmet but this gradually transferred to a fan-shaped extension on the top, like the crest of a cockerel. Later still this crest was modelled in wood or leather, held on with the same twisted wreath of cloth jammed over the helmet that kept in place the 'mantling' – the piece of cloth that hung down the back of the helmet to ward off the direct heat of the sun. All these items became important elements in the full achievement of arms. The heraldic picture is completed by the addition of a supporter on each side, upright figures of men or beasts, real or fanciful, who balance the composition. The lion and unicorn, already mentioned, are the most familiar example of all. In fact supporters were probably first introduced merely to fill the space on either side of the shield and helmet on circular seals, but as those who used seals to authenticate documents were themselves of the highest rank, supporters came to be used only on the arms of knights and peers.

The imagery of the crests and supporters is sometimes very odd or bizarre, even compared with the main charges on the shield, but they are quite important to our interest for they often become separated from their original families and coats of arms. It is quite heraldically proper to use the crest design alone as an emblem, perhaps on servants' liveries, carriage doors and horse harness, and many mysterious public house names probably owe their origins to the crest of the local landowner, or the first publican's previous employer.

It is usually suggested that heraldry's origin was purely practical and utilitarian, a method of recognising individual knights and soldiers under their all-encasing armour on the field of battle, but its rapid spread throughout western Europe suggests that it appealed just as strongly on the grounds of aesthetic pageantry as of cognitive utility. It was in existence soon after the Norman conquest, but was not formalised into a rigid system for another hundred years or so. Shields and flags had been decorated with odd designs for centuries, probably since the eagle standards of the Roman legions, but what

separated heraldry from random decoration was the acceptance of heredity, the idea that a symbol or sign belonged exclusively to one man and could be handed down as a possession to his family. During the thirteenth century heraldry became strictly documented and the rules were established and administered by officially appointed heralds, who came to exert considerable power in the granting of new arms and their use.

The rules of heraldry were laid down in the court language of the time, Norman French, and most heraldic terminology is still ancient French in origin. This is baffling to the layman but is a very precise trade language for the heralds, and makes it possible to describe or 'blazon' particular arms quite briefly but very accurately. If the rules are properly understood and followed it should be impossible to be inaccurate, or to confuse any arms with any others, even though there is considerable scope within the convention for artistic interpretation in the way the arms are painted or designed.

For example, the lion that supports the royal arms, opposite the unicorn, is 'a crowned lion rampant guardant *contourné* or, armed and langued gules'. This means, in order of description, that he (for all heraldic beasts are male unless otherwise stated) is crowned with the standard royal crown (or it would have been further described); is seen sideways rearing up, with one hind foot on the ground and with all his other legs spread out aggressively in a position of attack (rampant); and has his face turned to look straight at us (guardant). *Contourné* means his body is facing towards our right, that is to his left, 'to sinister'; for without this word all animals described face to their right, the dexter side. When describing a supporter to a shield, as in this case, the word would be unnecessary because he is the dexter supporter and would naturally be expected to face in towards the shield. 'Or' is the word for gold and is the colour of everything so far described; 'armed' refers to his teeth and claws, and 'langued' to his tongue. 'Gules' is the old word for red, so the last part of the description means that his claws, teeth and tongue are painted red.

Part of this description is unnecessary to the herald, for lions are always 'armed gules' unless otherwise stated, and much of the accuracy of the blazon depends on a knowledge of the usual convention; thus a lack of description often has a positive meaning. All animals are

This heraldic history of the male line of the Aston family of Cheshire was commissioned by Sir Thomas Aston for the consecration of the local church in 1636. The family tree, complete with leaves, runs clockwise from the top left-hand corner with the Aston arms (per chevron sable and argent) on the left of each shield impaled with those of each new generation's wife on our right. This is a slightly later copy on canvas of the one in the church, and hangs in the family house.

male and face to dexter, unless otherwise stated, and the lion's tail is always erect and waving proudly unless blazoned as 'extended' or 'coward'.

Many crests feature the head of an animal, and the way this dismembered head is to be shown is also blazoned. If the head is 'couped' or '*coupée*' the neck is shown cut across with a straight line, whereas if the head is 'erased' the neck is shown with a jagged edge as if torn off, an awful similarity of wording to the modern gangsterism 'rubbed out'. Poor-quality painting of this sort of crest probably accounts for pubs called the 'Bleeding Wolf' in Cheshire, which was the home ground of Hugh Lupus of Chester who used a wolf's head erased as his crest, or the odd 'Bleeding Horses' elsewhere in the country. It is also probable that bad heraldic sign painting accounts for some of the odder pub names, and that many 'Cats' started life as unsuccessful versions of heraldic lions or leopards.

Heraldic blazon is a technical language and would take a long time to use in any conversational sense, but it is quite fun. Heraldry has remained consistently popular and each of the many books on the subject, that variously venerate it as either art or science, have a glossary of terms to which the amateur can refer. There should be no excuse for getting it badly wrong, even if PUB SIGN painters often manage to do so.

The right to a coat of arms descends down the male line by primogeniture, that is by passing to the eldest son first, and then his eldest son before all others. Women can only inherit their father's arms if they have no brothers at all, and then they have to share that honour equally with any other sisters. However, all women have the right to use their father's arms, on a diamond shape and without the helmet, and they can choose to continue to do so when they marry. If they marry a man with a right to bear arms, the usual practice is to 'impale' the arms together by dividing the shield vertically, with his on the dexter or right-hand side of the shield seen from the soldiers' point of view, and with hers on the left or sinister side.

If the woman is the heiress of arms in her own right, then her children can choose, with consent from the official heralds, to 'quarter' their mother's arms with their father's and effectively start a 'new' heraldic symbol combining the two. Father's arms appear in the first and fourth quarters, the top dexter and lower sinister respectively, and mother's arms in the remaining second and third quarters. Should those children do something similar, however, perhaps marrying someone who also bears quartered arms, then the numerical progression of quarterings can very quickly get quite out of hand and visually confused. It is usual to drop some of the earlier quarterings for simplicity, but the house may have the full version painted on the wall in the hallway, or the church may have it on the family vault. Rich and decorative to the layman, it can be a detailed family history written in symbolism legible to those versed in the heraldic language.

At the head of the heraldic tree is the monarchy and the nobility, and their arms are distinguished by a crown placed on the helmet, with their rank within the hierarchy differentiated by variations in the design. It is the royal crown that appears in the popular arts, however, because its use is usually a token of loyalty to the king or queen or, by extension, to the country he or she represents. Over a crimson and ermine cap, a circlet of gold carrying four Maltese crosses alternating with fleurs-de-lis is spanned by two jewelled arches that support a miniature orb and cross at their junction. It is this crown that invariably appears on pub signs and processional pole-heads, painted in detail or cut out in silhouette.

The idea of giving a crown to honour an individual is very ancient, and the Romans used a wide range to honour a variety of deeds: olive leaves for athletes, and oak and laurel leaves for heroes and generals, as well as regular golden crowns for imperial rulers. In heraldry open crowns are found as collars around the necks of various royal animals to denote their ownership or allegiance. An example is the white hart badge of Richard II, the subject of innumerable pub signs, which is shown lying down with a crown around its neck, blazoned 'lodged' and 'gorged'. The Scottish unicorn is always gorged with a golden coronet, with a chain fixed to it passing between the forelegs and reflexed over the back.

The return of the monarchy with the Restoration in 1660 was welcomed with considerable relief after the rigours of the Puritan Commonwealth, and Charles II's escape and subsequent return to the throne are celebrated with many signs of the 'Royal Oak' in which he was supposed to have hidden to evade capture. His return also

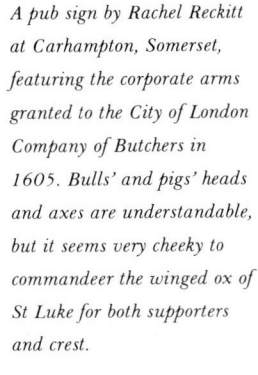

A pub sign by Rachel Reckitt at Carhampton, Somerset, featuring the corporate arms granted to the City of London Company of Butchers in 1605. Bulls' and pigs' heads and axes are understandable, but it seems very cheeky to commandeer the winged ox of St Luke for both supporters and crest.

heralded the revival of the maypole, banned by the Puritans as frivolousness bordering on idol-worship. Many newly erected maypoles were surmounted by images of the royal crown as a token of loyal thanksgiving. Chambers' *The Book of Days* in 1864 mourns their passing, but one maypole crown still survives in Audlem church in Cheshire.

One of the rules that particularly controls the visual effect of heraldry and all its descendants, sanctioned or not, is the 'rule of tincture'. Only a limited range of colours is allowed, and yellow and white are always referred to as the metals gold and silver ('or' and 'argent'). In heraldic painting these colours are very often actual gold or silver leaf applied to the surface, especially gold which is incredibly ductile and can be beaten into gossamer-thin sheets without losing its beauty or permanence (part of the reason why it is so sought-after and expensive). Silver is not so good because it is more difficult to work and tarnishes very quickly without protection, so it is more common for argent to be represented by white, despite its name. The rule of tincture states that no metal shall be placed over metal, or colour over colour; for example, if the background colour of the shield is gold you cannot place white designs on it, and if it is red you cannot use green.

The theory is that the rule was introduced to ensure clear recognition of the charges at a distance, which it does, but it also ensures a boldness of colour scheme that, though strong, remains aesthetically tasteful. The colours allowed are red, blue, green, purple and black (respectively gules, azure, vert, purpure and sable in old heraldic French), which by their nature are all mid-toned or dark. The rule of tincture therefore ensures the use of light against dark or dark against light, and sensibly avoids a clashing confusion of like against like. The

designs remain bold but rarely gaudy. There are some heraldic exceptions to the rule, and very occasionally other colours creep in, but they are rare and not worth considering in this broad generalisation.

There are, however, a group of 'furs' to be noted. These are patterns that cover the whole of an area with one conventional design and can almost be regarded as additional colours. The two commonest, and the two that bear most relationship to real animal furs, are 'ermine' and 'ermines', painted respectively as black spots on a white ground and white on black. Each spot is usually painted as a tiny fleur-de-lis with three dots round the base. Another design, in blue and white, is meant to represent squirrel skin, called 'vair'. It was a confusion of this word with 'verre', the French for glass, that gave Cinderella her uncomfortable slippers in the English pantomime.

Heraldry's successful survival and use since Tudor times has depended as much on trade and commerce as on an élite aristocracy. After a couple of hundred years of use in battle and tournament, heraldry had acquired the respectability of age and custom, and institutions such as the colleges, cathedrals and guild companies applied for their own arms in a desire for something of the same respect. Towns, cities and counties acquired coats of arms, some re-using charges from their local lordly landowners, but many adopting local references or legends for the shield and supporters, thus widening the range of heraldic symbolism. They also widened the range of possible usage, for these arms could now express a loyalty to a smaller geographical area or to a specific trade without acknowledging subservience to a particular man or family. In the eighteenth and nineteenth centuries civic and corporate heraldry offered a range of venerable symbols that could confer instant dignity on any new organisation that could find an excuse to include some heraldic arms in its public image.

The emerging friendly societies and trade unions were just such organisations, and did much to spread the use of old-fashioned heraldry through their new democratic institutions. Some of the earliest membership cards, painted BANNERS and printed certificates or 'emblems' were nothing but the old coats of arms granted to the craft guilds in the sixteenth century, perhaps with the addition of the motto translated into English. It was only a short time since these worshipful companies had tried to represent the interests of all the workers within any given trade, but as modern capitalism got into gear and master craftsmen were bought out by, or turned into, factory owners, the trade guilds ceased to have much relevance to the craftsmen. The arms remained honorable, however, and lots of the brand-new organisations immediately claimed several centuries of existence and used the guild arms as the basis for their new union trademark.

If there was no obvious guild candidate, then the answer was to invent one by choosing some suitable emblems for the shield and supporting it with appropriate figures on either side. A couple of fellow workers, were chosen by some organizations holding some of the tools of their trade, whilst others sought to express their higher aspirations by choosing emblematic female figures of Hope and Justice, with their usual accoutrements of anchor, sword and scales, to guard the shield.

As the nineteenth century progressed, depiction of a heraldic shield on banners or printed emblems tended to decline in importance, but the concept of supporters on either side of a central panel became steadily stronger. They were combining with the architectural ideas developed at the same time from the classical triumphal arch (as discussed in chapter 6), and several supporters in the heraldic sense gradually became more like statuary on pediments, or in alcoves; truly pillars of the union establishment.

A heraldic influence can be seen on church BANNERS as well as those of the more militant unions. But there was a third group of banner marchers, the friendly societies, which were possibly more influential than either of the others for a while in the middle of the nineteenth century. Their imagery touched a huge proportion of the population. Much of it came from the emblem books of the sixteenth century, via the Freemasons of the eighteenth, but the heraldic layout of central 'shield' or picture panel, with a motto on a ribbon below it flanked by emblematic supporters, underlies most of the societies' certificates and banners, giving a sense of solid security by its association with the antiquity of medieval heraldry. The members were very proud of their organisations and showed themselves in full regalia, marching behind the club banner and flags several times a year. Their purpose was not only to have a good time but to advertise themselves, for new healthy young members were the financial lifeblood of a 'sick and burial club'. (*To p. 54*)

POLITICAL MURALS, NORTHERN IRELAND

THE POLITICAL and religious differences that led to the present troubles of Northern Ireland have also resulted in an upsurge of public art, a recognisable genre of images and situations that now deserves a special section in a modern history of popular art.

Isolated examples of murals, particularly on gable-end walls of terraced houses in rather run-down inner-city areas, constantly spring up throughout the British Isles, often just prior to demolition or as an attempt to up-grade an area to avoid demolition, but they usually fall into either the playscheme or the professional category. Children's work, usually under the guidance or practical assistance of an adult, appears on all sorts of walls and temporary hoardings during holiday playschemes, and the results, though crude, are often cheerful, amusing temporary additions to the townscape. However, they rarely have much relevance to the place or time in which they are created and their design often has more to do with how far a ten-year-old can reach than with the architecture. When the novelty wears off, the effect may indeed be more like graffiti and detrimental to the area instead of life-enhancing.

'Playscheme' in this generalisation can also include the results of community arts projects where, although the subject-matter may be more serious, the participation of local people in making the artwork is just as important as the artistic quality of the end result. It may be fun and important for the minority who did it, but is less likely to be popular with the people who have to live with it.

A wide range of unionist imagery used in east Belfast to create a striking mural. The heraldic red hand of Ulster dances on the Irish tricolour whilst the emblematic women proclaim messages of freedom and defiance. Were it not for the Union flags behind them, they could be mistaken for versions of Marianne, the mythical heroine of the French Revolution; the visual language is the same, even if the message is different.

Republican murals overlooking a car park in Londonderry, 1989. The text of that on the left is an emotional poem about the lonely symbolic mother of Ireland, mother of the mythical hero Cu Cuchalainn. That on the right needs no text.

A gable-end mural being painted in the Falls Road, Belfast, to mark the twentieth anniversary of the arrival of extra units of the British army in Northern Ireland. A strong statement boldly treated, and an interesting use of photographic images blown up and overlapped to become the letterform itself, an enlarged version of a photocopied newsletter cover.

The professional approach, as the name suggests, employs a trained artist to design and co-ordinate the painting of the wall, even if he or she does not apply every brushstroke personally. If the artist is good, the results are more likely to suit the architecture and the environment and to be generally acceptable in the longer term. The best work is terrific, but formal training and teaching have intervened, as well as scaffolding and the local authority, and the mural is less likely to reflect local concerns and local tastes. Just occasionally the two approaches blend, and a strong artistic guide can help the less-experienced locals towards a result satisfactory in all ways, but this is unfortunately rare. After all, everybody needs some practice to improve, and few people paint wall pictures every day.

In Northern Ireland, however, particularly in the inner-city areas of Belfast and Londonderry, the gable-ends have become a visual extension of the ideological battle between Loyalists and Republicans, and to some degree between them and the British army. Twenty years of practice has led to a strong language of symbols and design.

The artistic success of this battle seems about equal on either side, although the design weapons used are subtly different. The unionist Protestant side relies heavily on the style of a military badge, with a central emblematic image like the standard picture of William III on his horse set against a huge pair of crossed flags. The Union flag and the Ulster flag are commonest of course, but this group also uses the Scottish emblems, the St Andrew's cross or the rampant lion of James I.

The formality of the arrangements has a number of design advantages. It controls the colour scheme within the historic heraldic limits, keeping them strong but with good tonal contrast, and directly picks up and plays with the emotional, patriotic, sectarian response that these flags have in Northern Ireland – far more so than in the rest of the British Isles. The symmetrical arrangement of flags plus image is quite consciously reminiscent of the heraldic achievement of arms of a gallant military past, and suits very well the Protestant message of pride in history, particularly in William of Orange's success at the Battle of the Boyne in 1690. It expresses a continuing romantic military steadfastness in the face of all change, a truly conservative response, and a visual resistance to anything that might alter the status quo.

The Republicans, however, are setting out to change everything, and whilst the religious differences between Catholic and Protestant are often stressed in the media, and were of course the historical well-spring, the huge political changes demanded by the modern Republicans are often overlooked in the daily response to the horrors of killings and security operations. Difficult revolutionary ideals have little chance of rational explanation in the aftermath of a bomb in a shopping street, and newspaper headlines have always played up to the immediate anger of the innocent law-abiding people caught up in apparently never-ending violence, and probably always will.

The wallpainters of the Falls Road, however, do have more time to make their case, and some of the murals reflect a much more international and progressive attitude compared with the insularity of the unionists' use of flags and badges. Messages of solidarity with the freedom-fighters of Africa, memories of Che Guevara, and pleas for independence appear alongside walls which stiffen resistance to the British army, or those that respond to recent local events, like a huge newspaper hoarding. Not unexpectedly the Irish flag of green, white and orange appears regularly, but the simplicity of these three stripes of colour is often used as an abstract design and suits the architecture of brick wall and gable-end very well. Combined with strong images in black and white, or with a restricted palette of bold colours, these basically political statements are sometimes well designed as architectural decoration for that particular space, and are true murals.

Much of the work, however, on both sides of the divide, merely uses any convenient wall as a noticeboard for a message or a memorial, and is as little concerned with the architecture as any other advertisement hoarding. Just occasionally the designers, painters and physical spaces combine to create massive artworks that are a positive enhancement of the urban environment, if only the observer can remain sufficiently detached from the violent sectarian politics that underpin the literal messages of the murals, to see the art. But the worm in the apple is often the hatred expressed, and the art gets used to harden old attitudes instead of taking any steps to soften them.

Saddest of all, both literally and in terms of seeing a way out of the impasse, are the large number of memorials to the dead that constantly reiterate the death toll of the fighters on both sides, as well as the innocent bystanders. These are reminders that go back well beyond the troubles of the past twenty years to the risings and resistances that led to the Irish Free State in 1922.

Most chilling of all are the paintings of hooded figures in the secret armies of the IRA and the UVF, who pose like comic-book heroes or advertisements for violent videos on the walls of many side streets. They are so similar in their faceless, hideous heroics that the uninitiated visitor must look to the background colours or the location to understand which side is being promoted. Extra elements of accidental violence are often given to these wall paintings by the explosive patches of paint that have been thrown on them by their opponents, so that even the most peaceful murals are sometimes marred by grotesque action painting. That too is a pity, for many are strong and exciting pieces of visual decoration and enhance their drab surroundings. If only all this creativity could be released into normal everyday living conditions, instead of needing the seemingly interminable bitterness of violent minorities to bring it into existence, what a colourful world it could be.

One of the commonest designs in Protestant Belfast is the vaguely heraldic 'trophy' layout of central badge and flanking flags, seen here on the side of the local UDA headquarters in Newtonards Road. In a town where every unattended car is a potential bomb, the 'No parking' sign really means what it says.

One of many painted memorials in Belfast. A very plain gable-end is given instant dignity, and made structurally interesting, by the addition of some comic-book classical architecture to frame the Loyalist badge.

Flags are also an offshoot of heraldry, and thus follow many of the same rules of colour and design. On the medieval battlefield the individual knight had a pointed or swallow-tailed 'pennon' flag attached to his lance, whilst the higher ranks of nobles and princes bore square 'banners' on theirs, carrying their coat of arms. A quick promotion in recognition of some feat of bravery on the battlefield was effected by cutting off the points of a knight's pennon, and creating him a 'Knight-Banneret' or baronet. 'Standards' were much larger flags, and the higher the owner's rank the longer the standard, carrying his own arms, badge and motto, and often St George's cross as well. The red upright cross of St George on a plain white background was by far the most common flag in military use. It remained almost synonymous with England from the time of the crusades and the Knights Templar in the twelfth century until the addition of the Scottish St Andrew's cross by James I in 1606 created a new Union flag. The rule of tincture forbade the charging of a red cross directly on the blue ground of the St Andrew's flag, so a thin outline of white remains around the St George's cross to separate the colours. A similar principle was engaged when the red St Patrick's cross was incorporated in 1801 and the present Union Jack came into existence.

Flags are a common motif in popular art, and are valuable to the artist and to us for several reasons. The first must be patriotism, of course, the immediate visual link with the home country and national pride expressed by showing the flag. Britain is lucky in having such an attractive and powerful design, for quite apart from the strong heraldic colours the tension of all those centrally converging lines creates a very powerful explosive or implosive symbol, drawing attention to the centre or radiating influence like a conventionalised star: ✳ . Cartoon characters swear unprintable oaths with asterisks, and that exclamatory poke in the eye is only partly reduced by confining it within a rectangular boundary. Perhaps it is the aggressive power within the design that appeals so much to certain extremist groups, for since the 1970s the Union Jack seems to have been hijacked to represent extremist nationalism, whether in Northern Ireland or on British football terraces. Items produced in the past to reflect a general, gentle love of country, are now invested with an unintended hard-edged political jingoism which, once introduced, is hard to shake off. A pity.

The same tension of converging lines, like the central point in a perspective drawing which attracts the eye inexorably in towards itself, is the basis of many designs and layouts which use flags as ingredients. Portraits of popular heroes are often surrounded by flags, and the favourite design is to have a radiating spray of flagpoles jabbing out from behind the picture, with the graceful drapery of the flags themselves pulled in towards the middle in a series of curves, like sections of an orange. It was a tremendously popular formula during the First World War, and masses of commemorative pottery and commercially embroidered greetings cards from the Front used it to great effect. Britain's allies had flags too and absolutely anything saleable was decorated with their bold heraldic colours in order to boost the spirit of the war effort, as well as profits. Japan was particularly welcome to the souvenir designer, for the concentrated power of the Japanese rising sun made an ideal design counterfoil to the criss-crossing of the Union Jack.

When that war finally ended the commemorative pottery industry had a last fling before the next coronation by depicting Victory enthroned, often heavily disguised as Britannia and again surrounded by the allies' flags. This design is close to the origin of the 'trophy' format, used in pictorial or sculptured work. A 'trophy' is defined in an old dictionary as 'a pile of arms taken from an enemy, or the representation of such a pile in marble, on a medal or the like'. When this pile was formally represented it usually had that same symmetrical arrangement, with the directional lines of the guns, swords,

A photograph that carries its own detailed caption within it. July 1989.

Flags seem well suited to embroidery in both colour and texture, and both soldiers and sailors employed them extensively to frame photographic portraits to take home as presents, or as souvenirs of their service. The picture also includes, at the top, a framed selection of commercially produced embroidered postcards. They were made in France and were particularly popular with soldiers during the First World War. They may also have contributed to the amateur tradition.

spears and flags of the vanquished focussed inwards to the centre of the pile. By a careful choice or change of the objects depicted, we are soon well on the way to a pictorial allegory of war and peace; or, with the addition of beehives and cornucopiae, of industry and prosperity. So, the trophy as a designer's concept arrived, the main feature of which was that sharp central focus. A portrait placed at that central point is a very powerful visual formula for success, for the figure is framed by a colourful design that enhances the picture as well as offering more generalised information about the individual.

PUB SIGN painters frame national heroes with flags and ensigns, they are used on trade union **BANNERS** to express international brotherhood, and for anything that features a royal portrait, like coronation or jubilee china, flags are essential. Sailors' nineteenth-century **WOOLWORK PICTURES** usually feature flags, both on their ship

The seasonal illustration for October in Thomas Miller's All Round the Year *of about 1835 in which the thatched rick is finished off with a little central finial of straw in the shape of a crown. Thatched haystacks have gone but there is a resurgence of interest in thatching houses, both old and new, and straw pheasants placed on the roof as a finishing touch are increasingly common.*

portraits 'dressed overall', or as a decorative surround. As photographic portraits became more common, sailors, and later soldiers, concentrated their embroidery efforts on making beautiful frames for their own pictures, or those of their loved ones. Once more the clear-cut colours and designs of flags and heraldry were perfect material for a neat colourful design, fairly easy to execute and yet telling the story of his travels and his service in symbolism which was immediately understood.

The use of flags, and of the Union Jack in particular, has received quite a boost in Britain in the 1970s and 1980s. The patriotic red, white and blue always comes out in force for coronations of course, and that of Elizabeth II in 1952 was no exception, especially as it was reinforced by the national spirit of the Festival of Britain. That sort of flag-waving went out of fashion for the following twenty years, and it needed a combination of influences to bring it back to popularity. The fashionable images of the 'swinging sixties' started it, and the commercially led 'I'm backing Britain' campaign of the early 1970s, that sought to promote British pride and products at home, continued the push.

The queen helped by allowing her silver jubilee to become a high-profile national event, supported in turn by Prince Charles stepping into the forefront of royal affairs. When he got married and had babies the delight of the popular press was unbounded, and the cohesion of royal family and public loyalty was once again very strong. Some of that modern loyalty was reinvested in the national flag, and the increasing influence and power of the European Economic Community made the population more conscious than ever of its British nationality. A quick successful war in the Falklands brought the Union Jack full circle, and photographs that appeared in the press of small houses draped with flags and bunting to welcome back the conquering heroes were strikingly similar to the same scenes enacted forty years before. Depending on the viewpoint, this was encouraging or bitterly depressing.

But much had changed in art and design, if not in spiritual values, and much of the present popularity of the Union Jack is simply that its powerful colours and proportions are in tune with current taste. Simple stripes in bold colours became a key feature of eighties designs, on clothes, in shops, on advertising packaging, and on coach and lorry liveries, and if the colours chosen just happened to be red, white and blue the designer immediately plugged into some of the underlying associations of the national flag.

The Union Jack appears on objects ranging from the greatest to the humblest, from the tailplanes of British Airways' jets to the milk cartons on the supermarket shelves, and although this is the world of the advertiser and some way from popular art, this common application is a factor that affects the flag's use elsewhere. Not only does the signwriter want to use it for patriotic or decorative reasons, but because it is fashionable as well! No wonder it gets painted increasingly on new lorries, whether they are international hauliers or not. The fairground painter, always chasing the latest trends, again incorporates the Union Jack, either as a continuous pattern or, more traditionally, as furled flags in the trophy position flanking a coat of arms on the waltzer cars. Meanwhile the Punch and Judy man still operates his puppets in a booth on the seafront with the royal arms surrounded by flags over the proscenium arch. Heraldry and its influence is with us for a long time yet.

STAFFORDSHIRE POTTERY FIGURES

ONE SUBSECTION of the British pottery industry is regarded as an important part of popular art: the mantelpiece ornaments produced in huge numbers in Staffordshire during the nineteenth century. Two features aimed the trade at the working-class market, the price and the subject-matter. Mass production techniques kept them cheap, whilst a fast response to topical events and customers' interests kept the figures selling well, and they now provide us with an endearing catalogue of popular taste. We have a gallery of heroes and villains who became famous enough for long enough to be worth commemorating with a saleable pottery figure, and little groups that illustrate the enduring problems of life in whatever century – love, family quarrels or drinking too much, all difficulties which can be helped with a little good humour.

The potters wanted to compete in the lucrative market for imported Chinese porcelain that was white, very hard, slightly translucent and very fashionable. However, they had a number of disadvantages. The Staffordshire Potteries came into prominence in the early eighteenth century because both clay for the pots and coal to fire them were found in close proximity locally, but the clay was reddish and relatively soft when fired and the finishing glaze was transparent. The potteries had given us the beautiful 'Thomas Toft'-style dishes of the late 1600s, with designs trailed on the plate in lines of contrasting coloured clays. This is the technique known as slipware. It demands confidence, and the results have a strength and freshness that make these 'chargers', with their lacework of lines and naive portraits of kings and queens, masterpieces of their time and extremely valuable collectors' items now. But they were in total contrast to the delicacy of Chinese porcelain, which was setting the fashionable standard.

Another partial answer developed in the seventeenth century was delphware, in which the red clay body was totally covered by a tin-based white glaze before any additional decoration was applied by brush, often in blue and in an oriental style. In Staffordshire the potters kept experimenting with mixtures of pale-coloured clays from the West Country, burnt flints and bones and different firing temperatures. Finally whitish clays were used almost exclusively, and the coloured glazes applied to them at last retained their brightness against the light body colour. To compete with the delicately modelled ornaments of Chelsea and Derby, the Staffordshire Potteries began to make a range of small figures in pale earthenware and stoneware decorated with the limited range of colours then available for underglaze firing. The figures were still aimed at the moneyed market, however, and their subjects were the fashionable Arcadian shepherdesses and pastoral musicians, although some humorous groups and rumbustious Toby Jugs offered a foretaste of what was to come.

Two Staffordshire pottery versions of William Hogarth's painting of David Garrick as Richard III, painted in 1745 but made more popular by publication of an engraving of it in 1746. By the mid-nineteenth century, however, the mercurial Edmund Kean was a more famous and more recent actor. He had played the part to great popular acclaim in the 1820s, so the potters gave Garrick a moustache and called him Kean. It was more topical and more profitable.

As the nineteenth century progressed, changes in society were echoed in the pottery industry. Living conditions and wages for the newly emerging urban working-class improved at last and many small potteries began to produce a range of downmarket ornaments for the mantelpieces of cottages and smaller town houses. In a period that started roughly with Victoria's accession, a flood of cheap and cheerful figures poured from the Staffordshire Potteries into shops and onto the trays of the itinerant image-sellers travelling the villages. The figures were modelled without much three-dimensional detail, and as they were designed to stand on a shelf against a wall they were more or less one-sided. For this reason they are often called 'flatbacks'.

They were cast from plaster of Paris moulds in great numbers on a production-line basis, dried and given a first biscuit firing before decoration.

A group of typical nineteenth-century flatback pottery figures from Staffordshire. They use a limited number of glaze colours, including the very typical cobalt blue of the gentlemen's coats, painted onto a white china figure.

A bold Highland hero certainly, but no name other than 'The Lion Slayer'.

By now more colours had been developed that could be painted on before the final glaze, the lead-based coating that fuses with the clay during another firing to give the overall glassy covering that makes earthenware waterproof. Finally more 'overglaze' colours could be painted on, but they needed yet another firing at a lower temperature to fix them. All were skilfully applied but at great speed, and some of the Staffordshire figures' charm is the daring brashness of the colours and brushwork, combined with the extreme fineness of the painted details of eyes and lettering or the 'sprigging' on a lady's dress or curls on a spaniel's coat.

The figures had a long lifetime, for several were still in production well into the twentieth century, and their subject-matter is a useful list of ordinary people's interests and obsessions during the period. Products showing animals have always been a favourite, both domestic animals – like sheep-with-trees groups or cow-shaped milk jugs – as well as the fairly fabulous ones like camels or zebras, or a patriotic British lion. Pairs of dogs in the standard Staffordshire pattern are still being made. Most of the figures, however, are human, with patriotism high on the list with portraits of royalty or military heroes like Nelson and Wellington. The idea of the simple rural life still appealed, and rustic lads still woo dairymaids, or both ride 'Off to market'. The seamier side of life is represented by several sensational murders that made national news, with depictions of the villain, the victim, and even the place where it happened. Actors act, Jenny Lind sings and lots of contemporary politicians and reformers declaim, many modelled directly from newspaper illustrations or popular engravings of the time. Folk heroes like Robin Hood or Dick Turpin seem to have been steady sellers throughout. Thankfully a large number of these pottery figures survive, both in museum collections and on many ordinary mantelpieces, as little icons of popular taste.

NATIONAL HEROISM AND POPULAR VILLAINY

IF THIS chapter were simply to list all the famous and infamous people who appear on PUB SIGNS and BANNERS, and as POTTERY FIGURES and SHIPS' FIGUREHEADS, it would already be getting too long. A quick glance at the index of the modern edition of Larwood and Hotten's *English Inn Signs* reveals over two hundred names that could rank for a listing, excluding kings, queens, princes and saints! Such a list would not be very useful, and would be pretty boring. What is intended here is a closer look at a few well-known examples that can be regarded as important or typical, in order to try and arrive at some useful and interesting guide-lines through the mass of names and history that have some relevance to popular art. Let us begin with words from some of the very old mummers' plays that are still in good voice all over the British Isles.

Room! Room! Brave, gallant boys,
Come give us room to rhyme.
We've come to show activity
Upon this Christmas time.
Acts of young and acts of age,
The like was never acted on the stage.
If you don't believe what I say,
Enter in Prince George and he'll clear the way.

Much as our heraldic lions were real beasts elaborated by the fancies of the heralds, some of our legendary heroes are the result of the same sort of transformation. Real people doing real deeds get transmuted by time and retelling into the sort of archetypes we need, both heroic and villainous, to illustrate and clarify life as we experience it or as we would like it to be.

A third-century priest converts the heathen in North Africa, and is finally beheaded for his beliefs by the Romans. He is canonised, and later his image is carried on Christian knights' shields and banners to the Holy Land during the crusades. From being the knights' saint he becomes a saintly knight, and as the crusaders slaughter heathen infidels, so he slaughters the dragon of evil and ignorance, incidentally saving the soul and honour of the ravaged country, personified emblematically as a young woman. Reworked versions in the thirteenth-century *Golden Legends*, in Spenser's sixteenth-century *Faerie Queen* and innumerable ballad sheets and chap-book versions in the eighteenth and nineteenth centuries give us the modern St George of children's stories and PUB SIGNS, an armoured knight on a white horse, thrusting a lance into a villainous dragon writhing underfoot. A pretty girl may be an additional embellishment. The power of the image is the simultaneous representation of several sets of opposites – good and bad, life and death, light and dark – and the lady adds the tension between pretty and ugly and man and woman. The combination of these parts certainly makes a strong symbol.

The only thing missing to make the knight a truly popular hero is a bit of human frailty, for nobody really loves a clever-clogs. This is no great problem for the George of the rumbustious MUMMERS' PLAY, for centuries of oral transmission and added topical comments have turned him into an image of strutting bravado, with some lively though barely comprehensible speeches to declaim. His character and name have merged with that of the English king, and he is called variously Prince George or King George, perhaps at the time an allusion to the heroism of George II in 1743, the last English monarch to lead an army in the field of battle.

Many a giant I did subdue;
I run my dagger through and through;
I taught them all courageously;
And still I gained the victory.
Here I draw my courageous hand,
Show me the man who dare me stand.

Enter the Turkey Champion, of whom more later.

Robin Hood, who also sometimes appears in the **MUMMERS' PLAY**, adds a more robust flavour to our perfect hero by treading an interesting moral tightrope. He is an outlaw from society for unspecified crimes, and for holding unpopular or unfashionable opinions. At that level he can represent anyone who feels they are the victim of tyranny or oppression. He lives, apparently very comfortably, in the forest as a free spirit in communion with nature, another attractive concept for urban people provided it never rains or gets cold. His background is mysterious, as befits a romantic hero, and no one is sure whether he is a nobleman in disguise or a yeoman who has made good simply by being strong, brave and very skilful with his weapons.

So far, so good, but the moral problem is that he goes about robbing people for a living. It is true that he then goes about disbursing the spoils to the needy, but we are left with the uncomfortable question of how much good is needed to balance the evil. We all know people richer than ourselves who could make do with a bit less – this is common justice after all. The dilemma is the definition of the line between richer and poorer, the politics between who should have more and who should have less and how to balance the account. The jester suggests to the disguised King Richard in *Ivanhoe* that 'The merry men of the forest set off the building of a cottage with the burning of a castle, setting free a poor prisoner against the murder of a proud sheriff'. Perhaps the ideal hero should be distanced above active politics after all, and his fallibility could be expressed by his occasionally losing a fight or falling in love with the wrong woman.

The outlines of a perfect hero are beginning to emerge. He needs to be a man of action and ability, a man of the people who rises by his own exertions but who is respected by both his master and his men. He must win battles, but carry some scars of mortality; he must fall in love with a beautiful woman, but the course of true love should not be too smooth even for him. If he could die at the moment of his greatest triumph the mythmaking would be complete. All that is needed is for him to say something memorable, invent a catchphrase like 'England expects that every man this day . . .'.

The life and career of Horatio Nelson were remarkably successful, but the survival of his name and reputation after his death is an even more remarkable phenomenon. His immortal memory can be divided into three main threads – what he did, what the country needed, and what the country did to him afterwards.

What he did was to become the most brilliant and well-respected naval commander in the country, respected by both the government and the sailormen serving under him. What the country needed were some decisive victories against the French, the traditional English enemy, who seemed frighteningly invincible under Bonaparte. Admiral Nelson's successes at Aboukir Bay in 1798 and Copenhagen in 1801 were tremendously heartening, and he was rewarded by being made a viscount, and quite rich. National pride and relief were almost unbounded after the victory at Trafalgar in 1805, for by decisively defeating the French at sea Nelson removed the immediate prospect of an enemy invasion and ensured a British supremacy at sea that lasted unchallenged for a century. But alas, the hero of the hour had been sacrificed on the deck of his aptly named flagship *Victory*, and the flavour of success was bittersweet. But what a death at the moment of triumph! What poetry in the pathos of last words uttered against a background of the smoke of battle, the pageantry of uniforms and flags, and the loyal bravery of bleeding men and powder monkeys! Here surely were all the ingredients of a bestseller, and so indeed it proved to be.

The Nelson memorial industry came into full production. Paintings of the death of Nelson appeared, and engravings after the paintings, and POTTERY FIGURES after the engravings. Cheap printed memorials were produced in great numbers, often featuring Britannia herself mourning her favourite son, whilst stone columns and towers rose all round the country, culminating in the creation of Nelson's Column in Trafalgar Square in 1843. Even this monument was not finally finished until the most famous animal artist of the day, Sir Edwin Landseer, had completed his four mighty British lions for the base in 1867.

When the ship retired from active service she too became an extension of the Nelson memorial business, and remains so to this day in Portsmouth dockyard. She is a fine ship and it was a fine victory, but still the niggling doubt exists whether this pyramid of sentiment and respect would have come into being if the hero had not lost an eye and an arm, had not been romantically linked with Emma Hamilton, and had not died at his apogee of success. No matter – the combination was irresistible, and more pottery was made to commemorate Nelson than anyone else except Queen Victoria.

It was a hard act to follow. Supremacy at sea may have been assured, but the land battle still had to be won and it fell to the other archetypal military hero of the nineteenth century to defeat Napoleon finally and decisively at Waterloo in 1815. Wellington, too, rose through the ranks, serving his time as a professional soldier in India before making his reputation in the Peninsular War, but it was his success at Waterloo that made him the most famous general and perhaps the most popular man in Europe. What Nelson had done for the image of the British sailor, the duke did for the soldier, and Tommy Atkins joined Jack Tar to become the folk heroes of the lower ranks.

Wellington did not die at Waterloo and he had to endure the indignity of being made first a diplomat, and then prime minister for two years, when he descended to being possibly the most unpopular man in the country. But he outlived that battle too, and remained commander in chief of the British armed forces for the rest of his life. He died in 1852 , a grand old man of eighty-three, adviser to the queen and a national heroic legend.

The death of the Iron Duke released a whole tide of public mourning which turned his funeral into a black pageant of extraordinary proportions, an occasion of national loyalty and lament that was not

An eighteenth-century chapbook illustration of the archetypal hero Robinson Crusoe. Daniel Defoe's book was first published in 1719 and became a bestseller very quickly. It spawned many other stories on the same theme of civilised man surviving wild nature and isolation, and obviously touched a very deep nerve of sensibility at the time.

equalled until the queen's own death half a century later. Business and Parliament were suspended for the day of his funeral, which took place two months after his death to allow time for the elaborate arrangements to be made. His body lay in state for three days; Temple Bar, gateway to the City of London, was transformed into a black-and-gold-draped funeral arch; and the interior of St Paul's Cathedral was equipped with tiered seating and had gas lighting especially installed. Most extraordinary of all was the creation of a huge, ponderous funeral car for the coffin's last journey: 10 tons (10.1 tonnes) of bronze and elaborate drapery encrusted with trophies, heraldry and allegorical figures of Victory to be used on this one occasion and kept

in perpetuity, as much a memorial to Victorian sentimental hero-worship as to the hero.

This national spectacle, seen by hundreds of thousands of people on every pavement, window and rooftop of the processional route, was intended to bestow an equal honour on the memory of the land hero of the Napoleonic war as had already accrued around that of the sea hero Nelson, but perhaps in their attempt to equalise the honours the organisers went too far. It was now virtually impossible to surpass such an honourable event or eclipse the heroic memory regardless of the achievements of any successor, and even the royal Prince Albert's funeral was a rather more subdued event ten years later. Despite Lord Robert's bravery and success in South Africa at the end of the century, the threat could not be compared with that from France all those years before, and Baden-Powell's Mafeking could still not be compared with Wellington's Waterloo. Britain had to wait for a different Battle of Britain in a different sort of war to find an equivalent sort of hero in Winston Churchill. (*To p. 66*)

(Above) *This delightful oil painting in the Museum of English Naive Art in Bath refuses to conform to any of the usual categories of ship picture. It is a portrait and a history in so far as it records the notable victory of the frigate* Indefatigable *over the French ship* Droit de l'Homme *in 1800, but it was surely designed to serve a more symbolic purpose as well to warrant such a panoply of mythological supporters at the event. It is neatly painted and lettered by a careful workman, but the drawing of the figures is naive and simplified to a surprising degree. A puzzling masterpiece.*

(Below) *A tribute to Nelson, published very soon after his death. It is an engraving printed on paper stuck to the back of the glass with an oil medium. When dry, the paper was damped with water and largely rubbed away, leaving only the ink and a very thin film of paper on the glass. Oil colours applied quite crudely to the back would then produce a very cheap and cheerful picture, with bright colours, clear lines, and a very long life if the glass did not get broken – as happened to the lower left corner of this example.*

SHIP PORTRAITS AND PIERHEAD PAINTERS

SHIP PORTRAITURE is a separate class within the generalised subject of sea pictures, for the sense of the ship as a symbol is less important than a factual account of the sum of its parts. Portraits of ships were painted for an initiated experienced customer, one who as owner, skipper or crew had a reason for requiring a record of that particular craft. The quality could range from the most academic to the most naive, from storm-tossed theatrical romanticism to drawing-board clarity, but if the number of sails was wrong or the ship flew the wrong flag it was a bad portrait and the customer would reject it.

This branch of ship portraiture was established in the eighteenth century but it reached its peak alongside the booming shipping trade of the

(Left) *A composition by Paul Eathorne of three ships belonging to Stevenson's fishing fleet of Newlyn, Cornwall, painted on the side of one of the company's refrigerated, articulated lorry trailers. As this book went to press he had completed painting eight separate vehicles, each with a different picture, and more work was promised for the future. The lorries are used to deliver fish to the rest of the country.*

(Above) *East Anglian herring drifter* Ocean Gift *at work. This is a watercolour painting by the prolific Great Yarmouth pierhead painter Tom Swan, most of whose paintings date between 1895 and the First World War. His paintings are now well known in the area, and this is a typical example of his recognisable style; but little more is known about the man than is expressed in his delightful, lively pictures.*

nineteenth century, when an increasing number of craft both large and small, tiny brigs and barges as well as the transoceanic clippers, carried an increasingly huge amount of goods. Each ship had its owner and crew, and each required a proud pictorial record painted by an artist. The trade survived well beyond the time when photography could have been expected to supersede it, for the last painters in this tradition were still working to the middle of the twentieth century.

Just as the boats varied in size and profitability, so the money available to record them was variable. Whilst the boardrooms of the large companies could afford several hundred pounds to employ a specialist seascape artist, the barge captain might be hard-pressed to find a few shillings to express his pride in his ship. But the market existed and increased, and a supply inevitably followed. There was a flood of stereotyped ship portraits that became a separate section of British popular art, the simplest of which form part of the folk art of the seafaring community.

In many ports around the country, and indeed all round the world, the 'pierhead painters' plied their trade. For an affordable sum they would supply the captain with an accurate portrait of his vessel to take home, and in most cases would supply it at great speed before the ship left on the next tide. Such specialisation and such speed led inevitably to slick formulas of technique and composition but, as with commercial craftwork in any field, certain combinations of master and craft sometimes led to art which was beautiful by any criteria. The majority of the pictures, however, were repetitions of a set technique of representation, one that could be easily learnt and copied. A large number of these paintings still exist.

Some of the artists remain anonymous, although modern research and enthusiasm has established many names and biographies. Some of these painters are known to have been ex-seamen, a great help in understanding and delineating the complexities of masts, sails and rigging of which the customer would have an intimate working knowledge. Mistakes in these practical details would be instantly criticised and corrected even if the sea and weather were painted in a surprising way, and many paintings are now very valuable

In Cornwall the ship portrait tradition has been turned into a striking and original company livery for the lorries belonging to Stevenson's trawler fleet. Each vehicle carries a different painting of one of the company's ships, worked up from a small snapshot and painted directly on the body by Paul Eathorne, an artist-cum-coachpainter from Falmouth. The cost is high but everyone in the firm, from the lorry driver up to the boss, is very proud of the paintings so one hopes this new, localised tradition will go from strength to strength.

'documentary' evidence of the working gear aboard ship. Many of the artists were self-taught, or were housepainters or sign-painters who apparently turned a hobby into a trade, and the directness and simplicity of their view, uncluttered by academic conventions of composition or historical significance, is certainly part of the charm and appeal of their work to modern eyes. A few aspired to a higher rank in the artistic world. Some success in a provincial port encouraged them to paint with a more historical maritime approach, and submit paintings to the Royal Academy. Most stayed at home, however, and continued to pour out paintings the popular way. Some are recorded as producing several hundred pictures a year.

The standard layout has a side view of the ship under full sail on a nice day. Occasionally a pair of pictures were produced, one in fair weather and one in foul, but generally single pictures commemorate a vessel under her full cloud of canvas. She will probably be close-hauled so that the viewer sees the full glorious area of all the sails and gets the benefit of the flags, ensign and name pennant streaming out astern, helping to hurry the ship forward to her mythical destination. The light is generally high and from for'ard to show up the sensuous curves of the billowing canvas to their best advantage, and the repeating pattern of sail piled on sail becomes the main abstract design of the composition.

The sea too is sometimes painted as a neat repeating pattern, this time of wave shapes, particularly in the simpler work. There may be a lacework of white-horse breakers across the lower part of the picture. Identifiable landmarks or lighthouses may be included in the background, restating the souvenir nature of the pictures. A considerable number of the early ones include another view of the same ship in the distance, showing the name and carved work around the stern as well as making a more interesting composition. Only a minority show an actual incident, a dismasting or a rescue, and these may establish a connection to the older votive pictures and models of the Mediterranean, tokens of prayer and thanksgiving presented to a church by a crew who felt that Divine Intervention had saved them from some catastrophe. It may be that the whole tradition started in this area.

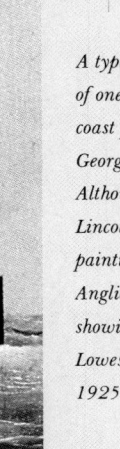

A typical example of the work of one of the most prolific east coast pierhead painters, George Race (1872–1957). Although originally from Lincolnshire, most of his paintings are of the East Anglian herring fleet, showing vessels like this Lowestoft steam drifter from 1925.

Many of the paintings of British ships in British collections were actually produced in foreign ports, for the trade was truly international. Shipping artists of the South of France, Italy and China, for example, were renowned among the sailormen but it follows that the more distant the origins of the paintings the more likely they are to be of larger, long-distance ships. Conversely, the smaller the vessel portrayed the more likely the artist is to be a local man with a corrrespondingly high understanding of that particular regional craft, and certain areas of Britain developed a more individual local school of painting.

Reuben Chappell of Goole in Yorkshire, for example, was particularly well known for his many paintings of Humber keels and sloops. The East Anglian fishing fleets of Yarmouth and Lowestoft supported several painters who specialised in recording the local fishing boats, and their work is especially interesting in continuing a sailing-boat tradition throughout the days of the steam drifter. The last pierhead painters will disappear only when boats stop going to sea and crews stop being proud of them, but the combined forces of photography, poor trade, and ugly steel boats have now virtually brought this lovely trade to a halt.

However, a foreign battlefield did provide the setting for the creation of one of Britain's enduring archetypal heroines. Great honour was awarded to Florence Nightingale for her pioneering services to nursing and to the wounded soldiers of the Crimean War, but perhaps her greatest battle and achievement was to overcome the entrenched forces of the male-dominated establishment. Any woman who could make progress against those odds was newsworthy and a populist romantic imagination, fed on centuries of female stereotypes, could be relied on to make her image beautiful and graceful. Even her name was eminently suitable. All that was needed to complete the picture was some symbolic attribute. The nightlight used to inspect her patients after dark was perfect, a light of knowledge and cleanliness dispelling ignorance and dirt. The concept of the Lady of the Lamp was born, one that still holds considerable power as a dual symbol of gentle nursing and practical female emancipation.

She held the middle ground for the female image whilst Victoria herself remained in command at the head of society. From young queen through devoted mother and distraught widow to venerable monarch, the titular empress of a quarter of the whole world, her general popularity grew throughout her reign, although she hardly qualifies as a heroine as here implied. She never had to overcome hunger or poverty, or to struggle bodily for a place in history, which was certainly the common lot for most of her subjects. One year after her coronation another young woman, four years her senior and born in the year of Waterloo, achieved fame and greatness as a popular heroine of the first order, for she certainly did come from the ranks of humble society and certainly earned her reputation.

On a September morning in 1838 Grace Darling and her lighthouse-keeper father launched their small boat into the storm to save nine people from the wreck of the steamer *Forfarshire*, bound for Dundee. It was a skilful act of bravery and judgement by William Darling and his daughter, and the journey had to be made twice to pick up all the survivors – although Grace was only needed for the first trip. Their courage was instantly recognised and it made newspaper headlines for months, but as the story was retold the part played by the father was conveniently reduced and the role of the heroine elaborated.

Popular songs of the time have her arguing with her father to force him to go to the rescue against his own judgement, and paintings depict her rowing alone through the storm. In recognition of her part in the rescue she was granted £725 and several gold and silver medals, but one wonders what her father's feelings were on these occasions. Pride in his daughter of course, and gratitude for his £175, but he could be forgiven if he felt somewhat overshadowed, for his daughter's fame seemed to undervalue his thirty years of service and the many other lives he had already saved.

Grace Darling became a national celebrity. She was plagued by visitors for the rest of her short life, and was even offered a well-paid engagement as an actress in a play called, predictably, *Wreck at Sea*; but with the true grit and self-effacement of the true heroine she remained at home, unmarried, to work with her father. Four years later the final chapter of the rich mini-saga was written, for she contracted tuberculosis and died in 1842. Her image could now be portrayed not only as the female archetype of bravery but of self-sacrificing purity as well. Her moving story, like that of Nelson, interweaves so many strands of basic emotion that it still has the power to support a museum to her memory, and a souvenir industry.

Once more, the separate strands are worth examining. The bravery of the act itself is understood, and underpins the image, and this quick analysis of the other elements of the heroine figure should not be read as any sort of denigration of the real achievements of real courage. But it is these other elements that turn that one act into a myth of enduring popularity, and differentiate it from thousands of other daily acts of selfless courage by thousands of other men and women.

Grace was an attractive young woman, part of a poor hard-working family unit, and had been brought up in the Christian beliefs so she personified several officially supported ethical standards straightaway. Like Miss Nightingale, she even had as pretty a name as could be wished for by a music-hall singing star. She was unmarried and so she was, it could be presumed, a virgin, a pure maiden unsullied by base passions or male corruptions, and her tragically early death preserved that purity in perpetuity. There was, however, one final attribute that was of paramount importance, and that was her connection to the sea and boats.

The British are an island race. We were all told so at school, and our first history lessons were probably about Vikings and Normans invading by sea or about Drake and Nelson defending us. We were also told that the sea and the navy had protected Britain from the ravages of war and occupation for centuries, unlike most other European countries which were regularly invaded by their neighbours, and this partly explains our general insularity and our inability to understand why foreigners do not understand us, even when we shout quite slowly at them. Until very recently the ship was the only way the British could get to foreign shores, to trade or to conquer, and the sea was what stopped foreigners getting to us. Not too surprising, then, that historically the ship – any ship – had a special significance for the British, and that Britannia is not complete without Neptune's trident in her hand and a ship offshore. A young woman in a boat performing an outstanding act of bravery is immediately a living emblem of Britannia, an acolyte of the national goddess.

Nelson and his men performed something of the same duty to Britannia as well. 'The wooden walls of old England' was a very popular phrase, for as well as describing the reality of the floating defence of the navy it also likens the country itself to a ship, anchored off the European coast, calm in majesty and power, but dangerous should any foreign upstart rattle her anchor chains. Britannia ruled the waves, and almost any picture of any ship could be construed as a proud British boast. Inside the wooden walls were the 'hearts of oak', another gentle nationalistic *double entendre*. It refers to the stout-hearted bravery of the sailors, who certainly did not disappoint the population during the Napoleonic wars – Jack Tar became and remains a symbol of bravery and efficiency, if with a touch of romantic raffishness. However, it was also a very apt metaphor and easily assimilated by the whole population, because English oak was simply the best timber for building houses and furniture as well as ships, and familiar to everybody. Oak trees grow for hundreds of years, and seasoned heartwood can last for a thousand, so what better expression to describe the hopes we had of our sailormen? The Hearts of Oak Friendly Society, instituted in 1842, drew on this imagery to decorate its membership certificates, and many other badges and insignia include some acorns and oak leaves as hints of what great oaks are still to come.

The fishing smack Daring *under full sail, a picture-model by George Burwood, a well-known Lowestoft pierhead painter and modelmaker. Undated, but probably from the 1890s. Making this sort of low-relief picture was also a popular hobby amongst seamen, and the works survive in satisfyingly large numbers.*

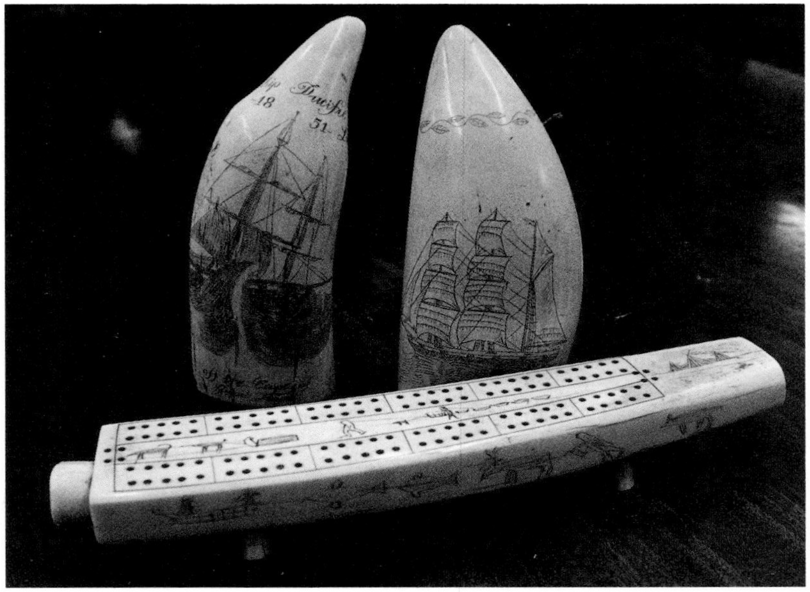

The cribbage board made from a walrus tusk has very simple drawings and may be the work of Eskimos, made for trade, but the two teeth are typical whalemen's ship portraiture. The ship Pacific *on the left is about to be overwhelmed by a huge wave; presumably this was an actual event as the precise location is given, but we can also presume the crew survived the storm to engrave the tooth.*

The sailor himself, of course, has a rather different attitude to the ship than the seaside visitor gazing dreamily at it from the cliff-top. His knowledge of his ship is intimate, from every ratline and yardarm to the rat-infested bilgewater; it is his home and his living, however temporary; and it is what keeps him out of Davy Jones' locker. Self-respect and the orders of the officers over him demand a high standard of work, and like any well-used craftsman's tool the ship has special characteristics of its own, and soon becomes an individual character to be cherished or, possibly, despised. The ship becomes a 'she' and her journeys give her a history. The crew becomes part of that lifetime, like a brother, a lover, or, in the case of a captain serving with his ship for a long time, like a husband. She has a name, and possibly even a pretty figurehead, and shares the same job and weather as the crew, so when there is time to make presents and mementoes for the loved ones at home a portrait of the ship is a natural choice.

The enforced idleness of certain parts of any long sea voyage encourages a number of time-consuming hobbies aboard ship, and we have a fine legacy of folk art from sailing ships. SCRIMSHAW, the engraving of drawings on whalebone and sperm whale teeth, developed almost to an industry on the North Atlantic, and much of the work includes a portrait of the ship. SAILORS' WOOLWORK also offers us some very spirited ship pictures, but some of the liveliest examples of the art of the seafarer are in the many sailormade ship models.

Full models, half models, or picture models set back in a seascape-painted box frame – all express a respect and love for the ship and the beauty of the sails and the wind. David Copperfield describes a wonderful hermaphrodite model-picture in Mr Peggotty's house that surely must be from Dickens' first-hand observation '. . . a picture of "Sarah Jane" lugger, built at Sunderland, with a real little wooden stern stuck on to it; a work of art combining composition with carpentry which I considered to be one of the most enviable possessions that the world could afford'. Boatbuilding details may be perfunctory or out of scale, for the artistic purpose of the hull is to support the mass of sails and rigging as the ship skims over the sea, not to plough through the water with the mundane load of coal or corn that was actually paying the wages. It is as much a poetic expression of the seaman's knowledge and trade as a portrait of a real ship. (*To p. 71*)

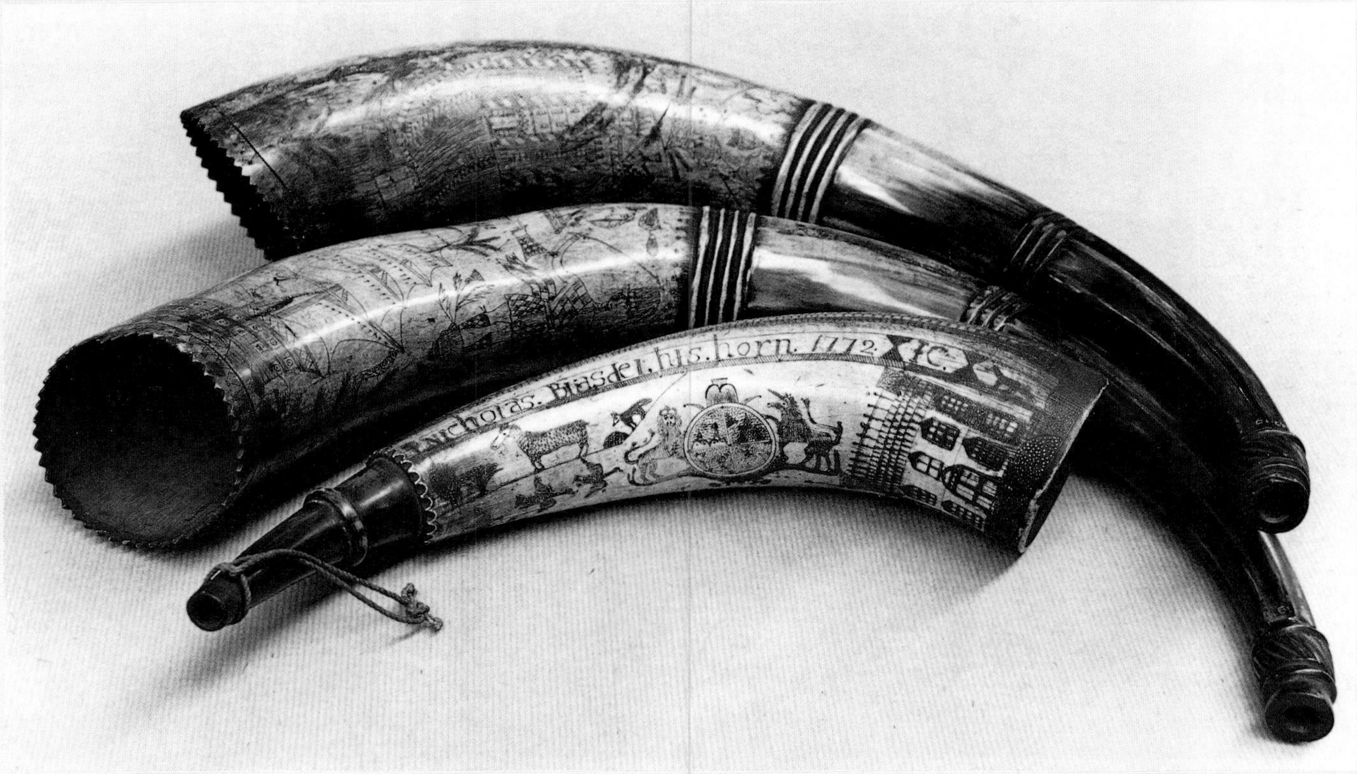

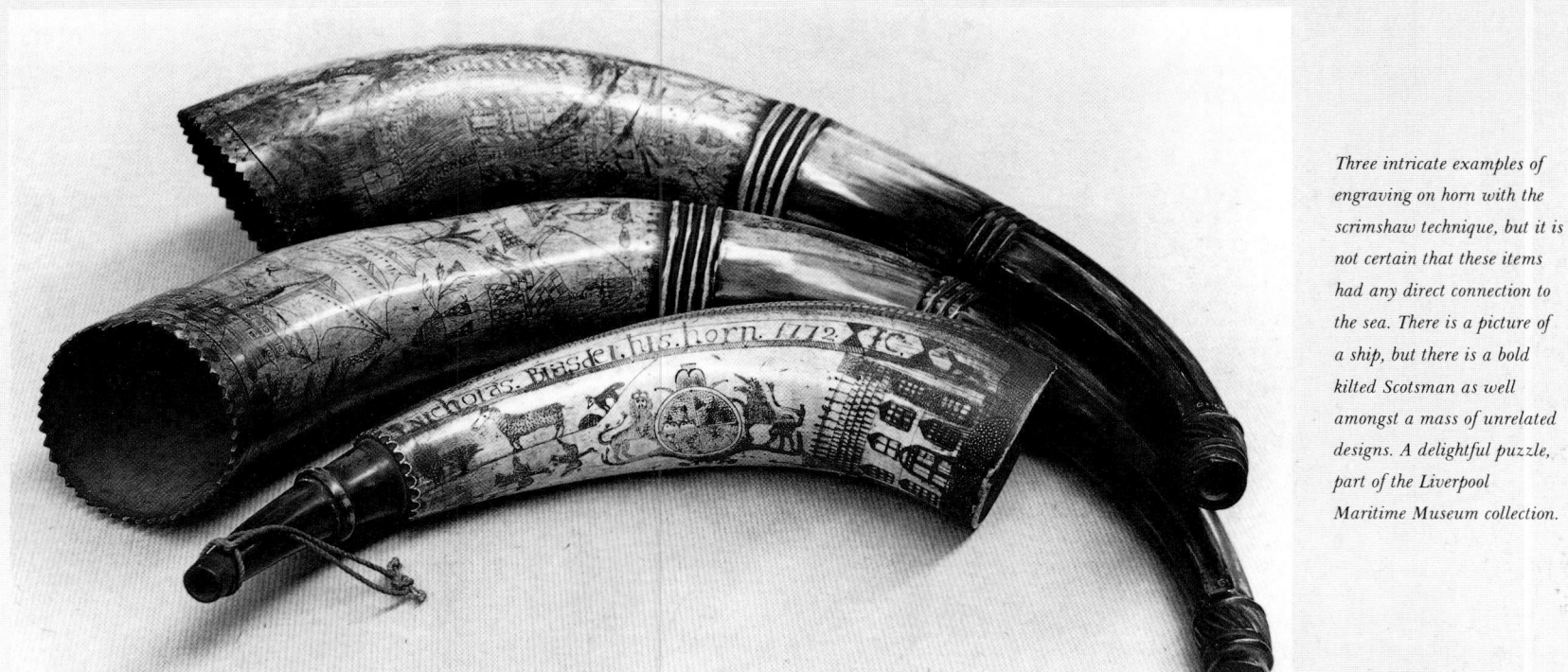

Three intricate examples of engraving on horn with the scrimshaw technique, but it is not certain that these items had any direct connection to the sea. There is a picture of a ship, but there is a bold kilted Scotsman as well amongst a mass of unrelated designs. A delightful puzzle, part of the Liverpool Maritime Museum collection.

SCRIMSHAW, THE ART OF THE WHALING TRADE

IN THE early nineteenth century a new craft was recognised and named amongst the seamen engaged in the whaling trade: the art of scrimshaw. The origin of the word is obscure but it came to mean carving and making objects out of whalebone or the ivory teeth of whales and walrus, and especially the engraving of pictures on them.

No individual part of the mixture of material, men and situation was new, except perhaps the pictures. Carving wooden trinkets and love tokens for those at home was a common hobby during the lazy periods at sea, and there were a lot of those on a round-the-world voyage that could last as long as three years. The use of bone inlay in that woodwork was well established. Carving in elephant ivory had been known and admired since the Middle Ages but it was, perhaps, an increasing familiarity with printed pictures on posters and in books that gave the whalers fresh inspiration and some patterns to copy.

As trade expanded a larger number of potential artists were brought together with an ever-larger quantity of available material. At some point before the 1820s, when the first dated examples appear and 'scrimshore' or 'scrimshandering' is mentioned in ships' logs, the craft had become a regular hobby, encouraged by the skipper as a valuable pastime for idle hands. It also became popular at home, and the whaler's sale of scrimshaw work became a useful bonus to add to his paypacket.

The peak of the tradition was at the zenith of the sailing-ship trade in the first half of the nineteenth century. As bigger steam ships were developed the number of men employed fell, and unplanned slack periods were less common on the more efficient mechanised whalers. Nevertheless the number of whales killed continued to rise and the scrimshaw hobby and trade declined only slowly. It continued well into the twentieth century, and modern examples are still available in the Azores.

Scrimshaw is an international folk art belonging to a trade more than to a country, although the Americans, whose whaling industry soon eclipsed all others during the boom time, claim it as one of their own indigenous arts. The Scandinavian fleet was also very large and, as there was a considerable mix of nationalities amongst the whaling crews, it is often difficult to ascribe particular pieces of work to particular ships or nationalities unless they are inscribed and dated. The British fleet came to concentrate on the North Atlantic, hunting whales for baleen as much as for oil. Baleen is the tough, fibrous, horn-like substance inside the whale's mouth that frays into a fine comb which strains small sea creatures from the huge mass of water taken into the mouth. Some British scrimshaw is worked on brown baleen as well as on the beautiful ivory-white teeth from the lower jaws of the sperm whale, and on the tusks of walrus.

Some of the carved objects had previously been shaped in wood – kitchen utensils for example, 'swifts' for winding wool and yarn, trinket boxes and stay busks – but to these were added the whale teeth and walrus tusks in their natural shape, simply presented as ornaments. Some of these carry the best artistic attempts, for the pictures are then the main reason for the object and absorb all the time and skill expended.

The compositions are designed to fill the tapering tooth shape. Straightforward portraits of ships are common, and we can presume that most are of the artist's own ship. Many of the most interesting ones show whaling in progress: pictures of ships, catcher boats and crews with the whale blowing or thrashing the water with its tail, all depicted with great spirit, for these are subjects drawn directly from the scrimshander's own experience. Ship portraits are often accompanied by emblematic figures of ladies representing Peace or Justice, along with the ever-popular Britannia with her trident and shield, or Neptune driving sea-horses. They were common nautical or patriotic images, almost obsessions, but they usually leave an impression of a second-hand interpretation of figures made familiar through engravings, membership certificates, or the transfer-printed commemorative pottery of Sunderland and Liverpool. However, some do have the direct and simple charm of the true naive artist.

Many of the designs engraved on scrimshaw work were from magazine illustrations of the period. They were transferred to the ivory by pricking the design through with a sharp needle or fine drill, or by pasting the paper to the tooth and cutting directly through the paper onto the scraped and polished surface. A finely sharpened jack-knife could do most of the work, but Herman Melville describes some of his whalemen in *Moby Dick* as having 'little boxes of dentistical-looking implements specially intended for the skrimshandering business'. The complete engraved drawing was rubbed in with ink, paint or lampblack and the surface was then cleaned and polished again.

Some of the more personal designs decorate objects that were clearly intended as presents to specific people, love tokens to the wife or girlfriend, and one particular practical object suited both this intention and the material of baleen or bone very well. This is the stay busk, a once-common item now lost to us in the history of costume. A busk is a flat, slightly flexible batten of whalebone or wood, 12–14in (0.3–0.35m) long and 1–2in (25–50mm) wide, that slipped into a long vertical pocket in the front of the working woman's stays. These may be described as a cross between a corset and a waistcoat, were worn over a thin shift, and without them the woman was not regarded as respectably dressed. The busk kept her tummy flat and the top of her corsage high and supportive, and provided the sailor with an intimate but perfectly respectable ground on which to express his affection.

Busks exhibited in museum collections display some of the very best of the sailors' art and, because they were treasured as such personal presents, they have survived in reasonable numbers (far more than the stays). One in the National Maritime Museum in Greenwich, and another obviously engraved by the same artist in the Hull Docks Museum can be interpreted almost as codebooks of the personal messages hidden in the imagery: the sailor's ship at the top, the romantic little cottage at home (real or just hoped-for?), the sanctity of a church, security of a castle, birds and flowers for grace and beauty, and a pair of pierced hearts resting on what looks, sadly, like the capstan used for weighing anchor before leaving again. One has the initials A. R. engraved in the design whilst the other bears A. M. L. Let us hope, for the sake of romance, that they refer to the same lady before and after her marriage to the artist, and that they are not from different ports.

Marine art is such a large field that it is easy to lose sight of the wood for the trees, and not see the ship for the shipping. At the base of our respect is the idea of the boat, the concept of creating an artificial shell which floats, to which mankind then trusts his life by travelling in it across stuff he would otherwise drown in. This is still big magic, and however sophisticated and distanced we get from that first discovery, we are still affected by the wonder of the floating object, the visible equilibrium between wind and water, between breathing and drowning, a wonder rediscovered in every lifetime through the bobbing plastic duck in the baby's bathwater. Small wonder that our forebears insisted on crushing up old eggshells so that witches couldn't use them for boats. A floating object responds to the movements of the water and the pressure of the wind, and immediately has a life of its own in tune with both. The sailor, who can work these immense forces to his own advantage, was seen by a simpler society as performing a brave balancing act with supernatural forces. The only thing between him and the fishy jaws of death is his boat, and to a landlubber the seaman is adventurous bravery personified. The ship can represent a much bigger idea, nature harnessed perhaps, or imperial power, but beneath the image there is always that balance between air and water, the tension between life and death. When Grace Darling rows her cockleshell into the storm those elements are starkly obvious, and her courage for the sake of her fellow man is dramatically heightened.

There is another less dramatic idea inherent in any picture of a ship under sail, for the picture has to be one frozen moment of a journey, somewhere between starting and finishing. It does not matter where to or where from, for these answers can be supplied by the imagination of the viewer; all the artist provides is a transitional moment that can be contemplated at leisure, a visual metaphor for time passing, or for the journey through life. This may account for the ship's widespread adoption as a decorative device on grandfather clock dials, especially on the inset dials that show the phases of the moon. The spaces between the moon faces, when the nights are dark, are usually painted with a seascape and ship on one side, and a landscape with a ruin on the other – simple temporal images of passage and decay.

That simple romantic symbolism takes second place, however, as soon as a ship is used as a setting for a story, or when a specific

In Cheshire, salt used to be made by heating large open pans of natural brine, pumped up out of the ground, until the solution became so concentrated that the dissolved salt crystallised out. Anything dropped into the concentrated solution as it cooled would collect a layer of salt crystals, which could be built up by subsequent immersions and coolings. The practice developed of making special armatures of wood and string, particularly depicting ships, to build up complex crystalline ornaments by this technique. The model of Alfred *shown here is a prime example of this very localised folk art, and is now on display at the Salt Museum in Northwich (photograph supplied by Cheshire Museums).*

occasion or action is represented. Then some prior knowledge of the event, some education in effect, may be necessary to share the artist's intention. When Turner painted his famous '*Téméraire* tugged to her last berth' in 1838 he was playing with both symbolism and historic sentiment. He was documenting the end of an actual ship's life that had included the Battle of Trafalgar and Nelson's finest hour, but his ships and sunset are also touching our sensibility with the intimation of our own end. Luckily popular arts rarely philosophise, and their ships usually set a course for the future with full sails and a fresh wind.

Concern for the future is also inherent in the idea of the Ark, the first boat ever built according to biblical mythology, and certainly one of its most potent images. Its prime purpose is to be a container, and the Latin origin of the word means a chest, equally applicable to the Shittim-wood box for the sacred writings as to Noah's big box of gopherwood for all the animals of the world. If we dare think of ourselves as enlightened and good, we can think of the Ark as a refuge for ourselves against future calamity. Religious imagery often equates the Ark with the church, ready to carry the faithful through the deluge of Armageddon, but a less self-righteous humanist is more likely to see it as a receptacle for ideas and values to pass on to the future.

Simpler still, and reinforced by generations of toys, is the idea of a complete miniature world where all the animals apparently lived in harmony with their neighbours, ready to come out, repopulate the world, and recreate the peacefulness of the Garden of Eden. It is a short step for a self-confident maritime nation's imagination to see its own ships as Arks, carrying goods or people, or even ideas, to the furthest corners of the world, helping to create a new golden age of peaceful civilisation. To do this Britain built bigger and better ships from the native oak trees, and fitted them with bigger and better guns with which to spread the word. Britain came to be represented by her ships, in reality and in image, in the high art of the maritime artists or the humble art of chap-books and cheap engravings.

In the nineteenth century a new image of the ship arrived. A mid-Victorian dictionary explains that a 'dreadnought' is a thick garment to keep off the rain, but HMS *Dreadnought*, launched in 1875 and one of the first iron-clad warships without sails, created a new and powerful advertising tradename, expressing everything brave and British and nautical in one word. Iron-clads and *Dreadnoughts* appeared in advertisements until the Second World War when the old warships were superseded by the sleek grey battleships and destroyers of the 'Senior Service', but the original *Dreadnought* still appears on England's Glory matchboxes and she still sails alongside the fully rigged ship *Britannia* behind the sailor's head of the Player's Navy Cut trademark.

The improvement in cheap colour printing in the second half of the nineteenth century had a considerable effect on all the popular arts, offering patterns to copy and new standards to emulate as it introduced more and more coloured pictures into everyday life through advertisements. As business expanded commercial artists were desperate for new designs to promote their products. They mined every well-established popular pictorial vein that could be expected to appeal to a broad public, ideas and images that had a proven track record like the monarchy or the national flag, and particularly Jack Tar and the wooden walls of England. Dependable clean sailormen started to advertise everything – matches, chocolate, soap, biscuits, mustard and, of course, tobacco in all its forms.

Grown in exotic colonies and imported in ships, tobacco seemed to have a natural affinity with the sea that was consistently exploited by the manufacturers, and sailors of the Royal Navy with their duty-free allowance and special techniques of binding it up in rope for preservation became the firm favourites of tobacco advertising. From the 1880s to the 1970s Navy Cut became synonymous with tobacco, and John Player's trademark became a portrait of a bearded sailor, with his hatband proclaiming him from a ship called *Hero*. He is a true survivor, for he first appeared in 1891 and is still going strong. Is this an example of the tenacity with which we hold on to the popular image of Great Britain ruling the waves, the inherent power of pictures of sailors, ships and the sea, or is it simply advertising's good luck? The trademark certainly struck a sympathetic chord with many people in the 1930s, when the sailor was popularly supposed to be a portrait of George V, sometimes known as the sailor king; and it certainly became a small but extraordinary part of the CANAL BOAT PAINTING traditions of the Midlands. It is only the unpopularity of tobacco that is now finally erasing that particular 'Hero' from popular culture.

A 1902 version of the famous trademark of the Imperial Tobacco Company, first registered in this form in 1891. Much pre-First World War advertising used the navy and its sailors as a sales image, but only this one survives unchanged.

To discuss heroes we have to discuss villains, for otherwise the see-saw won't work. We revere the hero and heroine because they exemplify what we would like to be like, how we hope we would behave in a situation that requires cool judgement and self-sacrificing courage. We take courage from heroic examples because they show what humans are capable of, which is uplifting; we fear, however, that we would be found wanting, which is a profoundly depressing thought. How can a villain help the situation? His deeds are also examples of what humans are capable of, which is a depressing thought as well, but we also know that although we are all capable of that sort of vileness, most people do not behave that way. We can compare ourselves to Jack the Ripper and decide we are quite nice people after all, which is a comforting thought to raise our spirits again. Either concept, hero or villain, can be read optimistically or pessimistically, and given the variety of private moods that are found within each of us, we probably need images of evil as much as images of good to keep us on a sane middle course. 'There, but for the Grace of God, go I', as the old saying runs.

King George's first heroic act in most of the English mummers' plays is to kill the villain, the Turkey Prince or Black Knight. The pivot of the play, the main action common to all, is the comic resurrection of George's opponent by the doctor, for otherwise the whole cycle of mummers' life stops. The same Staffordshire potteries that were making heroic figures of popular kings, generals and politicians were simultaneously making portraits of famous murderers. James Rush, who murdered two men in 1849, is featured and so is William Corder, who murdered Maria Martin in the Red Barn in 1828. In this case you could buy separate figures of the murderer, the victim and the judge, and a model of the scene of the crime. The printers were pouring out broadsheets on the latest murder, illustrated with a crude woodcut or two, and the more gory the story the better it sold. If it featured dismemberment as well it was a bonus for the illustrator. If not, one of the standard murder cuts could be employed again. Each murder is a news item, but the murderer in general is the constant factor of fascination.

The outer boundaries of this morbid fascination are marked by these stories of cold-blooded murder in the catchpenny prints, or the legendary wife-murdering Bluebeard of the chap-books. However, the emblematic villains that stay in something like 'affectionate' memory are those who are more enigmatic. They sum up some of the paradoxes of being human by showing at least a few traits that make their generally bad behaviour more forgivable and more believable, and their symbolism more relevant. Just as the character of Robin Hood is strengthened by being constantly on the edge of the law, so Dick Turpin is remembered for the amazing speed of his ride from London to York, rather than for the fact that he was trying to escape justice for one of several murders he had committed. Once again the highwayman is a gentleman in disguise and is, in the popular memory, a gentleman joining the commoners to redistribute wealth in a fairer if illegal way. In fact, although the murder was real the ride from London to York was pure fiction. (*To p. 76*)

SOLDIER AND SAILOR WOOLWORK PICTURES

MEN DOING embroidery seems odd to anyone who was brought up with the common historical belief that, traditionally, men hunted and women spun. We know that women were taught the fabric arts as soon as they could walk, and a working-class wife was expected to sew, knit and darn her family's clothes in every available moment, even during those which were nominally her leisure time. It is therefore not too surprising that her creativity should have emerged through embroidered and knitted designs for smocks or ganseys, and as her class or income rose she still used fabric and thread as recreation in her leisure time.

A typical but fine example of sailor's embroidery – an accurate ship, a strong formal framing design and a spirited rendering of the sea in stitchery. HMS Crocodile *was launched in 1866 especially to serve the British troops in India, and continued in that service until withdrawn in 1894.*

But the man's extra physical strength, as well as convention, had him out using heavier materials to earn a living: stone and wood, or the plough and scythe, and so there is unexpectedness about horny-handed working men using delicate needles to make pictures and pincushions. By the nineteenth century, however, British sailors had established a beautiful tradition of embroidered art which continued to the middle of the twentieth. Alongside this tradition, or possibly stemming from it, is that of soldiers' embroidery. Many keepsakes which were made for loved ones back at home survive from the First World War, but this may now seem to use the apogee of soldiers' work simply because there was an unprecedented number of deaths to be remembered by their handmade mementoes. The tradition continues in the modern practice of embroidering large regimental badges for the living-room wall. The surviving evidence of the 1850s, however, points towards a narrower fashion for just embroidering pictures of ships, the tradition now usually termed sailors' 'woolwork'.

Why was it so widespread? Some of the underlying reasons for the portraits of specific ships must be the same as those which demanded the work of the PIERHEAD PAINTERS, but the choice of materials may be more practical. They do not take up much space, and needles, coloured wools and a piece of cloth can be rolled up into a corner of the smallest kitbag, although some form of rigid tapestry frame must have been necessary too. Embroidery had been given a significant boost in popularity by the craze for Berlin-work in the early 1800s, when Germany developed a new range of dyes for worsted threads and started a significant export business, of both threads and designs, to England. This, of course, was a hobby for leisured ladies rather than working women, simply because it was so time-consuming, but time was exactly what soldiers and sailors wanted to consume with their pastimes; time off watch on long sea voyages or off duty in the barrack room. Their work was framed and took pride of place in many small homes; the result of so much effort was worth more in a poor household than a seat cover or a fire-screen in the big house. Many survive intact, perfect apart from some faded colours.

The usual sailor's woolwork picture covers the entire canvas with coloured stitches, which by

Neat craftsmanship on a neat version of the 'trophy of flags' formula around this sailor's photograph, which was taken before 1900 to judge by the uniform, although straw hats continued in use in the tropics for a few more years. Visually good for focussing attention on the central portrait, the flags also supply bold colour and perhaps a list of the countries visited.

The St Tudno, *a woolwork picture made by a member of the crew in about 1946. The ship ran a regular service from Liverpool to North Wales and is pictured here off Llandudno, one of her ports of call.*

their nature 'paint' the surface with a directional texture. If this technique is used sympathetically the pattern accentuates the movements within the subject, the bellying of sails and the wave pattern of the sea, and gives the picture an extra 'Expressionist' power that was only later to be seen in the brushstrokes of Van Gogh or Edvard Munch. The short strokes of each stitch can also give a sparkle to the colouring, like the broken brushstrokes of the Impressionists. But the main charm of these pictures is the simplification of subject-matter that has been forced on the untutored artist by a mixture of needlework technique and lack of academic drawing skills. Having been pushed so far from naturalism and towards an abstract pattern, the design will often incorporate other purely decorative items to fill the space: other small boats, or a border of flowers, or the ubiquitous spray of flags with the ship's name on a ribbon. As the century progresses the central image gets smaller and the borders and surrounding flags gain importance, until by the turn of the century the picture in the middle may be replaced by a photograph of the artist, and the picture becomes an even more personal memento, especially if the artist failed to return from active service.

As the design becomes more self-conscious and the picturemaking less important, the embroidery is just employed for the imagery – the flags or flowers for example – leaving the background cloth, chosen for colour and quality, as an important part of the design. The material is then more usable in a practical sense, and embroidered ships appear on cushion covers and sideboard runners. Working in the opposite direction, from utilitarian to purely decorative, during the same period is the heart-shaped pincushion. That developed its own language of love from at least the time of the Crimean War, being a present from both soldiers and sailors to their sweethearts at home. They used the padded heart as a base for such elaborate decorations of embroidery, beads and sequins that it was entirely useless for its nominal purpose. Some still express their real meaning, however, protected by the glass cases that preserved the memories of dead heroes, for their widows.

Most emblematic of all is Mr Punch, for he has been nothing but a glove puppet for a couple of hundred years, but despite a very bad press in the past few decades for his wife-beating, murderous character, he still has an important role in popular culture.

There are surely few husbands or fathers who have not been driven to distraction at some time by the arguments of a wife or the crying of a child. Never mind who was right or wrong – it happens, and is part of the balance of experience that is married life, a temporary frustration that is generally amply compensated in the longer term by conjugal love and the pleasures of family life. That does not alter the passion of the moment. When Mr Punch is faced with a nagging wife he knocks her down with an impossibly big stick and brushes her out of the way. It is a terrible thing to do and we join the children in booing him. We may not like it, but we understand it.

News of murders and murderers was always in demand from the sellers of catchpenny prints in the eighteenth and early nineteenth centuries, and each single-sided sheet would be headed with a simple woodcut illustration. To maximise the use of a printing block depicting a public execution, a space is left under the gallows to drop in additional blocks depending on the sex and number of the condemned. This one was used in London in 1823.

Then the consequences of his action come to haunt Mr Punch and he has to knock them down too and compound the crime. But the figure of the law is also something of an enigma, a fearful figure of punishment and dread who might want to catch us for the things we have done wrong, and it is something of a relief when he joins the body count in this black comedy. Finally Mr Punch cheats death and murders the hangman who has come to get him. 'That's the way to do it' says Mr Punch, and how we all wish it were as easy as that. He has become a hero of sorts by taking direct action and knocking all the problems out of the way, including death, and remains the same untrammelled hideous old man as he was before his troubles began. He is as immortal as St George and the Turkish Knight.

To complain that this ludicrous show is likely to encourage wife-beating or that it promotes violence as the answer to our problems is just as silly as saying that we can cheat death, or that Punch and Judy are not wooden puppets and unhurtable, however big the stick. The show is not a moral tale but an entertainment, a set of emotions made manifest, and made fun of, and made easier to live with. The fact that the show, only slightly altered, has stayed in popular existence for two hundred years merely goes to illustrate just how universal these emotions are, and how much popular art could be on the edge of supplying some universal help.

It has already been suggested in this book that there is likely to be more than one reason for the continued popularity of any particular image, and the same is true of a traditional custom or event. Traditional celebrations can be revived and restored by hard-working enthusiasts for a short time, but they will only take on a new life of their own if they are right for their new time and place. They need to strike some more powerful chord in their participants and audiences than that of being historically correct or a reminder of the good old days. Traditional customs that survive will have changed and adapted to their new age, but a strong tree has several roots and there has to be more than one influence at work to support an annual celebration continuously over several centuries. Ceremonies on the shortest day or the longest day are understandable, and special events for spring or the harvest, but nearly four hundred anniversaries for a failed political plan seems excessive. Bonfire Night is just such an event, however, centred around the image of the archetypal villain Guy Fawkes.

There are several strands to be unravelled from this still-popular festival of barely controlled anarchy. There is the Gunpowder Plot of 1605, certainly, when a group of fanatical Roman Catholics planned to blow up the Protestant king and Parliament. The general relief at their failure led to an annual holiday and a special church service which was not abolished until Victoria's reign. The anti-papal slant of the day was reinforced in 1688, for 5 November was the day when the future William III landed in England to depose James II and the date became a significant Protestant milestone.

However, the most violent anti-Catholic feeling dated back much further, to the Protestant martyrs in the reign of Queen Mary in the 1550s. Guy Fawkes was hanged for his part in the 1605 plot, but his effigy was always burnt. Was that in memory of those who were burnt at the stake? Perhaps, but burning was also the traditional punishment for witchcraft, and the fifty years following the Gunpowder Plot was a bad period for witch persecution. As that became discredited and the practice officially frowned on, something else was needed to fulfil the desire for public expiation and ritual cleansing. Public autumn bonfires to burn effigies of evil-doers may have been part of the answer.

There is another significant bonfire fact to take into account, one that stretches back to antiquity. James Frazer's massive work of anthropology *The Golden Bough* isolates four seasons of the year when ritual fires were particularly significant to the Celtic people of Ancient Britain, and one of them falls on the day that was later Christianised as All Saints' Day, 1 November. The previous evening, the eve of All Saints', or All Hallows Day – Hallowe'en as it is now universally known – was the most commonly accepted time for the spirits of the dead to return, and for witches to be abroad making mischief. By Guy Fawkes' time these old beliefs were being discouraged or repressed, but an officially sanctioned holiday to light fires and burn effigies

A Bowles and Carver engraving of about 1790, celebrating Bonfire Night, still recognisably the same tradition two centuries later.

found an immediate popularity with the same people who were being discouraged from lighting pagan bonfires or believing in ghosts. What did a few days' difference make, when there was still the satisfaction of making a massive source of light and heat at the end of the productive year, before the dark and privation of a cold winter?

Bonfire Night became a popular national festival, and has remained so ever since. In 1864 Chambers' *The Book of Days* remarked that Guy Fawkes' Day was unlikely to pass into oblivion as it

> . . . is observed by English juveniles, who still regard the 5th of November as one of the most joyous days of the year. The universal mode of observance through all parts of England, is the dressing up of a scarecrow figure in such cast-habiliments as can be procured (the head-piece, generally a paper cap, painted and knotted with paper strips in imitation of ribbons) parading it in a

> chair through the streets, and at nightfall burning it with great solemnity in a huge bonfire. The image is supposed to represent Guy Fawkes in accordance with which idea it always carries a dark lantern in one hand and a bunch of matches in the other.

The lantern and matches also appear in a late eighteenth-century catchpenny print from Bowles and Carver, but the paper cap with ribbons is an interesting detail, with its similarity to the strip-paper costume of the **MUMMERS' PLAYS**. The chairs of both illustrations are rigged on poles like a poor man's sedan chair, and are another interesting continuity, for Hogarth portrayed a very similar arrangement in his engraving called 'Burning ye rumps'. In this engraving stuffed scarecrow images of members of Parliament are being paraded and burnt at the time of the Restoration. Hogarth may have been recording a common form of contemporary political protest, an act that finds an interesting echo in the flag-burning of modern political demonstrations.

One of the reasons that Bonfire Night remained popular with the 'juveniles' was that, like the Mayday revels of the chimney sweeps, it was an accepted time for thinly disguised begging. As *The Book of Days* puts it, 'One invariable custom is always maintained on these occasions – that of soliciting money from the passers-by in the formula "Please to remember Guy!"' In more recent days that has become 'Penny for the guy, mister?'—and the request would be far more fruitful if a bit more effort were put into making the usual shapeless bundle of old clothes dumped in a pram look more human.

Chambers goes on with more interesting information about mid-nineteenth-century guys:

> . . . the 'Papal Aggression' in 1850 gave a new direction . . . Instead of Guy Fawkes, a figure of Cardinal Wiseman, then recently created 'Archbishop of Westminster' by the pope, was solemnly burned in effigy in London . . . In 1857 a similar honour was accorded to Nana Sahib, whose atrocities in Cawnpore . . . had excited such a cry of horror throughout the civilised world. The opportunity is also frequently seized by many of that numerous class in London who get their living no one exactly knows how, to earn a few pence by parading through the streets . . . gigantic figures of the leading celebrities of the day. These are sometimes rather ingeniously got up, and the curiosity of the passer-by . . . is generally taxed with the contribution of a copper.

Many of these threads of tradition, history and superstition are still present in modern Bonfire Night celebrations, but nowhere are they more obvious than in the spectacular torchlight processions, bonfires and exploding guys of Lewes, the small county town of Sussex. Anti-papal feeling has always been particularly high in Lewes because seventeen Protestant martyrs were burnt to death in the town in the 1550s, and some very old 'No Popery' banners reappear on the streets every year. Statues of the pope as well as of Guy Fawkes are ritually blown up, alongside other more topical figures whom the 'Bonfire Boys' of Lewes decide are against the spirit of toleration that they now officially espouse. All the collections go to local charities. The violent factionalism of the original religious fervour has been gradually diluted into a more broadly acceptable, anti-dictatorship stance. Much as old pagan festivals were absorbed into Christianity, and mid-winter Saturnalia became Christmas, so the flaming anti-Catholicism that remembered the martyrs has been gently shaped into a memorial to all who died to protect national freedom. The date is near to that of Remembrance Sunday, and all the processions begin their evening by moving to the war memorial and laying wreaths to the war dead. However, the extraordinary spectacle of pretend bishops officiating at a mock service, surrounded by flaming crosses held by fully costumed Viking warriors, Red Indians or Genghis Khan, is difficult to accept even for an English visitor with some historical forewarning. Then the set pieces explode, the streets fill with smoke and noise, the bands strike up and the Viking hordes, troops of eighteenth-century sailors and bands of war-painted Indians march away down the narrow streets under flaming torches and banners that proclaim 'Death or Glory', or 'No Popery', amid firecrackers and red flares. Foreigners and non-Anglicans have every reason to be totally confused, and not a little scared.

That, of course, is part of the intention – to create the scaryness of a ride on the ghost train or the thrill of a horror film, but on an enormous scale, live and rather dangerous. The public and participants can experience the bangs and flames of war and destruction, and can burn human figures without anyone actually getting shot or burnt at the stake; aggression is expressed without hitting anyone. Many people now argue that this is a celebration and encouragement of violence itself, but the opposing argument claims a sort of communal catharsis, a public release in a harmless way of tensions and emotions, feelings of anger and frustration that we all have at some time, and which need to be vented rather than bottled up.

Several things altered the nature of Guy Fawkes' Night in the 1970s and 1980s. The number of serious accidents made the government restrict the sale of fireworks to the public and draw attention to the dangers. This encouraged more large, public displays, designed and fired by professionals. Accidents at large civic displays are far fewer per capita than at small uncontrolled events, and costs in medical expenses and personal misery were cut dramatically. At the same time a network of companies grew which used the traditional festival as a starting point for multimedia theatrical events that blended the fireworks with music, lights, performers and puppets to create large, outdoor, seasonal shows. The bonfire was built to be the set and scenery, and probably the final spectacular funeral pyre for the villain; and Guy took on new roles all round the country, threatening the stability of the parish hierarchy or the international villainy of national power. Of course he has to be consumed in the flames each year, but each time the central source of power is challenged. Playwrights and actors always find it easier to create sinners than saints, to have more sympathy for the devil than the hero, and in the classical Bonfire Night scenario the members of the audience can momentarily allow their imaginations a world without government, without laws and without taxes. The enduring image of Guy Fawkes becomes an image of freedom from repression for one short, dark, anarchic part of the year, a release of frustrations that makes it easier to cope with reality.

There is, at the time of writing, another force for change at work which may have far-reaching effects. Bonfire Night has little significance outside Britain, and the Americans have always favoured Hallowe'en as their autumn festival. After draining Mothers' Day and Christmas of all possible profit, the formidable sales machinery of America is now trying to create a whole Hallowe'en season in which to spend money. Plastic bats, cobwebs and pointed hats are threatening to engulf the whole autumn period, with the fireworks simply pretty extensions to the party decorations.

Taking an even broader view, however, it may be that we are returning to the deepest root of the autumn fire festivals, filling an existing seasonal need that Guy Fawkes merely colonised for four centuries – though his annual death will probably live for many more years yet if the 'juveniles' have anything to do with it.

Lewes High Street in Sussex on Bonfire Night is like a mad pyromaniac's dream. Vikings, Red Indians and pantomime Zulu warriors hold flaming crosses aloft, and elaborate torchlight processions criss-cross the town before parading out to set fire to five massive bonfires on the outskirts. This photograph was taken at the beginning of the evening as the bonfire societies gathered at the central war memorial to consecrate the mayhem.

SHIPS' FIGUREHEADS

TO MOST people the subject of ships' figureheads conjures up a vision of a saucy carving of a full-bosomed young woman, bravely painted in heightened natural colour. There is some truth in this popular memory, but historically figureheads were just as likely to portray men as women, or horses and heraldic beasts, and many were plain white, ornamented with gold leaf.

The most elaborate heights of figurehead fashion were reached in the seventeenth and eighteenth centuries but very few have survived from that period, and much of our general conception of figureheads is derived from the numerous nineteenth-century carvings that are now collected in museums, or survive as signs on pubs or antique shops around the coast. Most of these are from smaller merchant ships and do feature pretty girls more than the naval figureheads, although the range of characters is still very wide. They are a better reflection of the popular taste of the time, however, for they were chosen by the shipbuilder or the private owner, whereas the complicated naval carvings were the choice of the Admiralty, designed as an emblem of the might of the navy or the prestige of the monarch. Not too surprisingly these followed and extended the classical architectural styles of their times, and allegorical groups of lightly clad gods and goddesses, tritons, nereids, caryatids and carved shells with their accompanying acanthus foliage spread all over the ship. Painted white for marble antiquity, or gilded for regal majesty, they may have been wonderful creations, but they could certainly not be called folk art.

The practice of painting eyes on the bows of a boat so that it can see its way ahead is very old indeed and was widespread amongst the Ancient Egyptians, Greeks and Phoenicians. However, this 'oculus' tradition is very different in spirit to that of making a separate representation of the ship's name and mounting it on the bows. In the first case the boat itself is the personage being given sight, the one whose powers are being extended, whilst in the second case the decoration is an additional emblem stuck on. It may later accrue personality or significance, but this was an intellectual investiture by the crew more than an inbuilt spiritual belief. The oculus tradition is still quite widespread, from the Atlantic where it manifests itself clearly on the prows of Portuguese fishing boats as actual eyes, or in a more sanctified way as little round religious pictures, right through to the China Sea where it persists strongly as part of the traditional decoration of Chinese junks. In Britain the idea centres around the anchor hawse-holes of coastal fishing boats and the inland river barges of the Thames, Humber and Mersey.

The figurehead tradition may owe some allegiance to this idea, but the more obvious ancestors are the Viking ships, whose bows reared up into carved dragons' heads, and the ships of William the Conqueror which are depicted on the Bayeux tapestry with lions and dragons carved at bow and stern. The introduction of the forecastle on bigger fighting ships enclosed the top of the stempost, and figureheads did not reappear until the development of the 'beakhead' – a low structure reaching forward below the bowsprit – in the fifteenth century. Then, for two hundred years, ever more complex and costly figurehead compositions of figures, fabulous beasts and foliage spread

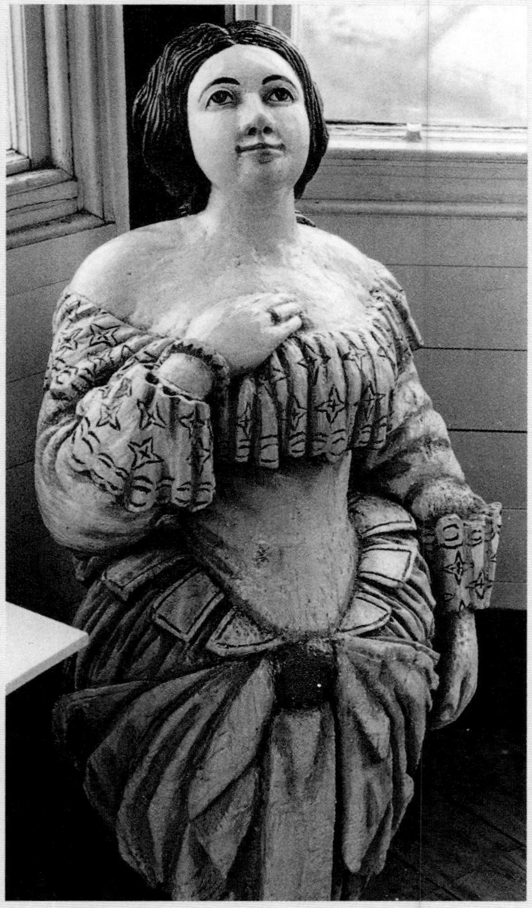

This lady, now standing more vertically than she was designed to do, graced the bow of the brig First of May *which was wrecked at Tynemouth in 1876. She now resides in the watch house of the volunteer brigade who rescued her crew.*

back around the bigger ships to meet up with more allegorical supporters and the royal arms around the stern galleries.

The fashion reached its extreme in 1637 when Charles I commissioned the *Sovereign of the Seas*, a ship half as large again as any that had been built in England before and truly smothered in gilded carvings, so much so that a lot had to be removed later to make her more seaworthy. She was a warship, but her weapons were as much the majestic display of splendour and royal might as her guns, humbling the enemy's spirit before a shot was fired. Unfortunately the cost was humbling the exchequer too, and there was a steady and sensible decline in the amount of extraneous decoration on all shipping from that time to the present day. But it only happened slowly and wooden sailing ships were always seen as attractive units to the end of their days, with the crisp black, white and gold leaf of the hull beneath a cloud of sails and rigging. At the time of Trafalgar the wooden walls of England were at their most refined and sublime, and the navy ships of that moment have become enshrined in popular culture as much for what they looked like as for what they did.

Heraldry, as one might expect, was a major design influence and the single lion emerged as the clear favourite figurehead image for European warships during this period. The low galleon beakhead was shortened and lifted up towards the stem, and the forward-leaning figureheads took up a higher, more vertical and 'rampant' position. Crowned lions, holding a shield before them or about to eat the French fleur-de-lis, were common images and one eighteenth-century example still survives as a pub sign in Martlesham, Suffolk.

In 1796 the navy ordered that all new ships should only be fitted with a billet head at the bows, a carved scroll like the top of a violin, but single figures kept creeping back. The ever-increasing merchant fleet was under no such constraint, however, and as warship figureheads retreated merchant ships went forth and multiplied them. The survivors form the bulk of today's collections and illustrate the highspot of the popular tradition during the latter part of the nineteenth century.

Heroes abound, either as specific people like Nelson or as generalised warriors like Highlanders, Turks, crusaders or Ancient Greeks, but as the century progresses the characters get more peaceful and portraits of the shipowner himself may appear. Wives and daughters are assumed to have provided the models for many of the female figures, although a classical allusion in the name allows the dress to slip off the bosom a bit and provide an acceptable pin-up for the crew.

But actual portraiture is only part of the carver's art, because the way the figure grows out of the stemhead scrollwork and the relationship of the swirls of clothing and hair to the whole sweep of the sheerline were just as important. As the faster clipper ships, with their raking bows, developed, the figurehead was again pushed forward and leaned out over the water. Many figureheads that now gaze piously at the sky were designed to stare ahead at the horizon. The 'trailboards' that linked the figurehead to the hull of the ship, both aesthetically and practically, were also an important part of the job, with running arabesques of ivy, vine, or acanthus leaves carved into them. A simplified version of this part of the tradition still appears on ships everywhere, from liners to **FISHING BOATS**.

Old ships' figureheads still survive in large numbers, collected and displayed in museums all round the country, but even these are only a tiny proportion of those that outlived their ships. Rescued from wrecks or breakers' yards they were stuck up as garden ornaments all over the place, and most just rotted away. Saddest, perhaps, are the nameless ones washed ashore after shipwrecks that left no one alive to tell their tale; and those

The skills of the figurehead woodcarver may also be seen and enjoyed on shopfronts in older shipbuilding areas, like this superb example in Tynemouth, Tyne and Wear.

(Below) *The drill hall and headquarters of the Roker Volunteer Life Brigade at Sunderland, one of the many shore-based life-saving organisations which came into existence in the middle of the nineteenth century. Their invaluable work has gradually been taken over by helicopters and an improved coastguard service, but a few brigades remain. Some have impressive collections of historic relics as well, and open their doors during the summer as private museums to raise much-needed cash. Roker has four figureheads, or 'wooden dollies' as they are known locally, and many interesting nameboards and photographs.*

(Right) *The figurehead of HMS* Satellite, *now on duty on the quayside of the Royal Naval Reserve shore station, HMS Calliope at Gateshead.*

used as memorials in churchyards, keeping watch over the bodies of the crew. Many, however, found a secondary use as shop or pub signs, and with continuous maintenance some still do their new jobs today.

The figurehead carver's trade never actually stopped, because as commercial demand faded away the restoration business began and new figureheads have been needed as replacements or replicas. The 'concept' of the figurehead has never died out entirely either and many shipping companies, large and small, passenger or commercial, emblazon their company insignia on the bows of their new steel ships. But it is a long way from the individual craftsmanship and imagination of the hundreds of ship carvers of the past, plying their trade in every shipbuilding port in Britain.

THE RENAISSANCE – A POLITE ROAD TO THE NAKED LADY

THE EFFECTS of the Renaissance were profound, and that word and the set of images that it introduced and encouraged recurs several times within this book. It is a complex subject, and many much better qualified authors than this one have defined and discussed it many times. However, this book does need to establish a few key dates in the development of the Renaissance and to mention some of the underlying concepts because they had a major influence on the arts at all levels of society.

The year 1500 is a memorable one from which to start, for many of the greatest painters of the Renaissance – Raphael, Leonardo, Michelangelo and Giorgione – were at work or just coming into their full creative flow in Italy, and several significant buildings by Bramante were complete and causing a stir in architectural circles. Then came the treatises by Sebastiano Serlio (1540) and Andrea Palladio (1570) which established the ground-rules of classical architecture, rules which affect the design of buildings, interior decoration and even furniture down to the present day.

At the centre of all these visible changes was a conceptual one, the idea that mankind was not perhaps so totally sinful that it always had to be represented as shameful, and that human beings and their works were worthy of respect for themselves. This new self-confidence started us proudly thanking God for what we are instead of constantly and humbly begging forgiveness. Whilst these confident thoughts were emerging, some of the most beautiful statues of the ancient world were being rediscovered and reinterpreted. Here were lots of different aspects of Godness expressed by representations of beautiful naked humanity, a historic legacy of art and government that had been ignored for over a thousand years by the Christian church's avowed fear of idol-worship. The time was ripe, a combination of prosperity and philosophy in a place where genius was at hand to build something new from the crumbling evidence of past greatness that lay all around. The late fifteenth and all of the sixteenth century saw the flowering of the Italian High Renaissance.

But Europe was a very large pond, and the cultural ripples from Venice and Florence took a long time to spread throughout the western world. Although the sixteenth century saw a number of buildings in Britain with classical pillars and porticos tacked onto the front of Elizabethan mansions, it was not until Inigo Jones came back from Italy fired by Palladian ideas and Sir Christopher Wren started his rebuilding after the Great Fire of London in 1666 that classicism became all-pervading. But having become a late convert, British architecture remained steadfast in its faith for the next couple of hundred years – until the eclectic Victorians added Pugin's version of Gothic to architecture again, and rediscovered Egypt and the East.

Underpinning this reverence for the art of the ancient world was the study of the classics, the study of the epic poems of Homer and Ovid in their original languages and of the philosophies of Socrates and Plato. These were the basics of a gentleman's education, and his thoughts were expected to be expressed to others of his class by reference to those classics. He would use allusions and allegories that

A ship's nameboard and stern carving now in Roker VLB headquarters, Sunderland. The vicious beak and claws rather negate the effect of the olive branch, but it is a strong piece of carving.

relied on a working knowledge of the myths of the pantheon of gods and goddesses of the ancient world; an allusion to one character or event in classical history could be philosophical shorthand for a whole set of attitudes and conflicts that the reader or listener was expected to have studied and understood. These characters and deities were waiting in the wings of the sixteenth century, waiting to be exploited by later poets, painters and sculptors as a valuable set of symbolic images.

With historical hindsight we can see that these philosophical and artistic changes were also entangled with the Reformation of the church and the emergence of Protestantism during the reign of Henry VIII. After a period of relative calm and prosperity during the reign of Good Queen Bess, the Puritans and the Civil War completed the cultural revolution. Their systematic destruction of all religious imagery changed the culture of the common people quite dramatically. What was swept away by that religious fervour is now quite difficult to assess. The dissolution of the monasteries in the 1530s had already removed some of the images related to the more blatant 'idol and relic-worship', but one hundred years later Puritan whitewash covered all the medieval wall-paintings as well and many more statues were defaced. Religious mystery plays were discouraged and anything that even hinted at pre-Christian celebrations, like the village maypole, was ruthlessly eradicated. As the whitewash is painstakingly removed by modern restorers it becomes obvious that the interior walls of the medieval church were smothered in colourful paintings and gold leaf and that a visit to church must have been a very rich sensuous experience, a ritual that blended music, incense, artistic imagery and intoned poetry, even if you could not understand the Latin. But the Puritan congregation was not going to church to enjoy itself or look at the paintings, but to prepare for death. *Memento Mori* – remember you die, so stop having fun whilst you live.

The intention is one thing but the result may be another, and removing the imagery does not remove the need that created the imagery in the first place. If you remove a whole panoply of saints from view and try to suppress the literature of saint lore without offering a substitute, there is bound to be something of a vacuum. Nature abhors a vacuum, says the physics book, and the imaginative capacity of mankind seems to obey something of the same physical rule. Remove the saints and their legendary exploits from everyday consideration, and their symbolic jobs will sooner or later be performed by another symbolic image. If what is available at the time is the fashionable pantheon of rediscovered, or reconsidered, gods and goddesses of Ancient Greece and Rome, then they will fill the vacancies in the imaginative needs of the people very well, thank you. As the Puritans removed religious imagery they created the opportunity for secular, historic and pagan imagery to dominate British culture for the next couple of hundred years.

The transformation was not as immediate and comprehensive as the foregoing sweeping generalisation might suggest, for the public has a long communal memory and many popular pastimes re-emerged after the Restoration. Many religious legends went underground to become part of folklore, but the pictures and pageants were gone forever. There was, and remains, a significant difference between the popular arts of insular Protestant Britain and those which grew under the continuous Catholicism of southern Europe. In Italy and France the classical art and architecture of the Renaissance enriched religious art; in Britain it tended to replace it.

Another piece of Renaissance culture that was imported from Italy was the emblem book. Once the idea had taken root that a human figure could satisfactorily represent an abstraction, it was a very short step to inventing new figures as emblems for contemporary concerns. With a knowledge of the Greek and Roman myths, the scholar could immediately identify an image of a woman with a plumed helmet and Medusa-headed breastplate as Minerva, the goddess of wisdom; brave but prudent, beautiful and virginal as befits such an ideal personification, but breastplated against the more squalid emotions that

ARS
Zeuxis ſæpius uvas pinxit, velut natura factas, quibus deceptæ advolabant aves. Eas Parrhaſius inſcio illo pingit velamento. Id Zeuxis animadvertens, credensque verum eſse velamentum, vult illud amovere. Ex quo apparet, Parrhaſium illi multo antiſtare.

TEMPUS.
Flurere interea pede tempora lapsa fugaci,
Tempora nec poſsunt lapsa redire tibi.

Art and Time, two out of over two hundred allegorical figures designed and engraved in the 1750s to illustrate the symbolism described in Ripa's Iconologia, *originally published in 1593 and continuously popular as a source of symbolic inspiration well into the nineteenth century. These illustrations are from the Hertel edition of the* Iconologia, *republished by Dover in 1971, which is recommended to the reader for the involved explanations of all the convoluted symbolism of mirrors, snakes, suns, moons, flames of inspiration and bare breasts of sustenance.*

An interesting confusion, probably wholly intentional, between Minerva and Britannia. Minerva, or her Greek counterpart Athene, is commonly used as a civilising and benevolent symbolic deity, and here she may be the personification of the wisdom of taking out fire insurance. The single pointed spear and shield and the aegis breastplate suggest this interpretation, but the British royal arms on the shield and the lion at her feet bring her back towards our national heroine. Or is the lion Leo, a zodiacal fire sign? Do note the calm rural serenity on the left and the panic of a disastrous industrial fire on the right, complete with horse-drawn fire engine at full gallop.

confuse normal human endeavours. With familiarity she stops being a character in a story and becomes just 'Wisdom' or 'Knowledge', and an extremely useful visual cypher. As the sixteenth century progressed, lists and descriptions of useful personifications began to be published as inspirational aids to poets and artists.

By 1600 the first edition of the book *Iconologia* by Cesare Ripa had appeared in Italy, a book which was immediately successful and became very influential. It was reprinted and translated continuously for nearly two hundred years, and spawned many copyists and competitors. Several other books of emblems appeared in England in the early seventeenth century, some of which were themselves reprinted many times to remain in circulation into the early nineteenth century. They describe hundreds of suitable figures and their accoutrements, to represent the virtues and vices, seasons and continents, and even emotional states of mind. The most useful and most popular books, and most plagiarised, were those that had illustrations to copy as well. These figures and ideas became a major influence on all the decorative arts throughout society, eventually affecting all classes. They have left us a legacy of images and symbolism, a portion of which still recurs in various branches of popular art.

Most of the more obscure imagery has simply disappeared into history as the fashion for understanding and expressing ourselves by this sort of convoluted symbolism has passed away, but there are still some remnants in use. Some symbolic images reflect our everyday experience or touch our emotions so directly that the symbolism is almost universally understood, and still relevant. The shape of an old-fashioned anchor is so expressive of its function, with huge hooks to dig into the seabed and save the ship from the rocks, that the image still expresses a hope of salvation even though the viewer may never have thrown out an anchor or even been to sea.

If the anchor is supported by a young woman in green who, according to Whittock's instructions to signpainters in 1827, should be '. . . looking towards heaven . . . a gleam of light from the dark clouds [to] give light to the face . . . ' the combined image is the standard representation of Hope. Her sister-virtue Faith is dressed in virginal white and carries a staff topped with a cross whilst Charity, in red, suckles one child and comforts a couple of older ones. Protestantism decreed that pictures of the Virgin Mary, the mother of God, should no longer be venerated, but her image and in some ways her attributes gradually became replaced by the triple deity of these three 'theological' virtues represented together. Faith, hope and charity were a particularly popular image of the nineteenth-century friendly society movement.

Death, and his close associate Time, have always had much of the best imagery – not surprisingly, perhaps, when the prime drive of religious thought is to prepare for death and so much of life is spent trying to avoid it. Death and Time each carry a scythe and although few people today have experienced a hand-cut harvest, with the rhythmically sweeping scythes slicing inexorably through a field of corn, the concept still has the power to send a shiver down the spine. The reality and purpose of that large, razor-sharp, curving blade is emotively clear to anyone who has ever cut themselves on the kitchen knife.

Skulls stare with brutal honesty out of many sixteenth-century wall-plaque memorials inside the church, and the death's head spread to the humbler gravestones outside in the seventeenth and eighteenth centuries. The skull and cross-bones then gradually give way to more polite classical euphemisms for death: the draped urns and broken columns still so familiar from hundreds of nineteenth-century municipal cemeteries. Another old graveyard image of time which still expresses its 'elemental' meaning quite graphically is the hourglass, with its trickle of sand pitilessly pouring away for its allotted span. It only had a very short period during the 1500s as a proper timekeeper, but it is reputed to have lived on as a guide for the preacher in his pulpit on Sundays. In the case of a very boring sermon this must have put the congregation in two minds about the passage of time. In its most emblematic version the hourglass is fitted with wings and time flies, but this seems to be a visual pun as much as a thought-provoking symbol.

The wings, however, are of fundamental importance, representing aspirations and concepts of a kind that are very difficult to express otherwise. Animals run about, eat, fight and procreate, all these being things that mankind can do, some better and some worse than his animal cousins. Fish can swim, and so can man, clumsily. On the other hand, birds can fly, but man cannot. Birds can escape into space, can soar and glide on the invisible wind, travelling up and down, over land or sea at will – but man cannot. All he can do is shoot a few, eat them and stick some feathers in his hair, but the act of flying is beyond him. No wonder that wings became the symbol of the desired but unobtainable and of magic and fairies, and the way that loved ones leave us in sleep, madness or death. Wings can symbolise everything that we want to be but cannot, and the places where we want to go but cannot. When heaven was thought to be up in the firmament, what was more logical than that the heavenly host must have wings?

Considering how many angels gaze down from the carved roofbeams in church, sing to us from the stained-glass windows, act as guardians and guides in thousands of religious pictures, and stand in mourning in most graveyards, actual biblical references to them are very few and far between. Even more surprising is how few of the references mention wings at all, and those that do give a description far removed from a pretty girl or a child, dressed in a white sheet with a pair of feathery wings. Isaiah's seraphims had six wings (Isaiah chapter VI verse 2) as did the angelic beasts of Revelations (Revelations chapter IV verse 8). Tobit's angel was indistinguishable from an ordinary man, and had to reveal himself as 'one of the seven holy angels', but Daniel was left in little doubt that he was in the area of the supernatural when he beheld 'a certain man clothed in linen, whose loins were girded with fine gold of Uphaz; His body also was like the Beryl, and his face as the appearance of lightning, and his eyes as lamps of fire, and his arms and his feet like in colour to polished brass and the voice of his words like the voice of a multitude' (Daniel chapter X verse 5). However did we arrive at the androgynous white wimp so beloved by the Victorian Sunday school, and still the standard image of the hereafter and the heavenly multitude?

White for unstained purity is easily acceptable, and a child for innocence when the angels are not avenging, but the wings are the significant addition. If God made man in His image then presumably He hasn't any wings either, so why should the angels be presumed to be like mankind, but with wings? In Ripa's *Iconologia* there are a number of allegorical figures who are winged, some of whom have angelic qualities. The Rational Soul, for example, is represented by a veiled woman who is nevertheless 'seen to be beautiful, since God, the

(*To p. 90*)

GRAVESTONES

THE HISTORY of British tombstones can be regarded as quite long or very short, for although the Romans introduced them during their occupation there was a gap of over a thousand years before the second phase of development happened in the seventeenth century. Finely carved memorials to members of the ruling class had appeared inside the church since the twelfth century, but outside gravestones appear quite suddenly in large numbers in the 1600s.

It is presumed that any earlier memorials were of wood and have long since rotted away, but why the fashion for stones took root so fruitfully and so quickly is still unclear. Many factors may have contributed, but prosperity probably ranks first – the beginnings of a middle class with the means to pay for some long-term memorials. The fashion certainly became part of the spirit of the time, and gravestones were common to all but the poorest graves by 1750. A new class of tradesman had also arrived, presumably from the ranks of the ordinary stonemasons, an artistic craftsman with his own traditions of technique and design in lettering and imagery.

A gravestone's most obvious job is to convey the names of the interred, and the style and quality of the lettering are the prime means by which the mason transmits that message. Borders, angel heads and poetry may be visual adjectives, but without at least the initials of the deceased the stone has no purpose. Some of the earliest have the most interesting layouts, although it is not always clear whether this is by design or default. Initial letters rise and fall above and below the line and letters may be joined together to form new lettering units; for example ligatures of N and D in 'and', or T, H, E written as one character.

Many layouts seem to be based on Roman stones, with spidery capital letters filling the space and nothing but a central dot to divide the words. There are plenty of ancient Roman examples in museums now, but most were recovered during Victorian excavations. It would be interesting to know whether our native seventeenth-century stonemasons were learning from local examples or historic designs introduced by post-Renaissance travellers and architects. Much lettering is badly spaced with the last word in a line crushed up to get it in, as if the sculptor had started chiselling away without any forethought, like a child with a piece of chalk. Surely he marked it out first? Spelling mistakes are more forgivable amongst a newly literate population, though odd or archaic spellings can lead a modern reader to think that these old craftsmen and their customers were of a much more ignorant or rural class than was in fact the case. What is amusing is the public admission of the spelling mistake by carving in the correction for all to see, forever.

From 1700 the average standard improves considerably, and influences from other contemporary lettering sources are apparent. The entwined penmanship of the writing masters' copy-books becomes obvious – particularly in areas where slate was available, upon which fine engraved linework was more practical – and the lower-case lettering of book typography becomes more common than capitals. Clearly these skills developed very unevenly across the country, for whilst high-

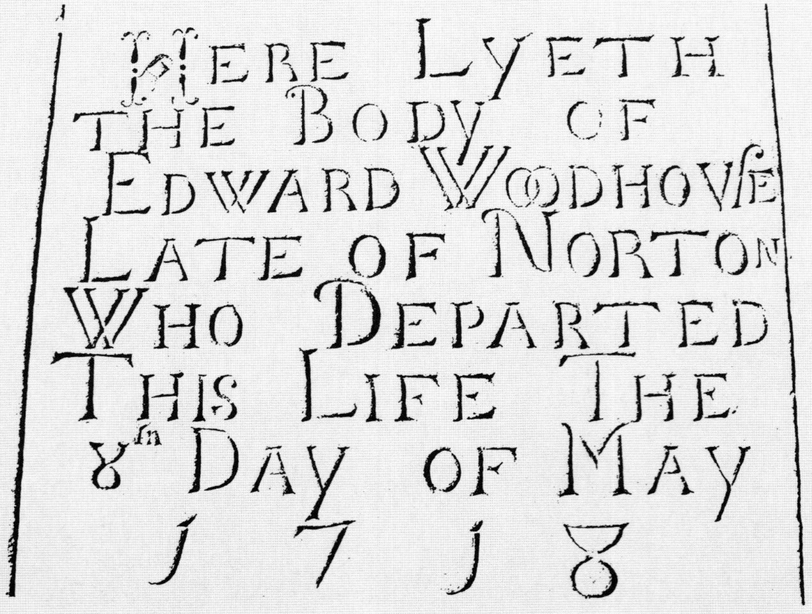

(Left) *How strange that a man capable of carving a permanent memorial in stone did not mark it out well enough in advance to be sure of getting in all his letters. Aston churchyard, north Cheshire.*

(Opposite page) *An attractive stone at Okehampton, Devon, although one more concerned with the successful naval career of the son who had it erected than the parents it commemorated. However, little extra letter-cutting was needed to add name.*

quality classical lettering was being produced in some places at the beginning of the century, extraordinarily naive and primitive designs were still being created, and presumably being found acceptable, in other areas at the end of the period.

By 1800, however, the standard is almost uniformly good, although it must be admitted that the whole subject becomes less exciting without the wilder eccentricities. The trade was by then organised more on a production-line basis, and continues only slightly abated to the present day, but we should not let familiarity breed contempt. The pleasure of discovering the very ablest gravestones can lead to a sort of selective blindness that ignores the huge mass of stonemasons' craftsmanship that is ranged round almost every churchyard in the country. The majority of these stones bear nothing but the lettering, and on their lettering they must be judged.

The commonest decorative addition is an engraved borderline round the stone, usually curving at the top to make an arch over the initial words 'Here' or 'In Memory', or it may frame an angel's head. As slabs give way to vertical headstones this concept of an arch or doorway gets transferred to the silhouette of the stone itself, which developed over the years into a wide range of ogee and wriggly Dutch gable-end shapes, eventually steadying to the standard lancet arch of the late Victorians. On the earlier square slabs the spandrel corners might contain any of the usual graveyard ingredients – skulls, bones, and hourglasses – or just bear a decorative device like a shell.

Occasionally the central space will contain an image that is directly relevant to the incumbent, a ship or a shipwreck for a sailorman or a basket of flowers for a gardener for example, but as the eighteenth century progressed another classical revival revitalised the imagery of the ancient world again and set new genteel fashions and euphemisms for death. Extinguished torches and broken pillars appear, and the funerary urn of a Roman cremation draped with a cloth – presumably the late patrician's old toga thrown over it in despair – is found almost universally. It is odd that this image found such widespread acceptance when the actual practice of cremation had to wait until the twentieth century before it became more than a fringe movement. The belief in a physical resurrection right there in the cemetery was widespread in Victorian times, and the scattering of ashes might therefore give God some insurmountable problems. It was even important to be buried so that you would be facing the eastern sunrise when you sat up in the grave.

By the end of the nineteenth century a new set of carved decorations occupied the top sections of gravestones: roses and lilies, praying or shaking hands, doves and Bibles. Anchors are not uncommon either, as a sign of a sailor's grave or a symbol of Christian hope. Larger free-standing monuments were in any or all of the architectural styles, but their cost and ostentation take them beyond the scope of this book. In towns even the simpler stones were really an expression of middle-class taste, for they all cost money. A huge proportion of the urban poor were buried in unmarked mass graves, only to be dug up within a few years to make room for more.

This nightmare of urban industrialisation, where most children died before they were five and most adults before they were forty, is in stark contrast to the calm and eternal peace we generally associate with the mossy stones and venerable yew trees of a country churchyard. Maybe it remained true in some rural districts. It is certainly true that the eighteenth century produced some beautiful examples of popular art and folk art on its gravestones, carved by local craftsmen in local stone, offering us a glimpse of a different relationship of life to work and to death. Then came imported marble, mass-produced designs and, finally, a limited choice of memorials offered from a catalogue. Today the little marble angels for a child's grave are imported from Italy, ready-carved, and the lettering is set out by computer and engraved mechanically by sandblasting through a stencil. Thank goodness the old stones were carved for eternity, and remain to us in large numbers.

Four Cheshire angels cut with the simplest possible line technique in sandstone graveslabs, dated between 1712 and 1774.

source of all beauty and perfection, created man in His own image'(!) She has wings to represent the 'lightness, the fleeting swiftness of the soul' and although the soul has no form or body 'it must be represented thus to men, who can perceive things only through their senses'. Old Man Time is winged, even when he is supporting the book of History, and his offspring Dawn and Dusk resemble cherubs, like the modern advertiser's New Year. The figures of Invention and Knowledge have small wings on their heads to symbolise the soaring power of the intellect, and Imagination has proper wings on her shoulders to 'suggest the spiritual, that is, mental, nature of imagination, for it is not earthbound'.

This powerful image of a human figure with wings has been in existence since classical times, and several gods and goddesses had wings as part of their personal equipment or symbolic attributes. Hermes had sandals with wings, almost a hieroglyphic for the attribute of fleetness of foot or speed. There were wings on the helmet of Hypnus, god of sleep – a very apt poetic equivalent for the drifting away of our waking control as we sleep. But the most probable inspiration for purely Christian angels, which first appear in the mosaics of the Byzantine church in the sixth century, was the goddess Victory, whom the Romans had inherited from the Greeks as Nike. Her wings are large and believable, and one gets the feeling that she would arrive amidst considerable sound and wind from those powerful, beating wings. She was the messenger who presented wreaths, representing the accolades of the gods, to human heroes and she has been a consistently popular figure ever since the Renaissance. With her pagan ancestry glossed over, she now stands mourning over hundreds of war memorials as the symbol of the Christian's hope of victory over death as well as the enemy. She can also be read as a symbol of war's victory over man's common sense.

The realities of biology or mechanics are not allowed to interfere with this image. The main reason that birds are worth eating at all is the breast meat: the powerful muscles of the chest, anchored to the deep keel of the breastbone, that provide the strength to fly. The power needed to force wings downwards and forwards against the upward leverage of the air at the wingtips is immense. Even the most cursory examination of a bird reveals a terrific wingspan compared with its weight, and wings large enough to lift a man in the air would have to be enormous, as well as requiring a breastbone sticking 2ft (0.6m) out of his chest. Also conveniently ignored is the fact that the forelimbs of the bird developed into wings, whereas the 'naturalistically' depicted angel has grown another set of limbs straight out of the shoulder-blades.

The response to this biological nit-picking is to insist that the standard angel image is solely a symbol, a line round a concept that does not need to conform to our biology or mechanics. This is fine, although it is still odd that so much care is taken to analyse and draw with accuracy real birds' wings, only to stick them unnaturally upon the naturalistic shoulders of angels and gods. On the few occasions when this common formula is varied, as on the impressed seal of the Freemasons where the arms of the supporting female figures become wings, or in Burne Jones' painting where he portrays Isaiah's seraphim as girls with six wings covered in eyes, the effect is bizarre and our conventional concept is severely jolted.

The shorthand version of Isaiah's vision in Renaissance art is to represent the seraphim and cherabim as infant faces with wings, sometimes with the full complement of six but more commonly with one pair, arranged either side of the head. These cherubs probably derived from a classical antecedent too, from depictions of Cupid and his playmates. The god of Love and the son of Venus, he was gradually demoted during the classical period from a powerful male spirit to a wilful winged boy, usually attendant on the affairs of his mother, or anyone else who was falling in love. He causes no end of human trouble by playfully shooting his arrows of desire at random, even blindfolded at times. He was often portrayed with other winged infants in antiquity, and the painters of the Renaissance came to use these little Cupids, or 'Putto', quite interchangeably in secular or religious art. If he has a bow and arrows he is Cupid or Eros, and is a comment on carnal love; whereas if he is merely gambolling in the clouds he is probably an angelic spirit singing the love of God. Even more confusingly he may become one with the clouds and represent the Four Winds, though a pretty, childish face with one wing on either side of the head was a common image in Britain by the 17th century.

Inside the church the winged angelic head is likely to ornament the memorial plaques of the local lords and squires any time from 1550 onwards, along with the hourglass and serpent of time and eternity, but it is not until about 1700 that it appears on the humbler gravestones outside. But in the outdoor examples a surprising and apparently retrogressive transformation has taken place, from sculpture to the simplest line drawing, and it took a whole century of graveyard fashion and development to turn the head back into three-

This solid cast-iron cherub angel mourns at the base of the memorial to Rebecca Price, the teacher at the local infant school for forty-four years, who died in 1889. There are several other iron graveslabs and memorials in this churchyard at Madeley, Shropshire, one of the iron-founding cradles of the Industrial Revolution, but iron monuments are unusual elsewhere. This fully rounded little cast angel may be quite unique.

dimensional sculpture again, albeit in low relief. The extraordinary naivety with which many of these angel heads are drawn poses a number of questions. Was it an entirely new trade staffed by beginners? This seems unlikely and unnecessary, considering the number of skilled stonemasons in business, yet there is a surprising contrast between the high-quality carved cherubs and anatomical skulls on the monuments inside and the simplicity of the engraved line designs on contemporary gravestones outside the church. No one expects a beginner or an apprentice to be as good as the master, but you do expect a similarity of intention, a sense of the one following and emulating the example of the other. These contrasting angels inside and outside are hardly talking the same language.

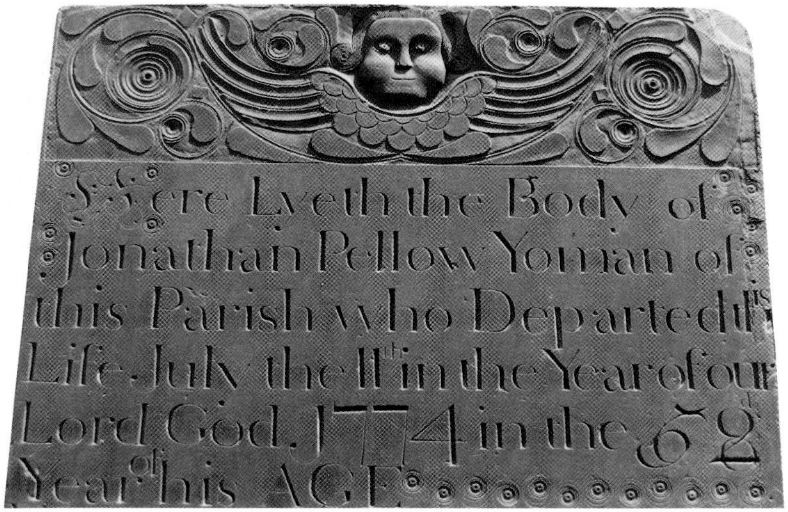

A very personal and powerful style of slate gravestone found over quite a wide area of central Devon. The mason obviously took great pleasure in cutting these bold whorls and scrolls as an extension to his angels' wings, and his style is instantly recognisable. He also seems to have invented a mechanical means to drill his little circular patterns, for they intrude into every available space. This example is at the church of St Thomas-a-Becket, Sourton.

Was there a pattern book for this newly emergent trade? It is quite easy to recognise the style of one craftsman or workshop in certain geographical areas, but the same basic formula of angel head and wings occurs throughout the country and, although there are variations, they do seem to have a common root. If there was indeed a printed book it obviously did not offer much advice on lettering, spelling or spacing, for in those elements there is no apparent similarity even to standard English.

The basic pattern has a full-frontal face occupying the centre of the top section of the headstone. A formalised pair of wings are spread out on either side, joined to each other below the chin by a frieze of feathers rather like a necklace, or a deeper band like a bib. The simplified faces stare out uncompromisingly and it is not really clear whether they are intended to represent the soul of the departed, a guardian angel or the spirit of the stone, or whether they are perhaps designed to deter grave robbers. The quality of the stone to some extent determines the fineness of the detail and how well the heads have survived, with slate leading the field in all respects.

As the century progresses the background is recessed more deeply so that the faces emerge in naturalistic, rounded, low relief. They become prettier and gain bodies, books, and trumpets, and rejoin the ranks of post-Renaissance, vaguely classical ornaments that form the mainstream of sepulchral sculpture for the next hundred and fifty years. But the earlier ones are still thought-provoking, and although many date from a century after the Puritan whitewashing of the church walls they seem to continue the linear emblematic drawing of the medieval wallpainter as much as anything else, without any noticeable influence from the rediscovered classical sculpture of the better educated.

Three angels are named in the Bible: Raphael in the book of Tobit, the originator of the idea of the individual guardian angel watching over us; Gabriel who announced the imminent arrival of John the Baptist and Christ; and Michael who appears in his most powerful role in Revelations. The annunciation, the moment when Gabriel announces the forthcoming birth of Jesus to Mary, was a favourite theme in medieval art and wall painting, and from the verse where Mary 'cast in her mind what manner of salutation this should be'

(Luke chapter I verse 29) the name 'Salutation' became a very common sign of hospitality and good news on inns and public houses.

The full depiction of Virgin and Angel was regarded as too Catholic an image for the Puritans, however, and some signs were converted to a secular meeting between a 'Soldier and Citizen' or a handshake; or the compound sign was simplified to 'The Angel'. Even so the angel may bear a scroll with Gabriel's words, 'Ave Maria, gratia plena, Dominus tecum' (Greetings Mary, most favoured one! The Lord is with you) as extra clarification of the origin of this most common **PUB SIGN**. 'Three Angels' may refer to Abraham's hospitality to three holy visitors in Genesis XVIII, but the multiplication of anything by three was a common way to differentiate otherwise similar signs: three crowns, three magpies, or three nuns. Like the 'Three Angels', the nuns were often used as a linen-draper's **TRADE SIGN**. Jacob Larwood and John Hotten, in their 1866 *The History of Signboards*, could see no good reason for this 'unless the long flowing garments in which angels are generally represented suggest their having been good customers to the drapery business.'

'The Three Living and the Three Dead' was a common church wall allegory, with three skeletons warning three kings riding by with some version of the regular graveyard rhyme 'As we were, so are ye, and as we are, so shall ye be'. It was one of a series of mural subjects that warned against vanity, like the wheel of fortune, or the dance of death in which the only certainty, regardless of riches, was death.

Above all, physically and metaphorically, was the Doom, a painting on the wall above the chancel arch. This showed the Last Judgement, in which the archangel Michael weighs the souls of the departed for admission to heaven. His emblem in this role is the set of beam scales, with a little naked figure on one side representing the human soul. The image was often elaborated by little devils trying to drag the soul side down, whilst the blessèd Virgin tries to tip the scales to the side of mercy with her sleeve, or a rosary. Here is another elemental image, this time of visible balance and equilibrium; an image immediately understandable to anybody who has ever used scales, bought potatoes by the pound or sat on a see-saw.

The other image of Michael is inspired by the book of Revelations, strengthened by Milton's 'Paradise Lost', in which 'there was war in

(*To p. 96*)

St Anne's Well, Buxton, in 1862, decorated to celebrate the arrival of piped water in the town twenty years previously thanks to the beneficence of the Duke of Devonshire. The detailed written description says the swan was 'made of the white rocket, extremely well modelled'. Presumably the 'two pretty white doves' on the oak branch were modelled in the same mysterious stuff.

WELL-DRESSING

MUCH OF Derbyshire is on high limestone hills. These provide fine pasture but no easy supply of water, and the older upland villages all developed around natural springs or a well. If it never dried up even in the hottest summer the villagers regarded themselves as well blest, and in return blessed the well and God with a thanksgiving service which, quite naturally, featured flowers as part of the decoration. Thus far there is little cause for excitement, but there are a number of features that make these 'well-dressings' very extraordinary indeed.

The first is the age of the tradition, for in one village it seems to date from time immemorial – or at least well beyond the living memories of those who described it as an ancient practice at the end of the eighteenth century. This points to a possible continuation of the old superstitious reverence for holy wells, whose waters were believed to cure all manner of ills, the sort of beliefs that the church and clergy were always having to denounce. Well-dressing may even be a continuation of pagan or Roman practice, especially as the early Christians had tried to absorb local customs instead of immediately stamping them out. Even if it only commemorates the village's survival through the Black Death in 1349, as is usually suggested, it is still a very old tradition.

The technique used to decorate the wells with flowers is also a surprise, for they are not arranged as sprays or in vases, but are pulled to pieces and the petals used to create elaborate pictures on wooden boards. The earliest commentators speak of wreaths of flowers 'placed in various fancied devices' but by 1826 Hone's *The Everyday Book* describes 'boards . . . cut to the figure intended to be represented, and covered with moist clay into which the stems of the flowers are inserted to preserve their freshness . . . arranged [so] as to form a beautiful mosaic work, often tasteful in design and vivid in colouring'. This is, in essence, the same technique as that used today. The boards, spiked with hundreds of small nails to provide a key for the clay, are soaked for several days in advance, spread with clay that has been puddled with a lot of water, and then covered with a mosaic of flower petals, leaves, grasses, alder cones and anything else that comes to hand, provided it is 'natural'. When the boards are erected their backs are covered in wet sacks to keep everything moist, so these beautiful coloured displays stay as fresh-looking as possible for the week they are on show.

The blacksmith William Wright and his friends pose by their handiwork at Tissington in Derbyshire in 1899 (photograph by courtesy of the Museum of English Rural Life, University of Reading).

The pictures are mainly religious in theme, as befits the thanksgiving nature of the ceremonies that now mark their installation. The relevant holy text is arranged around the design, with perhaps another entwined border beyond that. The boards are cut out in a series of architectural shapes that build into a temporary shrine around the spring or well (although most of the 'wells' are more like drinking fountains). Perhaps it is no accident that some of the oldest board shapes at Tissington strongly resemble Norman architectural details in the church, with added Victorian gothic details, for they have a strong flavour of a wayside chapel. Pagan altars or Shinto shrines are not far away in spirit either.

Possibly the most remarkable thing about the Derbyshire well-dressings at the end of the twentieth century is their increasing popularity, both

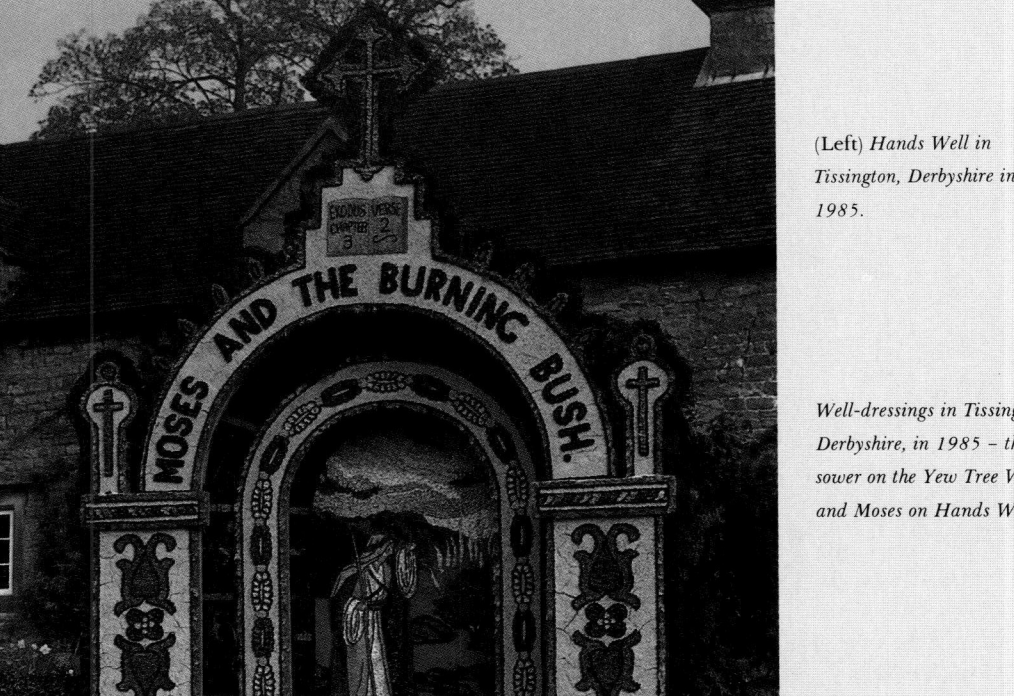

(Left) *Hands Well in Tissington, Derbyshire in 1985.*

Well-dressings in Tissington, Derbyshire, in 1985 – the sower on the Yew Tree Well, and Moses on Hands Well.

amongst the people who do them and those of us who go to visit. Tissington's ceremony was the only one regularly noticed in the 1700s but several more villages joined the tradition in the early 1800s. Some of these, like Youlgreave and Winksworth, were actually celebrating the arrival of piped water to supplant their erratic natural supplies, but they were truly thankful nevertheless and started decorating the sites of the new taps and stand-pipes. Between the two World Wars the number of well-dressing villages rose to fourteen and that remained the average until an increase of interest in the 1960s and 1970s doubled the number. Today there are even more, as more people appreciate the many worthwhile values that are almost inherent in the process. Each well-dressing requires a large number of people working together voluntarily with care and patience, and the creation of the decorated boards becomes an important social occasion. It can involve young and old, artists and non-artists, in an event that satisfies individual creativity and a sense of local pride. It may also be a bold public affirmation of religious belief. When one adds that a collection is usually made and donated to a local charity, the participants surely deserve a deep sense of satisfaction and our thanks.

heaven; Michael and his angels fought against the dragon . . . called the devil and Satan . . . [who] was cast out into the earth . . .' (Revelations chapter XII verse 7). Here was carte blanche for the artist, stirred by the poetic imagery of this apocalyptic vision, and the angel-warrior-hero emerges with wings and shining breastplate, wielding the sword of righteousness (perhaps even the flaming sword from the gates of Eden). What an inspiring image for Christian knights setting off on their crusades to the Holy Land in the eleventh, twelfth and thirteenth centuries; and what a fine model those helmeted knights, with their white surcoats bearing the blood-red cross of Christianity, offered to the artist for Michael, now canonised as the patron saint of Christian warriors, the church militant.

But the violence has to be tempered with fine judgement, and the sword of retribution in one hand is balanced by the scales of justice and mercy in the other in the complete picture of the archangel Michael. The elemental imagery is so good that it is no great surprise to find that the post-Renaissance emblem of Justice is a goddess-figure with sword and scales, and she still presides over many British law courts. There she represents the existing system and the power of the law and the government. However, on the trade union emblems and silk banners of the nineteenth century, where she was the firm favourite, she stood for the members' hopes and ambitions and was the embodiment of an ideal state towards which they aimed. In their eyes she was a very close relation to *Liberté, Egalité* and *Fraternité*.

One of the most significant images that the Renaissance/humanist revolution gave to the arts was classical clothing, or the lack of it. In particular, it provided an acceptable image of a naked woman theoretically divorced from any sordid idea of sex. Before the re-evaluation of classical statuary and ideas, the naked human being was only ever depicted as an object of shame, the embodiment of a sin, like Adam and Eve after the fall. The idea of accepting the body itself as beautiful, and capable of expressing some higher emotion without debasing the beholder by appealing to his more sinful emotions, was a difficult hurdle to jump but classical geography helped. Greece and Italy can be hot places and it was possible to imagine a way of life there, unlike northern Europe, that did not need constant clothing to maintain life and where one could publicly remove all one's clothes for reasons other than sinful behaviour. This was a good start. Then there came the conviction that the statuary was not really an attempt to depict real people but a series of idealisations, images of perfection towards which the viewer should aspire, and that these old outdated gods and goddesses must really be visionary parts of the One God.

Lurking beneath this was the concept of Arcadia, a pre-historical place of pastoral calm and balance, the golden age of Ovid's 'Metamorphoses' that blends in the Christian mind with the Garden of Eden before the fall, before shame and before the need for fig-leaf aprons. Whilst these ideas were becoming accepted, the emblem-makers were refining their symbolism, drawing their images from all these sources and finally defining nakedness as a positive emblematic state. Officially a nude woman need no longer be sexy, for in the *Iconologia* Ripa's Grace of God is 'a pretty agreeable Damsel, all naked . . . holding a cornucopia'. He explains that 'Her Nakedness denotes her Innocence that needs no external Ornaments. The . . . good Things she disperses, shew – that they all proceed from Heaven'. His version of Verity, or truth, is 'Naked, because *downright Simplicity* is natural to her'. Nudity is now expressing innocence and simplicity, instead of medieval sex and deceit.

The last rung of the ladder to respectability was Art. So long as paintings containing undressed people were disguises for poetic thoughts, expressing what were considered the finer qualities of human nature, they were art, and acceptable. It was not acceptable to paint a woman seducing a soldier, but if it were titled 'Venus overcoming Mars' it immediately became a beautiful allegory of the power of love over the misery of war; the viewer was no longer expected to see the flesh, only the poetry. There were a number of tacit rules for keeping within the bounds of respectability, chief amongst which was a degree of idealisation, expressing a striving for perfection and thus a homage to the spirit of humanity or to God.

A painting that expressed common reality was suspect, for if it was not aiming to elevate, to touch the finer sensibilities, it must be pandering to our coarser nature. This self-delusion and sexual double-think reached its most ludicrous stage during the Victorian period and on the walls of the Royal Academy, where innumerable maidens climbed in and out of Roman baths or were seen washing themselves

in streams, but woe betide the artist if the critics thought the girl resembled a real solid woman of muscle, bone and blood, to be looked at with anything less than clinical poetic detachment. The art world itself cracked open this delusion quite early, but the conservative world of popular art, and the art world as seen by the popular press, kept alive these conventions of what was decent and what was obscene for far longer. Nude pin-up photographs in the politer men's magazines of the 1950s still posed their models in raking light, stretched out to look like landscapes or reaching up to look like sculpture.

In terms of being used as an everyday image, the male nude has had a much easier time of it. Most artists, sculptors and imagemakers have historically been male so there was bound to be a generalised bias towards the attractions of the female. Men's bodies do not seem to promote the same sort of sexual response, even amongst women, and the almost completely naked man has always been an acceptable image of strength and pride rather than a source of shyness. His genitals dangling out at the front have always been a problem, and female readers may care to consider how modestly positioned are their prime sexual organs in comparison. But the man's area of sexual embarrassment is small and in art can be covered easily by the turn of a leg, a judiciously positioned shield, or the simple folds of a loincloth as on the conventional crucifixion. By contrast, women have breasts, and clothed or unclothed they are a key feature of the image of womanhood and make a much larger area of her body directly sexual, whether we interpret the word maternally or amorously.

If we ignore breasts' sexual attraction for a moment, which is what polite society tried to do officially from the Renaissance to the middle of the twentieth century, we are left with an image of motherhood, a source of nourishment, and – allegorically – a gift of sustenance. The emblem-writers describe all aspects of Earth or Nature as bare-breasted, 'for she feeds man and all things' or 'her naked breast symbolises the fountains of the earth'. Even the personification of Education is bare-breasted: 'A Lady at full Age . . . [who] . . . shews her turgid Breasts . . .' to denote 'the principal Part of Education to teach *candidly* and to *Communicate*'. Breast-feeding is likely to have been one of the first regular pleasurable experiences of our lives and one

This large painting on canvas is probably by A. J. Waudby, who did a lot of design work for the emergent unions in the 1860s. It may have been the prototype for the commercial bannermakers to copy, but it spent nearly a century in the office of the Operative Bricklayers Society as an artwork in its own right before becoming part of the collection of the Museum of Labour History, now in Manchester. Like the printed emblems sold to the members, and the old emblems from the Renaissance Iconologia, *every ingredient has a message to be decoded: the tools, scaffolding, quotations, moral pictures and, of course, the emblematic ladies. Truth is traditionally naked, honesty without any disguise and therefore so pure that a sordid thought should never enter our heads or hers; although it is more difficult to make a similar case for Science. Architecture is, of course, decently clothed in ancient classicism.*

unlikely not to have left a permanent impression on our psyches. Parenthood reintroduces the idea in adulthood in the opposite direction, and the image of mother suckling child is immediate and unambiguous. Even the early Christian church found the picture of the Virgin breast-feeding Jesus perfectly acceptable, the image known as the 'Virgo Lactans'. But it was too much for the Church Council of Trent in the middle of the sixteenth century which officially discouraged such unnecessary nudity, although the re-emergence of classical nudity was by then threatening to swamp many subjects with naked flesh and bare bosoms.

The final excuse for more visible flesh in art was a historical one, overlapping with geography again. Research revealed that clothing was indeed light and of thin linen in the hot countries of the ancient world, and that the 'himation' like a toga, and the 'chiton' like an underskirt, were often represented as blown close against the body or slipping off the shoulder in a moment of action. Artemis/Diana, chaste goddess of the hunt, may wear such a garment and the off-the-shoulder look, with one breast showing, gained an extra meaning as a symbol of action, of problems so pressing that the accidental disarray of her clothes, sexually revealing or not, has no importance compared with the vital business in hand. The apotheosis of this concept is Delacroix's vision of 'Liberty Guiding the People', in which a barefoot and bare-chested woman, carrying a rifle and the French tricolour, leads a gallant band of citizens over the dead and dying of the 1830 uprising. Her semi-nudity is nothing to them, nor should it be to us – except that, as we look at it in the contemplative calm of the art gallery, we can count up the layers of symbolic meaning to which we are heir: the comfort and sustenance of our mother, the expression of idealism in both ideas and physical beauty, of a sense of history and education, physical heroism and freedom from constraint.

One almost regrets to have to add that, beyond all these worthy sentiments, images of partially dressed young women are still quite nice to look at for half the population; that male half who were, until recently, almost entirely in charge of the official view of morality and aesthetics. One may wish that it wasn't so, but an overtly sexual interest underpins a great deal of the imagery of women in academic art, and more obviously in the popular arts. Whether this is a good thing or a bad thing is a question for the reader's own decision, and not for discussion here, but it should not be forgotten or disguised. At what point does admiration turn to lasciviousness, and visual enjoyment to titillation and lust?

Large naval **SHIPS' FIGUREHEADS** of the seventeenth and eighteenth centuries were very often elaborately carved allegories in the classical style, and included the appropriate nudity of sea nymphs. This set something of a precedent for the smaller but far more numerous nineteenth-century merchant ships, when single portraits became more common. Whether they are goddesses in classical undress or tight-buttoned-up-to-the-throat portraits of the owners' wives, their proud femininity suits the expression 'breasting the waves' very well.

The late nineteenth century saw the **FAIRGROUND** at its most extravagant, with its demountable gilded architecture exaggerating the decorative style of the French rococo of the eighteenth century, and loosely draped caryatids and atlantes support many organ showfronts. Their titillation was soon eclipsed, however, by the real dancing girls who paraded in front of the bioscope shows and peep-shows, suggesting that the customers would see more if they stepped inside. The superb book *Fairground Art* by Weedon and Ward (1981) describes 'Fine Art Galleries which included amongst their exhibits erotic tableaux posing as art', a convention that became enshrined in the Lord Chancellor's rule that nudes could pose in public, but were not allowed to move. If they pretended to be statues they were art, but if they fell off their plinth they were pornography.

Fairground Art continues, 'It is an extraordinary paradox that an age which felt obliged to cover even the legs of tables, could so freely ornament its public buildings and monuments with nudes of both sexes. Clothed in art, such figures were widely used in the fairground to decorate rides as well as showfronts. The hypocrisy went unrealised or at least unspoken.' Truly this is a version of the story of the emperor's new clothes, in an international artistic disguise. Even the angels in the churchyard completed their transition from messengers of God to post-Renaissance handmaidens by donning classical clothing, which of course obligingly slipped off the shoulder to reveal the bosom as the angel raised her trumpet. The confusion between the Last Judgement and the personification of Fame is complete.

SIGNWRITING

SIGNWRITING as a separate trade is relatively recent. It can be defined as painting lettering for outside signwork, and is really an offshoot of the signpainter's trade of the seventeenth and eighteenth centuries. There were then a huge number of carved, gilded and painted pictorial and heraldic signs in every large town, but they decreased in number and importance as literacy became more widespread and street numbering was introduced. What had been an extra became the mainstay, and tradesmen whose cards had added 'gilding and writing' to their main description of 'painter, decorator, and signpainter' became full-time signwriters by the middle of the nineteenth century. An increasing number of books arrived to cater for them, with ever more complex instructions for recreating the very involved decorative lettering of the time, and the business came of age.

The majority of signwritten lettering has always been simple, functional and rather boring. Today much of it is merely a large-scale version of designs done on paper in advertising studios, following a house style or a corporate logo, and although this copying needs a great deal of skill the amount of personal interpretation or addition by the tradesman is very limited. Much modern signwriting is also done very cheaply, in the fastest possible way, and creativity is constrained by this commercial pressure as well. However, the very speed and dash of the work of a well-practised writer always gives a personal character that adds some of the interest of handwriting, and immediately creates signs with some individualism, even if they are a bit rough.

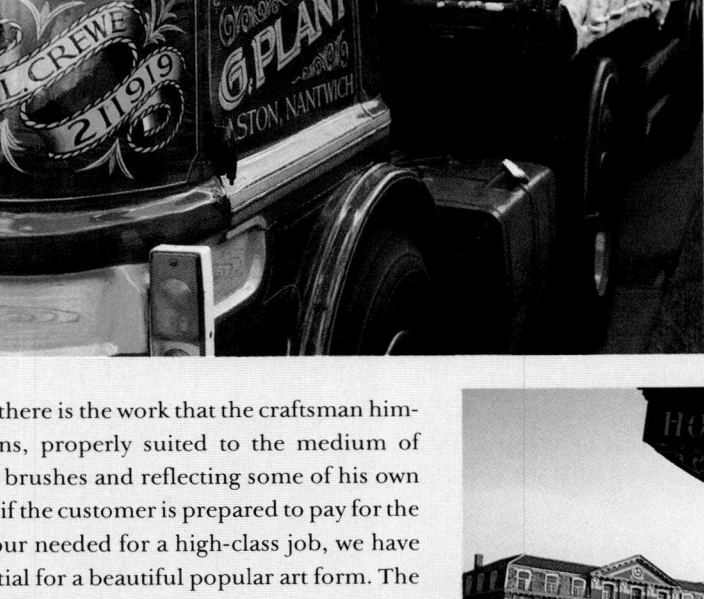

Traditional graining, lining, scrollwork and signwriting on a modern lorry painted by Saxon's of Sandbach, Cheshire, the home of Foden and E.R.F. lorries. The distinguished lettering is by the company signwriter Stephen Cranney.

An elaborate signboard by John Wagon of Dawlish adding a touch of exotic colour to the street outside the Queens Hotel in Newton Abbot, Devon, in 1985.

Finally there is the work that the craftsman himself designs, properly suited to the medium of paint and brushes and reflecting some of his own taste; and if the customer is prepared to pay for the extra labour needed for a high-class job, we have the potential for a beautiful popular art form. The craftsman still needs to have some artistic sense of his own but, as in so many of the traditional occupations described in this book, a young signwriter can be taught the tricks of the trade that avoid the worst mistakes. The artist-craftsman grafts his own ideas on a standard traditional practice that should shield him from disaster.

The majority of signwriters learnt their trade as apprentices, probably as part of a general painter's and decorator's training. Natural talent or particular interest led them to concentrate on signwriting if the opportunity arose, for it was better paid and provided regular work for the winter. There were a few large specialist signwriting

companies, but the majority of signwork was done by the one or two signwriters at the local painters' and decorators' firms in the larger towns.

In villages or rural areas one man could handle all the signwork over a wide area and some of these rural craftsmen, without interference or competition, have had a considerable influence on public art and design for miles around them. Personal touches or idiosyncrasies are added over the years to the basic core of knowledge and styles inherited from the master craftsman, or possibly from the man's signwriter-father, and a style develops that becomes part of the local culture clearly recognisable by the enthusiast, but accepted as the norm by the locals.

The apprentice system has almost collapsed since the Second World War and most of today's signwriters are self-taught or the result of shorter, intensive training courses. This has had the advantage of opening up the business to women, but it has rather broken the continuity of tradition that kept some very old lettering and decorative styles in continuous use until the late twentieth century.

The commonest letterform for signwriting is a capital Roman letter of some sort, with a noticeable contrast between thick and thin strokes, and with the end of each stroke widening out to form a serif. The possible variations are innumerable, and elaboration into almost unreadable complexity was a particular sin of the late Victorian writer who, with truly amazing skill, was constantly showing what was possible rather than what was sensible. Attempts to emulate fashionable three-dimensional letters in the early nineteenth century led to techniques of 'blocking out' and 'shading' painted lettering, a self-contained decorative technique which succeeded better than the real thing

The art of the signwriter emerges in the most unexpected places, in this case in a public lavatory in Southport. It would have been so much easier to do it straight, without flourishes, but it would have been so much more boring, both for him to do and for us to read for years afterwards.

and one which is still in regular use everywhere. With the excuse of these extra colours and tones the signwriter can create a colourful texture and design without losing legibility, and present an artwork as much as information.

This is a desperately needed approach, for the actual message of any signboard is only really required when it is read for the first time or until its meaning is learnt. For the following fifteen or twenty years of its natural life the sign is part of the street furniture, a considered piece of the human visual environment and as important as a mural or the architecture. A good creative signwriter deserves as much honour and credit as an artist or architect, although his work too often goes unnoticed.

As well as the lettering and the colours, a signwriter has several other design ingredients to deploy as necessary. The shape of the board and the layout of the lettering are important, and scrollwork and flourishes can be extensions of the alphabet or fill spaces between the lines. Painted ribbons can introduce swathes of colour across the board, curving lines of lettering can lighten the mood, and the signwriter might use the old decorators' techniques of graining or marbling for added interest in the background. Gold leaf provides long-lasting elegance, especially when the gold is applied to the reverse side of the glass, and many superb examples of Victorian craftsmanship still survive on shopfronts all round the country.

Unfortunately all these techniques are time-consuming and become progressively more expensive as labour costs rise, and few businesses can afford to give the craftsman a free hand. Happily, public houses increasingly see their lettering as part of their image of Dickensian Olde Worlde conviviality, and lots of high-quality old-fashioned craftsmanship has found a new home with competing breweries prepared to pay for it. Road transport firms, particularly in Scotland and the north of England, continue to use the lining, scrolls and deeply shaded lettering that they used to have on their horse-drawn vehicles, but in general signwriting has reached a fairly low ebb both in popularity and skill. There are still some natural artists at work, however, and some delightful unsophisticated artworks to be discovered as the illustrations show. The trade looks fairly secure, in its reduced form, into the new millennium.

HEART AND SCROLL

WHILST DISCUSSING mythological beasts and the emblematic way they can be drawn (see chapter 2), the zigzag line of the dragon's teeth was noted as an expressive mark, a sharp staccato and potentially painful bite:

This chapter's underlying theme is the zigzag's antidote, the curve, and more particularly the double curve that finally grows in on itself at either end to become a double spiral or a scroll.

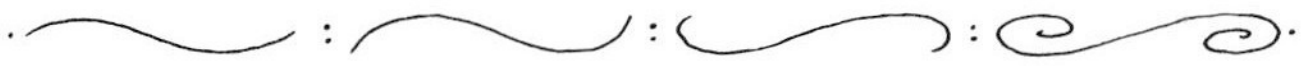

In 1753 William Hogarth, after a lifetime's work as a painter and engraver and years of consideration, published his *Analysis of Beauty* in which he stated his conclusion that one underlying principle of art was pre-eminent: the 'line of beauty'. This was actually nothing more than a graceful version of the diagram above. He was very well known by this time, although he never quite achieved the polite academic acceptance that he craved, and with his gift for self-publicity the arrival of the book caused quite a stir. Alas for poor Hogarth, his book was held up to ridicule. He was a hundred and fifty years too early for the serious consideration of abstract art but, as we rediscover this most basic motif recurring throughout decorative and folk art, we may owe him an apology. He had certainly touched upon a very significant and expressive key line, even if he went too far in asserting that so much artistic beauty must relate to it.

Part of his problem was that he only told half the story, for there is no contrast in that simple double curve to give it meaning or completeness. It is bland, a story without an action, St George without the dragon, and its smoothness demands some straightness or sharpness to give it its full graphic value. Connect two of these lines in opposition to each other and a tension is created, a contrast of angle and curve that is far more active and, for my taste at least, more positively interesting if not beautiful.

A series of curves cutting in from a straight line can be seen positively or negatively, as a series of soft bumps or sharp spikes, but for the purest satisfaction it is difficult to improve on two of Hogarth's lines of beauty meeting in the middle at a sharp peak.

It is a symmetrical balance of hard and soft, sharp and smooth, beauty and the beast, and this graphic equilibrium seems to be an important visual archetype. The spirit of this simple balance between curve and corner turns up in a number of areas of popular art and craft.

It is the shape of the ogee archway, much used in the architecture of Queen Elizabeth's time, and has appeared on a lot of simple furniture ever since as shelf brackets or as a decorative frieze along the top of a dresser. The classic example is the chamfering of the woodwork of nineteenth-century farm wagons, later taken to its most decorative and filigree effect on GYPSY CARAVANS. The corners of the woodwork are shaved away in a series of curves that leave the original face of the timber a more interesting shape, bordered by a design of contrasting curves and corners.

Basically a chamfer cuts off the corner formed by two surfaces at right angles to each other and transforms a square-sectioned timber strut into an octagonal one. This bevelling makes the strut more comfortable to handle and less liable to damage, as well as making the woodwork look much slimmer. Where timber frames meet at a joint they need to remain at their maximum size and strength, so the chamfer sweeps out to the original corner in a curve. The resulting surface shapes can add considerable beauty to the simplest utilitarian structure, for each original rectangular plane now has an elegantly dished outline with an added sculptural stress at each constructional corner.

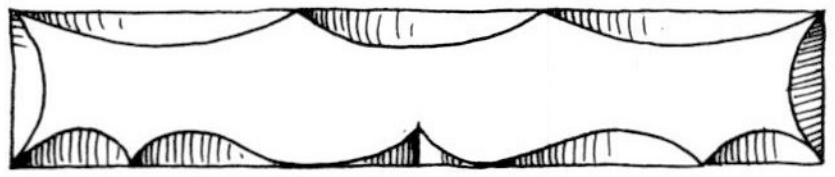

The usual reason put forward for this practice is reducing weight, but the proportion saved by this tremendous expenditure of skill and labour is tiny and one suspects that weight-reduction is an excuse rather than a reason. The real need is for grace and beauty, and a statement in pride of craftsmanship.

The traditional painting of wagons and carts also picks up on these curves and scallops. All the shapes may be picked out or echoed with coach-lining, thin lines of contrasting colour applied by small brushes with immensely long hairs that, in skilled hands, can paint a perfect line of even width and colour for several feet. This technique of lining transferred from horse-drawn to motor vehicles very well, and many carry small decorative designs on the cab or fuel tank that are direct descendants of the carved chamfering of wooden vehicles. The brushes control the design in some ways, for they cannot paint a very sharp curve without dragging the paint sideways and spoiling the neatness of the line. Decorative flourishes are therefore made up of a series of overlapping shallow curves, with the junctions between one line and another providing the sharp counterpoints. GYPSY CARAVANS, as one might expect, take the technique to glorious excess.

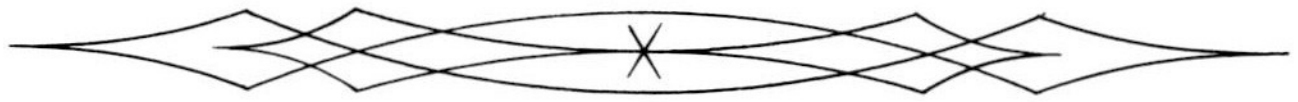

If this visual balance between curves and corners is recognised as a principle, a number of other decorative shapes in all sorts of fields can be seen to have a family resemblance. The central thin plank in the back of an ordinary kitchen chair, the splat, may well show a variation of the shape in its outline, as well as some central fretwork. The shapes of the tops of gravestones are often an elaboration of the ogee arch, the traditional stitching patterns on leather horse harness share the same basic patterns as coach-lining, and the horse-brasses fixed to the hames strap above the collar balance curves with points, inwards and outwards.

Farm wagons in certain regions had a very striking development of the idea on the frontboard of the wagon body. This was constructed of two layers of planking, but the outer one had a shape cut out of it to reveal the inner timber. It is purely a bold piece of decoration, unless there was some folkloric meaning which is now lost to us, and in its simplest and most common form the shape is two circles linked together by lines that swell out in the middle to form a peak at top and bottom. The design is known as the 'spectacles' decoration from its obvious similarity to these items. C. F. Tebbutt describes many variations on vehicles all over the country, from Scotland to East Anglia, in an interesting article in *Man* (1955). In its final and most degenerate form it was simply two circles painted on the frontboard.

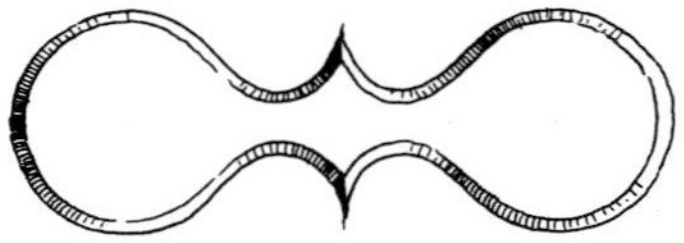

There are also a whole clutch of generically similar designs amongst the traditional paintwork of the CANAL NARROWBOATS. A few pieces of wooden boat equipment are actually chamfered, but the patterning is mainly in paint. The back of the cabin usually has a design strikingly similar to the top half of the farm cart 'spectacles', with the line sweeping down to the deck on either side like theatrical curtains, and strange little shapes combining curves and spikes appeared on the bows and rudders of many boats. The sliding hatch lids over the cabin entrance doors are usually bordered with bold scallops or chamfer shapes in green or blue, framing the resulting spiky centre shape which itself bears another symbol, like a charge on a heraldic shield. This may be a simple circle, a shamrock or, most common of all, a plain red heart shape. The reader should note that the heart is yet another subtle blend of curve and spike, and this visual balance may partly account for its eternal popularity. This point will not be belaboured any further.

The simple outline heart has been one of the most universal decorative symbols for centuries, and with the help of the Valentine card industry it is probably assured of a long commercial future. It is popular because people want to express love in its widest range of meanings, and to express it with one single graphic image. The heart can be a sign of love for lover, mother, brother, country or God. On car window stickers it is now advertising shorthand for loving one make of car, or Paignton or Torquay, but its commonest use is still as a courtship sign.

It is a sign that came into our visual vocabulary very early, perhaps before we even saw an ox heart in the butcher's window, and certainly before we read about Cupid and his arrows of desire. It was the first abstract symbol that some of us ever used, as we drew hearts, arrows and initials on the desk lid at school, or passed someone a grubby note ending 's.w.a.l.k.'. With adolescence we discovered how apt that sign could be – the heart beating faster in anticipation of a meeting, transfixed with a painful arrow of disappointment if we are refused. The heart symbol needs careful consideration.

There seems to have been a shift of emphasis over the centuries, and more particularly since the last century, from using the heart as a symbol of the soul to a narrower symbol of sexual love. Two hundred seventeenth- and eighteenth-century gravestones decorated with a heart for each of those interred below them have been recorded in one

A soldier-made memento in the Grosvenor Museum collection, Chester, with a decorative design created by a mass of patches, sequins and beads held on the padded cushion by steel pins. In this case the word 'pincushion' describes the way the item is made more than its purpose.

Late Victorian craftsmanship and letter styles on a fanlight window in the city of Bath. Gold leaf and paint carefully applied to the back of glass have a very long life but damp is the main enemy, and damage to this sign can be seen creeping in from the crack.

A tattoo design built with a series of overlapping emotive images – dagger, heart, flowers and blood, all delivered by eagle. This diagram is drawn from a full-colour design on the waiting-room wall of 'Saz''s tattoo studio, Warrington.

geographical area of Yorkshire by Peter Brears, who published his findings in *Folk-Life* in 1981. This appears to have been a regional design, developed by the local school of stonemasons, which finally became so elaborated that it blended with and disappeared beneath the fashion for rococo scrollwork and angels that flooded the country in the eighteenth century. The large concentration of heart-stones in one area is unusual, but the same idea crops up on stones in Devon and South Wales at least, and probably in many other areas besides.

By the beginning of the nineteenth century sailors were scratching hearts onto whalebone stay busks for their lovers at home, and rural swains were using them to decorate knitting sheaths, wooden spoons and other domestic objects as presents for their sweethearts. Wives and mothers used the heart quite often as a decorative motif in their elaborate embroidery on the collars and yokes of farmworkers' smocks throughout the century. The suggestion has often been made that the various designs reflected the occupation of the intended wearer, but there is no hard evidence for this belief and the hearts may simply be one element in a palette of designs available to the needlewoman. The heart rarely seems to be used alone as a significant image, but is repeated and outlined as a wide border design, or four hearts are arranged with their points together to take on the spirit of flower petals, or a group of leaves.

The heart-shaped pincushion, however, does appear to have had much more significance, although a heart stuck full of pins does offer some contradictory and peculiar messages. There may be elements of magic in its origins, for a number of real animal hearts pierced with pins have been found hidden in chimneys and under floors and they were undoubtedly being used in some magical curse or cure. In *Pins and Pincushions*, published in 1911, E. D. Longman and S. Loch assert that sailors were proverbially superstitious about bringing pins on board ship, believing they were little witches in disguise; but the same book also says that 'Sailors, when starting on a voyage, are still often given, for luck, heart-shaped pincushions stuck full of bead-headed pins in fancy designs' as a charm against storm and tempest. From the Crimean War until after the First World War it was a hobby amongst both soldiers and sailors to make large padded hearts to give to loved ones at home. (*To p. 107*)

MADE IN WOOD, MADE IN BRITAIN

ONCE UPON a time Britain had timber in abundance. We built ships with it, built houses with it, and – the beginning of the end – we started to smelt iron with it. Specialist woodworkers used timber to make furniture and vehicles for those who could afford them, whilst the majority of poorer people used it to make a wide range of domestic items for themselves. Because it was a familiar material and relatively easy to work, many homemade wooden objects display the extra care and decoration that lifts the purely utilitarian towards self-expression; the best examples, made with practised skill for practical use, sometimes as practical love-tokens, are folk art of the finest quality.

It is difficult to know where to stop in defining any of these areas of woodworking as folk art or popular art. Furniture-makers made tiny pieces for their children's dolls' house, or immaculate miniatures as emblems to be carried in trade processions, whilst the simple items of furniture produced in the hills of Wales or by the chair-bodgers in the woods of High Wycombe seem to be perfect pieces of folk art in their own right. Boatbuilders and shipwrights carved models of ships as a hobby, but so did sailors and canal boatmen, and the journeyman carpenter travelling light with only the essential ironwork of his tool kit had to create his own block planes and chisel handles before he would begin work. Some of these are far more decorative than practicality demanded. Trade skills often shade imperceptibly into a hobby, and into the pleasure of creation for its own sake, or for the pleasure of another.

Some of the larger-scale woodworking subjects are fairly easily defined and **FIGUREHEAD, FAIRGROUND** and **SHOP SIGN** carving are discussed in other sections, but the remaining mass of smaller wooden bowls, boxes, biscuit moulds, butter pats, ornaments and walking-stick handles are usually lumped together under the unlovely word 'Treen', coined by Spenser to describe something made from a tree. The term was adopted by the collector Edward Pinto, whose extensive collection of woodware is now housed in Birmingham City Museum, and since the publication of his books, *Treen* in 1949 and *Treen and Other Wooden Bygones* in 1969, the name has been widely accepted. Within the wider subject two particular subsections of amateur woodcarving have been collected and documented quite extensively: the knitting sheaths of England and the wooden love spoons of Wales. Taken together, with their similarities of size, material and intent, they provide a useful catalogue of British folk art designs and techniques.

Knitting sheaths are generally pieces of wood about 6 or 7in (152–178mm) long that are tucked into a belt or waistband on the knitter's right-hand side. The top juts forward and has a hole drilled in the end to receive one of the steel knitting needles used by countrywomen to make gloves and hosiery, an extremely important part of domestic industry throughout the eighteenth and nineteenth centuries in all the wool-producing districts of the north of England. The sheath is thus an extension handle for the needle and, fixed in the belt, an extra hand for the knitters. With this aid they developed a truly incredible knitting speed, and the income generated was a significant benefit for the family.

Three nineteenth-century carved wooden knitting sheaths, almost certainly from the Teesdale area of Durham where this pattern was most common. The outer ones are also a good illustration of chip carving, decorative patternmaking with triangles cut into the flat surface of the wood, which is common to much carved wooden folk art.

Utilitarian comfort shaped some of the sheaths to a flattened, curved blade of wood with the needle-holding part sticking out at the top like a dagger handle. Most have an angled, carved notch on the outside to catch the waistband and stop the sheath slipping out of the belt. Some were made by professional woodcarvers and turners, presumably available 'off the shelf' at the local shop, but the majority were made by amateurs, with a glorious profusion of decoration and symbolism for such a small item. They are clearly love-tokens, made by a local lad for his intended sweetheart, and many survived the death of the knitting trade because of their romantic associations for the owners.

Peter Brears writes very authoritatively about this subject in *North Country Folk Art* (1989), which has many splendidly clear illustrations, and there is a fine display in the Dales Countryside Museum in Hawes, North Yorkshire. The sheaths only survived in large numbers in the northern counties of England, but similar tools did occur in both Scotland and Wales and it can be presumed that they were used in the rest of England too, at some time. The sister-objects of carved wooden spoons, however, only seem to have taken deep root as a tradition in Wales. They too were generally carved as a courtship present to a young woman, but on the evidence of the surviving ones practical use was not an important consideration and many are entirely ornamental. The spoon bowl is usually fairly normal-sized and usable, but the handles may be very large, and may be pierced with intricate fretwork, or carved with low-relief leaves and flowers.

The form of decoration most common to both, and indeed common throughout Europe and North America, is that known as chip carving: cutting into the flat surface with a knife or chisel to remove small triangular chips of wood in patterns that leave the original surface marked with zigzag lines and criss-cross patterns, or other simple geometric shapes. Chief amongst these for curving contrast is a six-petalled rounded flower marked out with a pair of compasses, with all its interlocking variations. Words, or the initials of the loved one, are important of course and may be engraved into the flat surface with a pair of hearts or a formalised flower. In the most intricate examples of knitting sheaths, the message and the date is written on a tiny piece of paper behind a tiny piece of glass, inset into the wood and held in place with minute pieces of contrasting wood beading.

Marquetry is used, and inset patterns of bone or brass, and in both classes of love-token the most complex examples feature the amateur woodcarver's *tour de force* of patience and perseverance, a wooden chain carved out of the same continuous piece of wood. Closely allied to the chain is the 'ball and cage', one or more captive balls that move freely inside four corner pillars, again carved into the single piece of wood forming the spoon or knitting stick.

Beyond these simple categories the creative variations begin in earnest, using some or all of these techniques, and there is a huge richness of shapes, chamfering and sculptural carving that only a visit to one of the public collections can illustrate adequately. The Welsh Folk Museum at St Fagans, Cardiff, has a superb display of spoons, as well as much else of interest to readers of this book, and the Pinto collection in Birmingham has a few of both on display along with a wide variety of related items – boxes, stay busks, nut-crackers and gingerbread moulds as well as fine examples of all the various professional woodworkers' trades.

Butter moulds and biscuit moulds of various sorts used to be common throughout the country and are represented in most country-house kitchen collections and folk museums. Although they are probably the work of specialist woodcarvers, the imagery is often refreshingly direct and clear and, in the case of the moulds bearing human figures, sometimes amusingly naive. But they are purely museum pieces today. Walking-stick handles and shepherds' crooks are still cut and lovingly carved in some areas, mainly for the tourist trade, but sadly the amateur arts of woodcarving now seem to be firmly in recession.

The increase in entertainment accessible to all, particularly television, now fills much of our spare time and the availability of new materials has reduced our awareness of the qualities of wood. The problem is compounded by the difficulty of obtaining timber of good carving quality. Rural workers of the eighteenth and nineteenth centuries understood the qualities of holly, beech and sycamore wood, and knew where to find and how to season it. Today even the pre-war mania for plywood fretwork is becoming a mystery, and the Lord's Prayer painstakingly cut out of a single sheet of plywood in the 1930s has taken on some of the outdated charm of the wooden chain carved by a Welsh shepherd in the 1830s. Both are evidence of patience and of a love of elaboration and intricacy in wood. Will there be comparable examples in the middle of the next century?

A wooden biscuit mould from the Lake District of Cumbria, especially designed and carved to shape the traditional funeral biscuits of that area.

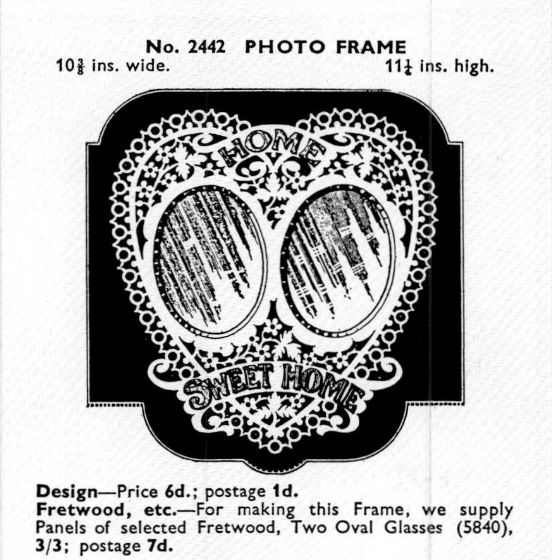
No. 2442 PHOTO FRAME
10⅜ ins. wide.
11¼ ins. high.
HOME
SWEET HOME
Design—Price 6d.; postage 1d.
Fretwood, etc.—For making this Frame, we supply Panels of selected Fretwood, Two Oval Glasses (5840), 3/3; postage 7d.

From the Hobbies handbook, 1947.

Those same soldiers and sailors also brought back some tattoos from their travels, and hearts have featured regularly amongst the tattooist's stock-in-trade of designs. Some are quite gently romantic, with 'mother' written on a ribbon entwined round the heart, or the name of the bearer's wife or girlfriend – although he often came to regret the indelible loyalty he declared on his arm to Marjorie when he decided later that he wanted to marry Dorothy. More recent designs often use the heart as a symbol of raw emotion or undirected passion, and a voluptuous red heart is stabbed through with a dagger, and wound round with 'death or glory' messages of bravado, with added tear-drops of blood like hideous exclamation marks. The designs can be very striking, the youthful bravado is understandable, but how one wishes that less violent imagery were sufficient to express this fervour for action and excitement, both so potentially creative.

In Wales in the eighteenth and nineteenth centuries young men developed a tradition of carving a wooden spoon as a courtship present to their intended. To begin with the spoons were probably strictly utilitarian, with a little fancy flourish cut into the handle as a personal message, but they developed in size and complexity until they could only hang on the wall as an ornament. Some of these spoons had wide flat handles which were pierced with fretwork designs, and not surprisingly the simple heart shape features very strongly. Half of the superb collection on display in the St Fagan's Welsh Folk Museum uses the heart shape somewhere: singly, in pairs, or multiplied into a pattern. Apart from its symbolism it is an easy shape to cut into wood, for two holes drilled side by side can soon be turned into a heart with a keyhole saw or a small penknife.

The same practical simplicity applies to the slightly curved, tear-drop shape that is also common on these fretworked flat handles, used in various combinations with hearts, diamonds and keyholes to ask the girl of the carver's choice to unlock her heart to him. Cut singly these tear-drop shapes are just space-fillers, but two nestling together is an ancient symbol of yin and yang, male and female, night and day. On the Welsh spoons, however, the commonest combination is a group of four spinning out from a central axis, to make the very potent and energised swastika design. This symbol, that has been so degraded by its annexation by the German Nazis, is another very

Hearts and horseshoes, and other traditional good luck signs, feature strongly in the button embroidery of the 'Pearlies' of London. This amazing tradition, only invented in the 1880s, raises huge amounts of money for local charities and seems set fair to continue into the future through the strictly regulated 'royal' families. Here Arthur and Emily Hayes, the Pearly King and Queen of Woolwich and Greenwich, display some of their homemade and immensely heavy regalia.

ancient sign and versions of it have been used in many different cultures and ages. It is visually powerful and it usually represents something positive and active, like a wheel or the energy of the sun travelling across the sky. From the sun it is an easy step to sanctify the sign as a symbol of God or Goodness, and from there to turn it into a good luck charm, and it is used in that sense to decorate Welsh furniture and wooden spoons. It turns up on the other side of Britain, in Norfolk, as a traditional painted symbol on sailing wherries.

The circle of the sun, and to a lesser extent the part-circles of the moon, underpin many of the designs that appear on decorative horse-brasses. The connection was probably strengthened by the image of the wheel with its radiating spokes, like the rays of the sun, because for centuries vehicles presupposed horses and their images were closely related. Harness has certainly been decorated for a long time, but the big face brasses and their cousins on extra martingale straps and back straps are mainly a nineteenth-century invention. It is usually assumed that their original purpose was superstitious, to ward off the evil eye, and although that may be so they soon took on an equally important role: expressing the pride and self-esteem of the carter or wagoner. Top of the list of favoured designs are various versions of the sun, or circular designs that can be construed as representing a sun or a wheel, but the range of images that the Birmingham brass-founders offered for sale was very wide. Birds and animals, particularly horses, and the whole catalogue of good luck charms like hearts and anchors appear, whilst the most simple and symbolic of all is a plain crescent hung with the points either up or down but never actually sideways like a moon.

A horse's head in profile is quite often framed by a single horse-shoe, and this same arrangement of horse's head looking out of a shoe, as if looking out of a stable door, is to be seen in **GYPSY CARAVAN** carving as well as on the cab doors of modern horse-boxes. The horseshoe, although apparently a cast-off from the image of the horse, actually has a whole body of mythology of its own. Heraldically, three horseshoes are the arms of the Farrier's Company, and many 'Three Horseshoes' pubs were really using the smithy next door as their address. A trinity of horseshoes also appears as a common horse-brass design. However, it is a single shoe that is widely accepted as a symbol of good luck, even today. The superstitious habit of nailing an old horseshoe over the door for luck is well known, but what is the quality that appealed so much that it became so common?

The blacksmith has traditionally been accorded a very important place in a village community because he is the man who makes the tools with which other men work. The ability to use raw fire and cold iron to make strong and beautiful tools and artefacts has always been respected, but in primitive societies with only stone-age or bronze-age technology a man with iron-working skills was a magician indeed. Did something of this awe attach itself to the iron objects he made, the commonest of which was the humble horseshoe?

The horseshoe's similarity to a crescent moon, the ancient symbol of the Romans' chaste goddess Diana and the Greeks' Selene, is usually cited as its main source of power. Some of that symbolism was absorbed into the medieval image of the Virgin Mary, who was sometimes depicted standing on a crescent moon as a symbol of chastity, surrounded by the stars of her crown as Queen of Heaven. Perhaps the seven nail holes in the common horseshoe were thought to refer to the seven stars or the seven virtues, for this magic number has several biblical connotations. All these interpretations, however, depend on some knowledge of the mythology and choose to ignore the real moon as we experience it, or as we did before street lighting. A bright moon does so much to banish the night-time horrors of our imagination that surely a little moon nailed to the door would deter a witch bound on dark deeds. But it is never fixed up as a moon waxing or waning, looking left or right, and there is a hint of the horseshoe as a symbolic container in the usual admonition to fix it with the horns up 'so the luck doesn't run out'. I suspect there is an equally deep-seated need purely for aesthetic symmetry.

One element of decorative art that appears consistently throughout history, although in many disguises, is the scroll ornament. In its simplest form it is a line spiralling inwards to an ever-tightening centre, but one that can simultaneously be seen as swinging away from the central starting point with the coiled energy of a snake or watch-spring. Alone it is like a simplified picture of a snail shell, but as one unit in a repeat pattern, with one scrolled curl growing out of the next, it becomes part of a wave sequence or a continuous growth like a climbing plant. It decorates the most ancient primitive pots, the finest classical architecture, the simplest popular arts and the most complex cast-iron railway station. There is a mass of scrolled decoration visible in Britain all the time, but the majority of it is a legacy from the past rather than modern currency. It does form an integral part of the designs on traditional **BANNERS** and **CANAL BOATS** but both are becoming rather anachronistic, and when it is used on printed work or furnishing fabric it is usually a nostalgic or historic ornament added to give period flavour to the design.

There are two areas of modern work and life, however, that still use scrollwork unselfconsciously and naturally: the **FAIRGROUND** and the painted work of the **SIGNWRITER**. In both cases the design is a continuation of standard historic practice, but there has never been a period of complete disuse so development has never stopped or needed to be revised. Signwriters have always used scrolls and ribbons with their alphabets on signboards, and old-fashioned flourishes still appear and still look as 'right' on the latest motorway juggernaut as they did on a nineteenth-century farm cart. The fairground artist, meanwhile, just absorbs influences and trends like a sponge, and the carved baroque scrolls of the 1880s have blended with a century of fads and fashions to create a swirling language of painted expressionism that belongs to the fairground alone.

Excluding prehistoric pots, the oldest direct influence on the scroll's continuity is from the architecture of Ancient Greece and Rome, and that influence is exerted on modern British taste mainly by the classically derived architecture of the Renaissance, and the eighteenth century in particular. But there were many earlier versions. Many Saxon crosses exist and some of these feature low-relief carving of running leaf scrolls, as well as strapwork designs that may hint at a Celtic influence brought over by the monks from Ireland. The invading Vikings certainly used rolling scrollwork in their decoration, and it was seen in the architectural remnants of the empire left by the

(*To p. 113*)

BRITISH COASTAL FISHING BOATS

A carved and painted nameboard on the wheelhouse of a North Sea fishing boat, carved by Harold Dickinson with paintwork by John Marshall of Cleethorpes. It is only a sideline, additional to John's main job of maintaining a fishing fleet, but he has painted quite a number of them and it is becoming something of a local tradition.

BRITAIN is surrounded by the sea; consequently it is also surrounded by a fringe of activities and industries concerned with the sea, and these trades still provide a necklace of traditional craftsmanship, colour, and even folklore right round the country. Fishing and boatbuilding, like other industries, have had to modernise and mechanise, and boats have become fewer and bigger and, it has to be said, generally uglier. But some regions still retain their indigenous craft, like the extraordinary beach cobles of the Northumberland coast, and many of the smaller trawlers are still built of timber and still retain the grace and beauty that traditional wooden shipbuilding demands. Certain things remain constant, like the power of the sea and the wind, and finally these still control the practical design of fishing ships. Nature takes a strong hand in their utilitarian design, and the smaller they are the less they can afford to ignore her demands.

Another natural factor that the boat has to accommodate is the crew, and a really efficient vessel will take those men and their traditions into account as well. The industry may have modernised, but the men are still likely to be the sons and grandsons of fishermen, and their regional and family conventions still need to be respected. The smaller the boat the more likely it is that the skipper is also the owner, and the boat's appearance will reflect his personal taste, pride and prosperity, or possibly his poverty.

The outside of the hull is the most obvious area of colour. Historically tar and black varnish provided cheap and efficient preservative coatings for bigger craft, but varnished woodwork has always been the most appreciated finish if the trade would allow enough time to maintain it afterwards. Small clinker-built boats are still usually varnished early in their life to show off the beauty of the wood and workmanship, for there are few secrets under varnish. When paint is used black and dark blues are most common, and show the marks of a hard life least, but brighter paints are becoming increasingly popular as they improve in durability and ease of application. The boats of the South West are particularly bright and cheerful. The cobles of the North East coast have traditionally been brightly painted for ease of recognition off the beach, and their wide planks painted in strong hues with bands of curving colour on the transom are still common.

Painting a section of planking of a traditionally built wooden boat immediately accentuates the curves of the sheerline, and most craft restate that gracefulness by picking out the gunwales or top rail in a contrasting colour. Most larger boats have a purely decorative 'cove' line cut in along the hull near deck level, perhaps ending in a spearhead shape near the bows, and when this is painted yellow against a dark hull, or even picked out with gold leaf, it adds a very crisp touch of distinction.

Many boats have white 'boot-topping', a band of paint at or just above the waterline between the top side colour and the anti-fouling paint, an abstract version of the wake of the ship under way. Initially it was a powdery paint put on to inhibit the growth of surface weed, and to make it easier to scrub off, but it is much more cosmetic nowadays. It usually widens considerably towards the stempost, or may be just a white triangular 'shark's mouth' at the bows like a stylised foaming bow-wave, probably the most common decorative addition of all. The most exaggerated version is seen on the cobles, where the white sweeps up at the bows, sometimes following the line of the planking, and curves down to the bottom of the deep forefoot below the waterline. It looks very handsome when the boats are drawn up on a beach.

These traditional wooden Northumberland cobles are very picturesque, but this graceful regional style of inshore fishing boat is a direct practical result of a need to work straight from the open beaches of the north-east coast. Their beauty is not lost on the local fishermen, who work them hard but maintain them carefully and with pride.

Fishing boats in the Gut at the mouth of the Tyne in North Shields with a variety of colour and bow scrollwork on display.

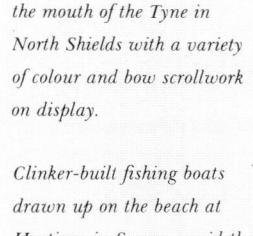

Clinker-built fishing boats drawn up on the beach at Hastings in Sussex, amid the utilitarian but picturesque clutter of the job. Clear varnished hulls are the tradition on this part of the coast, but there is plenty of colour inside and on the equipment.

Inside the smaller boats, and on deck on the larger ones, the equipment and separate parts of the vessel can be painted all sorts of colours in all sorts of combinations. Black and white are common of course, and will mix well with any others. Green is perhaps least common, as if the colour of vegetation is out of place on the water, although it becomes very popular with the inland barges of the canals and rivers. Wood is significant however, both as actual varnished work or oiled teak on the very best ships. It is represented in paint through a range of yellow-ochres and browns called mast colour and stone colour in the old naval painting manuals. Rich orangey-browns are provided by the translucent colours of artificial oak graining, with the most elaborate decorative panelling appearing on the plain steel of the wheelhouse in memory of the more gracious days of varnished wooden cabinwork. Plenty of navy blue and admiralty grey hint at emulation of the Senior Service (or at least the proximity of a naval dockyard and some cheap paint), but it is bright sky-blue and bright red that add so much to the cheerful picturesque quality of many fishing fleets.

The boat's name appears on the bows, usually executed with significant flamboyance and pride whether carved or simply signwritten, for the prow of a ship, big or small, is always the leading edge, seeing the way ahead. There is a world-wide practice, known as the 'oculus' tradition, of painting eyes on the front of a boat for her to see with. Although the rational mind knows this is nonsense, the irrational part that feels for the ship as an individual character, with a life and nature of her own, will accept the concept quite readily. We anthropomorphise motor cars and see headlights and radiator grilles as eyes and grinning teeth, and the stempost of a boat easily becomes a proud patrician nose with the anchor hawse-holes on either side being eyes, staring ahead. There are no actual eyes painted on boats in Britain, but the hawse-holes very often become the focus for a mass of scrollwork, on the tiniest fishing boats and the biggest Thames barges.

Sometimes a special nameboard will be carved and painted, and mounted either side of the stempost. The designs on these nameboards may be very graceful or very clumsy, but most are trademarks of the boatyards where the ships were built, a visual language to be read by the initiated. In origin they owe much more to the trailboards of the clipper ships and figurehead carvers than to the oculus tradition, and are yet another descendant of classical foliage, but boatyard simplification has reduced them to a different convention of naive decoration, the purest of modern popular arts.

On decked boats, the next most popular place

Lawrence Ferguson, a local signwriter and grainer who specialises in work on fishing boats, painting the registration number on Coquet Herald *during her annual repainting at Blyth in September 1989.*

for the ship's name is on the front of the wheelhouse, either signwritten directly on the structure on a painted riband, or executed on a separate, carved and painted nameboard mounted below the wheelhouse windows. These show an influence from Scandinavia, where they are more common, and may feature flags, carved rope borders or central paintings as well as the lettering itself. Flags sometimes feature amongst the bow scrollwork too, bearing the owner's initials or insignia. However, the wheelhouse ones are more likely to be Union Jacks, perhaps crossed with the flags of St Andrew or St George, with various shamrocks, thistles and roses added.

The signwritten boards are quite ephemeral, for most fishing boats get repainted many times throughout their life – once every twelve months for the best-maintained – but the constant demand produces a specialist supply. Certain workmen become the accepted boat signwriters and their preferred styles of lettering, colour schemes and scrollwork become an important part of the decoration of the area, another visual clue to the boat's origin and history.

Apart from the boat's name and home port, and the large fishing registration number on the side at bow and stern, the signwriter may also be called upon to write the name on the lifebelts. The care and beauty with which this is sometimes done, with swirling ribbons of colour and deeply shaded lettering, should be a reminder to quayside visitors admiring the romance of the fishing fleet that fishing is still the most dangerous job in the country, bar none.

Romans. Classical acanthus leaves and volutes of a sort still adorned the tops of pillars, but as the pointed-arched Gothic cathedrals soared ever higher these motifs either disappeared or grew into more realistic representations of natural plants to glorify and praise the complexity of God's natural world.

Symbolism of a more conceptual sort also had an influence. The grapevine and ivy, previously sacred to Bacchus, became accepted as Christianised symbols of the Eucharist, the blood of Christ in the wine, with the Trinity symbolised by the three points of the evergreen ivy leaf. Abstract tendrils of plants entwine the pages of the illuminated manuscripts and we can suppose that similar designs bordered the many wall-paintings of the medieval church. As praise of nature became praise of God floral patterns proliferated, and designs showing the energy of growing tendrils and leaves, budding and sending out shoots to fill any available space with an intense image of birth and rebirth, became increasingly useful and common.

If the design could fulfil a practical function as well, and suit the nature of the material with which it was expressed, then perfection was not far away. Some surviving church doors from the thirteenth and fourteenth centuries reach towards that standard, for the wrought ironwork of the hinges splits and tapers and curls into whorls that simultaneously strengthen and beautify the door, and the work certainly expresses the blacksmith's love of craftsmanship, if not of God. The ironwork still sets standards to which modern blacksmiths can aspire, and offers vibrant designs for others to use.

The main rootstock of modern scrolled decoration is, however, classical architecture – partly, as already suggested, through the remains left by the Roman occupation and drawn up into the gothic, but much more importantly by the massive reappraisal and reinterpretation of the ancient, classical values and ruins that came to be known as the Renaissance. In 1540 Sebastiano Serlio published a treatise in Venice that described five 'orders' of classical architecture, and thirty years later Andrea Palladio published another that became the rule-book for architects in Britain for the next couple of hundred years. Both based their texts on the only surviving written reference work from the classic period, penned by Vitruvius in the first century. He described three orders of architecture – the Doric, Ionic and Corinthian – but the scholarship and hindsight of Serlio and Palladio added two more, the Tuscan and Composite.

Each order precisely described the proportions and decoration of one of the accepted styles of stone pillar and its relationship to the beam and roof structure above it, called the 'entablature'. This is made up of the architrave, frieze and cornice. Each section and detail was carefully drawn and measured as a proportion of that particular order's 'module' – half the diameter of the base of the pillar – and this set of proportions and details had to be rigidly adhered to when creating a new building in one of the correct classic styles. The absolute rigidity of the system softened a little over the centuries but it is difficult to overstate the influence these academic studies and their successors have had on the daily lives of absolutely everyone, because the town hall and museum were probably designed to their rules, and the proportions of most town houses and shopfronts were controlled by

Exuberant ironwork on a thirteenth-century strongbox kept in Audlem parish church, Cheshire, still richly decorative even though nearly half the scrollwork has been broken off over the centuries.

In the eighteenth and nineteenth centuries, a working knowledge of classical architecture was regarded as essential to anyone working in the decorative arts with any pretension to good taste. This diagram is one of a series on the orders of architecture published in the Universal Decorator *magazine of 1859.*

CORINTHIAN CAPITAL.

them, right down to the mouldings and panelling of the living-room door and picture rail.

The new broom of classical architecture swept all before it, and the grace and beauty of its simple forms and elegant proportions of solids to space, and light stone to shadow, found enthusiastic devotees amongst the well educated. They were simultaneously reading Greek and Roman legends and literature and studying ancient philosophies and morality, and with hindsight we can see that the new architecture became a summing-up of a whole new set of attitudes. What was missing was the richness and complexity of the traditional gothic approach, the gold and colour and mass of texture and pattern, and something had to be found in classical architecture to supply that need for elaboration. This was met by the capitals, or wider stones, on top of the pillars.

The Tuscan and Doric styles are the plainest and least ornamented of all, but the Greek Ionic order has the capital carved with volutes. A volute is a line moving around and away from a central point, but instead of the radius increasing by a steady amount each time, which would result in a simple spiral, it increases by an arithmetic progression and the space between the curves grows wider, like the natural growth of a horn or snail shell. It is very graceful and powerful, but it is difficult to measure and draw, and studying and accurately drawing the proportions of the classical volute formed an essential part of any architectural student's training until very recently. The Ionic pillar has a pair of volutes spiralling out and down on either side like formalised ram's horns and the twisting vitality of these curves, with the textured pattern between each pair, has a disproportionate power when contrasted to the calm rigidity of the rest of the structure.

Contemporary with the Ionic was the Corinthian order, which was especially beloved by the Roman builders. Here the capitals are taller and carved with a pattern of foliage growing up and curling outwards from the pillar, below another set of tiny volutes. This mass of classical foliage provided the key prototype for much of the decorative art that followed. The Composite order blends the lot, and has far larger corner volutes springing out of a huge bunch of vegetation. It is the most elaborate stage of the development from the simple log huts of the primitives to the final stone flowering of the architecture of the Roman Empire, before the fall. But the seeds fell on fertile ground a thousand years later.

The plant used on the Corinthian capital is acanthus, a variety of thistle called 'Bear's Breech' in English. It is found all over southern Europe, and particularly in Greece according to Vitruvius. He also tells us that the Corinthian capital was the invention of Callimachus, an Athenian sculptor of considerable fame. He was inspired, so the story goes, by seeing a basket of fruit left on the tomb of a young virgin of Corinth as a memorial offering by her nurse. A thistle had grown up around the basket from underneath, and the leading leaves had been turned out and back by the projecting edges of a large tile that the nurse had placed on top to keep the birds out. This had suggested the curled vegetation turning into the corner volutes beneath the abacus of the classic Corinthian pillar. All commentators agree that this story is unlikely to be true, but it deserves to be for poetry's sake.

The same plant, with its deeply serrated edges and curled leading

points, was sometimes carved as a running scroll design on some of the mouldings that made up the entablature. It was therefore one of the relatively few decorative images that a classically minded designer could, with academic safety, use to add texture and intricacy to the new architecture. It grew everywhere, plastered on the ceilings, carved into furniture, and painted on the walls. Added impetus was given to the acanthus fashion by the rediscovery of ancient 'grotesques' – decorative figures of animals and humans growing out of arabesques of foliage – painted directly on the basement walls of ancient ruins in Rome, discoveries reinforced by the eighteenth-century archaeological surveys of Pompeii and Herculaneum. Acanthus scrollwork ruled supreme as a symbol of fashionable, well-educated good taste, and by the beginning of the nineteenth century it had percolated down to every level of society in some form or other.

But by then two further influences had helped to distance scrollwork from architecture: the work of the writing master and the older science of heraldry. The impact of heraldry on the popular arts was discussed in chapter 2, but one part of the full achievement of arms is particularly relevant here. The knight in armour wore, out of necessity, a piece of cloth draped over his helmet to keep the sun off his head and the back of his neck. This veil was kept in place by a twisted quoit of fabric jammed over cloth and helmet, now represented as the 'wreath' that supports the 'crest'. The cloth, called the 'lambrequin' in old French heraldic terminology or 'mantling' in English, became another item in the set of symbols that make up the language of heraldry.

The earliest pictures show the mantling as a quite small piece of material with a decorative scalloped edge, as was a common contemporary fashion. However, as time goes on the cloth gets longer and the *découpage* more involved, fringing the mantling with a deeply cut pattern of fleurs-de-lis that twists with movement and the wind to reveal the inside colour counter-changed with the exterior. Traditionally these colours are the main metal and colour of the shield, and in legend the deep cuts that create the ragged edge are the honourable results of battle. Painted in colour the explanation is acceptable, but represented in black and white engravings, or in monochrome stone on a monument, this swirling mass of drapery soon turns into an involved framing device. It surrounds the shield with a tangle of scrollwork which, under the influence of the Renaissance, becomes indistinguishable from its architectural acanthus cousin. The ragged edge takes on the same formality as the serrated leaves of the thistle and the main heraldic influence left is the layout: a symmetrical pattern of growth that starts in the centre of the top of any rectangular panel, swirls out towards the corners and trails down either side. The clearest examples of this layout are on the trade union and Sunday School **BANNERS** but it recurs on all sorts of certificates and signs.

Another area of popular art that blends these architectural and heraldic influences is that of **SHIPS' FIGUREHEADS** and their associated scrollwork. From a medieval heraldic beginning, featuring lions particularly, the sixteenth- and seventeenth-century warships absorbed all the fashionable Greek and Roman mythologies in their names and carvings. Acanthus scrolls swirled around the ships, and swept up to support allegorical figurehead groups at the bows. Time, the need to save weight, and financial restraint simplified the tradition to a single figure with a running scroll tapering back on the trailboards or the top planks of the hull.

Heraldic mantling has become indistinguishable from architectural acanthus scrollwork in this wood-engraved diagram from the Universal Decorator, *1859.*

Thames sailing barge scroll work on the transom of the Lady Daphne *of Rochester, built in 1923 but seen here 60 years later in St Catherine's Dock, London.*

Modern remnants of this tradition are to be seen on many present-day merchant ships, fishing boats and yachts. The transom sterns of Thames sailing barges usually bear a bold scroll cut in either side of the rudder post, and the variations became the recognisable trademarks of individual bargebuilders. Stylistically it is not obvious that these designs are truly remnants of Renaissance shipbuilding elegance, for they are generally rather graceless and lumpy, with more affinity to eighth-century Saxon stone cross carving than eighteenth-century acanthus. Some, however, are pretty, and most have a matching set of scrolls round the hawse-holes at the bows which certainly tie them into the mainstream shipping tradition.

The final recognisable influence was added by those who taught the art of copperplate writing. As literacy spread, so the need for teachers and examples to copy was felt. The increased skill and numbers of engravers provided part of the answer, and influenced penmanship in return.

The invention of typography and the printing press in the 1400s hit the trade of the old professional scribes very hard, for good-quality printing in 'Black-letter' – the style now loosely called 'Old English' – was virtually indistinguishable from that done by the pen. However, indirectly it did give some motivation for the development of a more graceful, cursive handwriting for gentlefolk that could not be emulated by printing. A neat, sloping handwriting that used a thin springy steel nib developed, but in the hands of exhibitionist writing masters it became an extravagant display of virtuoso penmanship, the words entwined with knots and flourishes and tail-piece drawings designed for the pen, images knitted onto the page in swirls and loops. This curvilinear design work, with its graceful variation of pen stroke from thick to thin, was ideally suited to engraving and to reproduction by engraved copperplate printing. The writing masters produced many fine engraved example sheets for their pupils to copy.

Copy-books began to appear in the early 1600s and increased in number and popularity for the following century. Their influence was not confined to the drawing-room, however, for public lettering reflected the fashion too. In districts where fine-grained, easily worked stone was available, particularly slate, all the swirls and flourishes of copperplate engraving were transferred to the local GRAVESTONES. Many superb examples of calligraphic design and scrollwork, translated into stone-cutting, are still on display in the churchyard. It never really went out of fashion, and elements of pen decoration formed part of the stone-cutter's repertoire throughout the Victorian period.

Copy-books were also perfect example sheets for the emerging trade of the SIGNWRITER, for both copperplate writing and its associated scrollwork are ideally suited to fine brushwork. Slim 'pen' flourishes remain popular with modern signwriters to link words together and add a touch of handwritten elegance. Combined with the heraldic and architectural influences, they become a valuable extension to the alphabet for the craftsman signwriter. Beautiful examples still enrich the simplest signs and the cab doors of the biggest lorries.

The scrollwork of the **FAIRGROUND**, however, is firmly architectural in origin, even though it is now often expressed in paint. When the fair reached its greatest height of prosperity before the First World War, it was providing escapist enjoyment for a large number of working people by framing its excitements in an illusion of grandeur and aristocratic opulence – and the popular conception of royal extravagance was the excesses of the French royal court before the revolution. Thus the glitter and intricacy of the crystal chandeliers and gilded rococo furniture of the royal courts of the eighteenth century provided the key patterns and images for a popular art of the nineteenth. As the eighteenth-century designs in turn had been exaggerated versions of the classical motifs of grotesques and acanthus leaves, with an occasional half-naked goddess slipped in, the Italian Renaissance of the sixteenth century was again directly affecting the popular arts at the beginning of the twentieth. Ancient Mediterranean exterior decoration had been transformed into the interior decoration of the Baroque and Rococo periods, only to be exaggerated again into an exterior architecture of fantasy. There was no subtlety this time though, no thoughtful note of texture against the simple masses of the pure architecture; this time the carved foliage smothered everything in an exotic jungle of gold leaf and colour which would at last rival the interior of the medieval cathedral in complexity and intensity of pattern and design.

This carved and gilded architecture spread to the homes of the showmen too, and their living wagons developed a specific style of layout and decoration of their own, rich with colour and carvings like the roundabouts and fair organs. The development had been steady, from Wombwell's travelling menagerie in the 1820s at least, and as the century progressed the wagons became heavier and more complex, and more were built by firms who came to specialise in this line of work. Later in the century the gypsies too began to move out of their traditional bender tents and two-wheel carts and into their own variations of the wagon styles developed for the showmen. The **GYPSY CARAVAN**, as it is now known and romantically loved, remained lighter and generally smaller than the showman's wagon, but both shared a desire for ostentatious display and the same late-Victorian decorative images and designs: the ubiquitous acanthus and vine leaf scrollwork. We have moved a long way from the temples of Ancient Greece, but the connection is clear.

At Knutsford in Cheshire there is a continuing tradition of drawing decorative designs in coloured sands on the town's roads and pavements on Mayday morning. What began as a local wedding custom has now become much more important as part of an event that is well known throughout the Cheshire and Manchester area: the Knutsford

Another design pattern sheet from the Universal Decorator, *and perfect opulent, rococo, inspirational material for fairground painters, caravan carvers, glass embossers and signwriters.*

A restored bow-top gypsy wagon built by Hirst Bros of Leeds in 1918, now part of the Romany Folklore Museum collection at Selborne, Hampshire.

Royal May Day festival. The sanding was started, according to local tradition, by King Canute emptying sand out of his shoes and wishing a newly married couple, who were passing by, heaps of happiness and lots of children. In fact history is not quite sure whether King Canute ever came to Knutsford, but it is a good story nonetheless.

The sanding was a well-established tradition in Knutsford in the early nineteenth century, but it was apparently not then the responsibility of any one person; everybody did some sanding outside their houses for high days and holidays as well as weddings. As time passed it became the province of a few specialists who became renowned as local folk artists. The present sanding team consists of the brothers-in-law Ray Veale and Alf Gilbert, both of whom learnt the job by helping their father-in-law, the late Ted Worrals. When he died in 1955 they took over, and they have continued the Mayday tradition ever since. Ray and Alf are now helped by their respective sons Colin and Jimmy, so the immediate future for this lovely tradition seems secure.

The design and message is first marked out with white sand poured through a funnel, and is drawn with large arm movements and sweeping confidence, with one finger stopping or controlling the flow of sand through the tundish. As soon as the basic layout is complete the other members of the team follow on, trailing parallel lines of different coloured sands alongside the first, producing fresh stripy patterns that reflect much of the movement of their creation in the rhythm of the designs. As with a spraygun, the hand must be kept moving steadily to produce a regular line – any stops result in a pile of sand, just as a spraygun would deliver a dribbling blob of paint.

Speed is also essential to get the job done at all, because upwards of fifty sections of pavement or road all around the town are decorated before the majority of the shops open for business. This necessitates a very early start and from 5.30am the Land-Rover containing the team and the buckets of sand moves from shop to church gate to pub forecourt, where the crew draw out the designs with swift military efficiency. The road or pavement outside the home of the new May queen is always decorated, along with that outside certain shops and pubs, including the 'Lord Eldon' which was the home of the first May queen in 1864. After that it is up to the sanders and the vagaries of the weather, for although the work will survive some gentle rain it cannot

actually be done in the wet, as the sand has to be absolutely dry to pour through the funnel.

The message most frequently used as the basis of the design is 'God Bless Our Royal May Queen', with the Christian name of that year's choice added. The letters are simple block capitals, outlined or 'shaded' with another colour alongside, with some multicoloured underlining to finish them off. It is the borders that frame the words and define the sections of pavement that are most startling. They make an elaborate frame for the message, a series of curving lines and spirals that outline the motto with primitive rococo jollity. A group of three spirals arranged rather like a fleur-de-lis will sometimes burst out of the border scrollwork and when they are extended, growing up out of a circlet of white sand, they are known to the sanders as the Prince of Wales' feathers, the heraldic device of three white ostrich plumes.

This is now the commonest design motif, and it may be significant that it was the visit of the Prince and Princess of Wales in 1887 that granted the town the right to call the local festival Knutsford Royal May Day. The sanding was outstanding that year and the streets were described as 'one continued arabesque'. It seems likely that the feathers were featured in that very royalty-conscious jubilee year in sand, just as they certainly were in flowers and pampas grass.

Regardless of any literal meaning or historical continuity the scroll or spiral is a very strong visual design, both active and attractive. It can be read as a meaningful symbol of life, death, or rebirth and it has certainly been used in that way in some systems of belief, but this need not stop our enjoyment of it as a purely decorative pattern, a pretty doodle of continuity. It is probably for simple aesthetic pleasure that it has appeared in such profusion in the elaborate embroidery of countrymen's smocks, the ironwork of church doors, the paintwork of canal barges and gypsy caravans, and as a tail-piece to this chapter. It is a visual archetype as important as Hogarth's line of beauty, and is of course a natural extension of it.

Sanding the pavements of Knutsford, Cheshire, early on Mayday morning, the day of the town's annual carnival, parade and big fair. Colin Veale, son and grandson of Knutsford sanders, is trailing a third colour of sand along the scrolled outline border to the traditional message for the May queen.

Knutsford church, Cheshire, with some of the results of the early-morning work of the 'sanders' on Mayday; a traditional message updated with the name of that year's May queen, topped and tailed with the Prince of Wales' feathers.

TATTOOING – POPULAR ART ON THE SKIN

AS A western art tattooing is quite young, for it only became common knowledge after explorers returned from the South Pacific in the seventeenth century. The practice had existed in our own distant past but the church frowned on it as an attempt to improve God's own image made manifest in man, and it was rare in Christian Europe from the eighth century onwards. There is some evidence of tattooing in Ancient Egypt, and plenty in China and Japan and among the American native Indians, but it was the designs of the Polynesians and of the Maoris of New Zealand that caught the fancy of the seafarers. Heavily tattooed men were imported to Britain and exhibited to much popular interest in the seventeenth and eighteenth centuries.

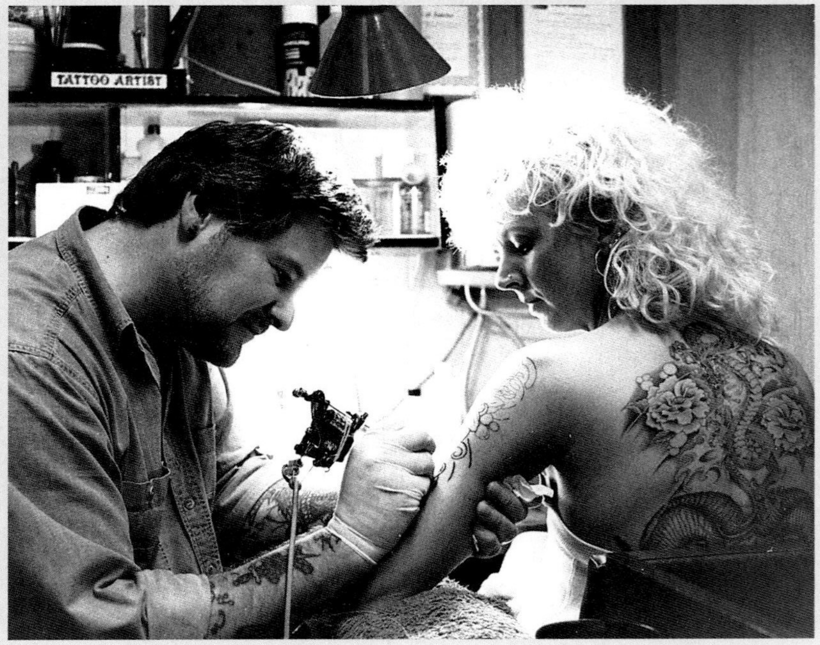

'Saz' working on a new shoulder piece, especially designed for his customer Tina Isherwood of Leigh to cover her first, small, four-year-old tattoo. From that small beginning her enthusiasm and her tattoos grew year by year. In 1990 she and 'Saz' won the trophy for the best lady's large tattoo at the annual tattoo expo, and some of it can be glimpsed on her back on this photograph. But that's only the top third of it!

Tattooing was still regarded as an exotic aberration, however, and it was not until the mid-nineteenth century that it became an acceptable part of the romantic image of the seafaring man, for it was sailors returning from the Far East who brought home tattoos as permanent souvenirs of their voyages. They started the fashion, and set the standards. Some of them set up shop on their own account in the seaports and tattooing became much more common, particularly amongst soldiers and sailors, and it remained very largely their province until after the Second World War and the ending of National Service. Since then it has become the indelible badge of rebellious youth, with ever more outrageous imagery proclaiming some allegiance to the violent reputations of punk rockers, motor cycle gangs or the excesses of heavy metal rock music. But beneath the changing imagery there are a number of traditional constants, a framework that supports the tattoo as an interesting modern popular art form.

A distinction can be made between the great majority of tattoo carriers, who have just a few designs usually on the forearms or on the outside of the upper arms, and the rest, who have many more, everywhere and anywhere. The first group wear their tattoos like badges or a bracelet, as a piece of permanent jewellery. The remainder are the more extreme enthusiasts who either have so many individual designs applied that these eventually join up to become an overall pattern; or they commission more ambitious pieces to begin with; pieces designed to cover the arm and shoulder, or the whole back, or the whole body. With this group, tattooing has become their hobby, or an obsession or fetish; the body becomes the artwork, rather than a large canvas for a small picture, and they form clubs and arrange meetings and competitions to display their body art to fellow enthusiasts.

These extreme exhibitionists are beyond the subject of ordinary popular art, but it is on their backs and bosoms that new ideas are developed, setting new standards for the professionals to adapt and follow. Faded pictures of men and women displaying their major 'body pieces' hang in every tattoo professor's waiting room. The enthusiasts' bodies also display the most extravagant versions of what have become the traditional tattoo designs, the oriental dragons, snarling tigers and exotic flowers and birds. These are now joined by late twentieth-century designs featuring horrific beasts, flaming skulls and motor bikes, but still the main features are writhing serpentine lines that echo and enhance the sinuous curves and muscles of the body beneath them.

The shop window or the walls of the tattooist's studio are always lined with framed sheets of tattoo designs for the customer to choose from, and they form an instructive catalogue of the favourite imagery. Hearts, flowers and bluebirds entwined with a ribbon bearing the name of a loved one are still available, as they were fifty years ago, and combinations of snakes, tigers and voluptuous women remind one of the fairground sideshow booths with their lurid but expressive showfront signs. Daggers, and mottoes of bravery and defiance, have become ever more bloodthirsty under the influence of adult comics and, more recently, the advertising graphics of the video rental business. Blood, skulls and staring eyes have turned the traditional spitting Chinese dragon into a quite restrained and tasteful alternative.

The imagery is always vehemently active. Panthers spring with claws at full stretch and satanic beasts with bats' wings snarl, with ferocious bared teeth dripping saliva. Even a soft red heart of love must be graphically pierced with an ornately handled curved dagger, with blood and roses exploding out from the twisting name ribbon. The more fundamental archetypal images that can be blended together, the better. The big-breasted naked girl will be entwined with a ravenous snake in the classic erotic combination, but she is better still if she carries a knife or a gun, and is in chains or a mask. The abstract linear quality of all these designs writhes expressively, and the colours have the brightness and boldness of the cheapest colour printing of the comic-books they resemble.

And yet, despite all this violence of intent in the origination, by the time they are transferred to tanned skin by the tattooist's needle, with his blue-black outlines and a limited range of colours, they become far more subtle than words or the wall charts suggest. Well placed within the confines of an arm, the average young man's tattoo has a rightness of place and colour that is aesthetically very satisfying, despite the grossness of so much of the imagery.

Women tend to be more careful about both subject-matter and position, and designs are chosen and placed as aids to beauty. Small colourful butterflies, birds and flowers are neatly tattooed on the shoulder or the breast, just above the bikini line, like jewelled brooches, with larger exotic birds and beasts on the upper thighs. By the time that point is reached, the true tattoo enthusiast has discovered herself and any further pieces are no more restrained than those of the male. The finest traditional work covers the entire body like a fabulous close-fitting oriental silk housecoat.

The underlying need for tattoos is hard to pinpoint. Enhancing the body to make it more beautiful or interesting is understandable, but the aggressive violence of so much of the imagery is hard to equate with any common idea of beauty. A degree of bravado and sexual boasting by the young to friends of both sexes is also understandable, and this clearly underlies the eroticism of the serpentine entanglements of women and beasts that are so common. But the obsession with images of death, decaying skulls and hooded ghouls, seems to cross the field in a totally different direction.

It is true that the young cannot be expected to have thought about death very deeply, and nor should they have to in an average situation, but most tattoos positively make fun of death and treat it with no respect at all. By combining it with sexual overtones the message becomes unequivocal – let's play now and not even think about paying later. This is reinforced by the basic concept of the more outrageous tattoos, for even an eighteen-year-old must realise that the fashionable imagery of today will not mean so much to him in two years' time, never mind ten or twenty years. They are a paradox, a permanent statement of transience. It is lucky for some that the perennial black panther is always available to cover an outdated image or declaration of undying love.

Not all tattoists are artists in their own right, although all the good ones are good craftsmen, accurately transferring to the skin the design chosen by the customer from the wall charts. The best ones are also scrupulously clean in their practice today, a welcome improvement brought about by the deadly threat of the AIDS virus. Most design some of their own artwork and will create a special piece for the individual customer according to his or her taste, perhaps working from photographs or magazine artwork. But the standard range of designs on offer is quite wide and the average customer can usually find something that appeals to an inner emotion. The tattooist's work then offers the customer a form of self-expression by proxy, and he leaves flaunting a permanent statement of passion, bravery or exotic beauty. But, for all the spitting fiery courage of the lion on his back, some young men have been known to keep their shirts on at home for years in case their mothers found out.

LANDSCAPE WITH ARCHITECTURE

IN THE seventeenth and eighteenth centuries a young aristocratic gentleman's education was completed by his Grand Tour, if his family could afford it, whereby he travelled and lived abroad for several months or even years to experience the culture of Europe at first hand. In particular he needed to go to Italy. With his knowledge of the Latin and Greek classics, he was expected to visit many of the famous sites of antiquity, study the architecture and maybe bring back some artistic or archaeological souvenirs for the country house back home. Some engaged in very useful research and study, and brought back valuable collections of antique art, whilst others had a wild time and came home with the very clever forgeries that were already being foisted onto these first British tourists.

Also needed were some visual reminders of the Italian landscape, and the rigours of the journey there through the mountain passes of the Alps. The latter demand was catered for by the paintings of Salvator Rosa and his followers, painters of rocky ravines and precipices with gnarled trees clinging to them, harbouring bandits and colourful peasants. These painters were catering directly to the need for pleasing horrors for romantic imaginations.

Having accomplished this arduous journey the visitor was then in a properly receptive mood for the southern light, the plains and trees and ruins of the classical fatherland. One painter stands pre-eminent as the recorder of the Italian landscape for the English visitors: the Frenchman Claude Gellée, usually called Claude Lorrain. Born in 1600, he spent the majority of a long life painting in Rome, developing a style of idealised landscape that found much favour during his lifetime and which remained consistently popular well into the nineteenth century.

There is something of a theatrical formula to his compositions, with three clearly defined planes building a sense of depth and recession. The dark foreground plane usually features some trees rearing up on one side to frame the more distant view in the middle ground, probably featuring a classical building as the visual centrepiece against a misty mountainous background. The nominal subject of the title is played out on the front stage by small figures enacting scenes of ancient mythology or Christian testament, but it is more truthful to say that the subject provides an excuse to paint the background landscape.

It is worth remembering that, at the time in which Claude was working, the term 'landscape painting' had not been invented and the practice had not yet been recognised or accepted as a worthy or separate subdivision of fine art. There was still a century and a half to go before the unashamedly natural landscapes of Constable or Turner. In the meantime the paintings of Claude and his many copyists had to serve as the aristocratic picture postcards of the period, and there can be few picture collections dating from the seventeenth or eighteenth centuries that do not include an oil painting 'after Claude', featuring dark trees and classic ruins.

Both types of topographical painting gained an extra level of importance in England as inspirations for new fashions in gardening.

There was a reaction against formal gardens, where shrubs and paths had been laid out as neatly trained extensions of the architecture; the garden was now allowed to be a part, however artfully contrived, of the surrounding landscape. One now stood with one's back to the house to admire the view instead of turning inwards to admire only the artifice of the architect. But the view could not yet be pure nature untamed. It had to conform to a number of accepted and civilised standards, and to that end prodigious amounts of labour were expended in the grounds of the country mansions to move hills, make lakes, plant forests and create architectural exclamation marks with temples and newly built ruins. What had to be created for the fashionable was a 'picturesque' landscape.

The word picturesque has reversed its meaning since it was defined by Uvedale Price in 1794, like a sock describing a foot instead of being shaped by it or keeping it warm. A picturesque landscape, or rather a vista or prospect as it would have been described in the eighteenth century, was one that looked like a picture rather than a view that might supply the subject for one; and the pictures that it had to look like were the idealised classical landscapes of Claude or Poussin, with perhaps a thrill of excitement added by some rocks by Rosa. The first English garden temples and ruins were built in the classical style, for the concept which was being promoted by these post-Renaissance garden improvements was the all-pervading superiority of Ancient Roman art and civilisation. The temples were built in emulation, proof perhaps that the new age could now vie with the ancients in understanding and construction of classic architecture, whilst the ruins were a more contemplative comment on the immense passage of time since the golden age described in Virgil's Aeneid, a time of pastoral calm and balance and of unhurried poetry and art. Both of these values were very attractive to the moneyed leisure class of an

A pair of typical commercial glass paintings of the nineteenth century, although quite where and when these works were produced is still unclear. The clarity of the colours protected by the glass and the slickness of the fast brushwork, particularly the feathery trickery of the trees, make them superficially attractive and they have become collectors' items.

WILTON CASTLE.

The sort of picturesque ruin beloved by the nineteenth-century romantic, with still a hint of eighteenth-century Arcadia in the unhurried sheep and shepherds. This drawing is from a late Victorian pot-boiler of a travel guide called England Pictorial and Descriptive, *and is of a ruin near Ross-on-Wye.*

increasingly prosperous and industrialised society, with an increasing population of urban poor clamouring for progress.

This Italianate influence was important, but another homegrown strand was creeping in during the eighteenth century to widen this concept of acceptable landscape much further. Poets and fashionable pundits rediscovered our own gothic architecture, particularly as so much of it had been reduced to ivy-clad mouldering ruins since the Dissolution and Reformation. Romantic sensibilities could now contemplate local stones to find their symbols for the distant past, for a glorious golden age of our own, when happy peasants tilled the fields to support these graceful buildings full of simple holy men praising God.

Writers and travellers were also discovering sublime and awesome scenery within the British Isles, in the Lake District in particular, and when both were combined – dramatic scenery and romantic ruin, as in the case of Tintern Abbey in the Wye valley – a whole new pursuit was born, the conscious search for the picturesque. Old castles took on new meanings redolent of ancient battles and chivalry, especially if they were juxtaposed with some humble cottages, and a shepherd with some sheep to add a simple pastoral note of homegrown Arcadia. All these ingredients were readily absorbed into the landscape gardening language of the country house, and mossy ruins, gothic follies and damp rocky grottoes – sometimes complete with a living anchorite for a final touch of atmosphere – spread into the parklands of the rich during the eighteenth century. The cold classicism of the Age of Reason was nurturing all the excesses of an Age of Sentiment at the bottom of the garden.

So far this catalogue of sentimental and romantic imagery seems to have little connection to popular art or the common people, but by the beginning of the nineteenth century a number of industries had developed which took their decorative ideas from the fashionable, and which by industrialisation and factory production disseminated the ideas downwards. Literacy was becoming more widespread and books were becoming cheaper. Illustrations became more numerous as woodblock printing took over from steel and copper engravings, and prints to hang on the wall were available to a greater part of the working population as wages rose and prints became cheaper.

In all these areas the artists and engravers were Academy-led, and subjects that found approval on the walls of the Royal Academy, the arbiter of educated taste in pictures since 1768, soon found their way onto cheap prints on cottage walls and *papier maché* tea trays. There was a well-meaning but ultimately hopeless tendency to try and give the people what was good for them, but this was fairly firmly counteracted by commercialism which finally only supplies what will sell. As always, the market tended towards a lower common denominator of general taste. Pious pictures were fine, and enchanting children, and sometimes the two could be combined. Sporting pictures and pictures of royalty were nearly as good as classical ladies showing more flesh than was usual in an English climate, but top of the list was a romantic picturesque landscape, and there it remained throughout the nineteenth century. It diversified to include cattle and sheep amongst Scottish mountains, and rustic workers near their thatched cottages, but the spirit was an idealised peaceful scene of rural tranquillity – perhaps in response to the increasingly frenetic urban life of the customers.

Sometime in the early nineteenth century a series of mass-produced paintings on glass appeared which developed all the essential ingredients of a saleable romantic landscape into a set formula. Many hundreds, and probably thousands, of these glass paintings were produced, presumably for the cheap end of the market. However, the disdain in which these flashy, not to say crude, productions were held by historians and collectors alike until quite recently has meant that their origins are still mysterious. No one is sure where, when or by whom they were done, but as they become increasingly valuable collectors' items more research will probably reveal their origins with greater accuracy.

They use the Claudian technique of foreground, middle ground and misty mountainous background, but in a very stylised way, like the cut-out scenery for a toy theatre. Dark masses of foliage in the foreground frame the view which will include a rustic cottage or two by a ruined castle or church, with one or two white-sailed boats on the distant lake which reflects the mountains. The scene may also include a bridge or a few perfunctory figures dashed in with a couple of practised brushstrokes.

The title page of an 1875 volume of Byron that captures the mood of romantic melancholy that his work did so much to make fashionable.

Most examples, it has to be admitted, are awful, but some achieve a pleasant balance of shape and tone and the colours are nearly as fresh as the day they were painted, protected as they are by the glass. Some are very crudely drawn, but most have the attraction of a professional dash and slickness from the obvious speed and confidence with which they were done. They are painted in reverse of course, with the finishing outline and details put in first, presumably working over a sketch on paper laid beneath the glass. When the outline was dry the blended

This picture was published in Life on the Upper Thames *in 1875, a reworking of the earliest illustration to show the canal population's tradition of painting pictures on their cabins.*

colours of buildings and foliage could be painted in, then the blocks of general colour for grass and trees, and finally the sky, mountains and water were painted over the lot in shades of blue. With the melancholy touch of an ivy'd ruin the best exactly reflect the mood of Byron's poem to Newstead Abbey, surrounded by trees beside its 'lucid lake', 'A glorious remnant of the Gothic pile' which:

> . . . kindled feelings in the roughest heart,
> Which mourn'd the power of time's or tempest's march,
> In gazing on that venerable arch.
> A mighty window, hollow in the centre,
> Now yawns all desolate: now loud, now fainter,
> The gale sweeps through its fretwork, and oft sings
> The owl his anthem, where the silenced quire
> Lie with their hallelujahs quench'd like fire.

If the paintings did reflect the work of England's favourite poet they probably date after his greatest period of fame from 1810. However, Sir Walter Scott had already opened a similar vein of romance in his Scottish tales and landscape gardeners had been giving instructions on how to create this mood of contemplative melancholy since the middle of the previous century. What was new was that it was now truly common currency.

In the Midlands the japanning industry was in full swing. It had started as an attempt to copy the glossy lacquerwork of furniture imported from China and Japan, but had by the turn of the century developed into a fully-fledged industry, decorating huge quantities of trays, boxes, buttons and furniture in *papier maché*, and all forms of domestic tinware like jugs, basins, coffee pots and even more tea trays. Japanning was a technique of baking a very glossy, hardwearing coat of varnish, usually black, onto the object but it is the subsequent riot of applied decoration that is of special interest here. Chinese patterns and willow patterns, classical Greek key borders and elaborate rococo scrollwork, masses of roses and assorted flowers, and all the most popular picture subjects of the day were copied or adapted by the japanning industry's decorators. (*To p. 129*)

NARROW BOATS

THE INLAND waterway network at the height of its prosperity in the early nineteenth century covered central England rather like a cobweb, with the Black Country coalfields in the middle, and the corners anchored in the river estuaries of the Thames, Severn, Trent and Mersey.

Water transport is so efficient compared with wheels that every creek and river around the coast was being used by some sort of boat or barge by the seventeenth century, and many rivers were being improved with locks and weirs to allow bigger boats to travel much further inland. The late eighteenth century saw the development of totally artificial canals, especially after the success of the St Helens' and Bridgewater canals near Manchester in the 1780s and the end of the century saw them spreading fast. By 1840, when railways became a serious threat to their prosperity, there were few places in England and Wales that were more than 15 miles (24km) from some navigable water. It was a transport system that was one of the foundations of the Industrial Revolution, bringing coal to factories and taking finished goods to the docks. At the heart of the system were the boats, and the new population of men and women who worked them, with their amazing traditions of decoration and bright paintwork that survived almost unaltered to the middle of the twentieth century. Instead of killing folk art, the Industrial Revolution seemed to breed an entirely new one on the waterways.

Canals built as extensions to rivers were constructed to accommodate the local river craft, but the interconnecting links crossing watersheds between rivers were often made to a smaller gauge to minimise the construction costs and the

The cigarette-packet 'Hero' reused as a popular patriotic image on a handbowl painted by Bill Hodgson of Stoke-on-Trent in 1937. This traditional piece of tinware was the cabin's washbasin-with-handle, and became part of the cabin decoration when not in use.

The 'roses and castles' decoration of the narrow canal boat people often spread over every possible piece of utilitarian boat equipment.

problems of water supply. The barges designed for these small canals were the long thin 'narrow' boats, horse-drawn craft that carried roughly 25 tons (25.4 tonnes) of cargo and were fitted with a tiny cabin at the stern for the crew of two, one steering and one driving the horse. As the new railway system expanded, the waterways were left as the poor relations, economic enough to be useful but not attracting any new money for development. They and their population were gradually left behind by industrial progress. The development of motor boats helped but the narrow boat traffic only really survived because of the cheap labour available, for many men used the boat as their only home and took their wife and family along as unpaid crew. In a couple of generations this had led to a complete society born and bred to the boating life. Perhaps to compensate for the restricted space of the tiny cabins, they developed a tremendous pride in the appearance of their boats, expressed with an ostentatious display of cleanliness, paint and polish. Bare wood was scrubbed white, painted wood was picked out with the brightest colours, and all brasswork was polished to a glittering brilliance. Certain outdated styles of dress remained in use on the canals long after the fashions had changed on land, and they symbolised the boat population's separateness, and their rich and independent lifestyle.

Another part of that lifestyle was a range of painted patterns that decorated every available space on the boats, inside and out, and included flags, good-luck hearts, stripes, patterns of diamonds, swags of flowers and as many paintings of romantic landscapes as the skipper could afford – a tradition now usually called the 'roses and castles' of the narrow boats.

The complexity and intensity of all this decoration makes it impossible to ascribe one origin to all of it, and some subdivision helps to make some sense of the mass. The bright colours picking out different parts of the boat are common to many vessels, fishing or cargo-carrying, and all the river barges have their regional styles and patterns that are still in use and contribute to the narrow boat tradition. Deep-sea conventions of fancy ropework and naval spit and polish also float into the city centre, but it seems that the further inland the boat can travel the more extreme does the standard become. The multicoloured diamonds, and the compass-drawn circles and six-petalled flowers seem to be the boatman's own contribution, although they may owe something to medieval heraldry on ancient ships; but the flower painting and pictures of castles seem to come from inland.

During the heyday of canal-building and canal transport there were many decorators in different trades who used these design motifs, and many examples of flowers and romantic landscapes survive on pottery, furniture, *papier maché* work and japanned tinware. Both the latter trades were firmly based in the Birmingham–Wolverhampton area, the hub of the narrow canal system. Painted clock dials, also produced in Birmingham, also show striking similarities to canal boat motifs. There was some very similar flower painting on folk furniture abroad, notably in Holland, and that too may be part of the origin; but it seems likely that it will always remain a mystery. By the 1850s the boat paintings had become a recognisably different tradition that belonged to the boats alone, and the boatmen and women, with the aid of the boatyards, held on to it proudly as part of their own special culture.

The boatbuilder was a key figure in this culture, for he not only built the boats – and developed some extraordinarily graceful craft, considering their utilitarian nature – but also painted, decorated and lettered them as part of his job. Some of the working boatmen did the traditional painting as a hobby, but spare time was very limited and the majority of the work was carried out by professionals at boatyards. Most of the painters were boatbuilders first, but constant practice with a paintbrush soon led to a neat decorative technique that was fast and simple, and could be taught to the apprentices without any need for academic art training. A few were naturally gifted artists, and their work sometimes produced masterpieces of folk art, but the majority merely carried out a decorative technique that they had learnt from their master craftsman, or their father, to achieve a satisfactory and reliable result. Cost was always a consideration, so the faster the painting could be done without sacrificing too much quality the better, and much of the charm of canal boat painting is in the attractiveness of the brushstrokes, the slickness of the technique that gives much of the work such dash and flair.

Unfortunately, this is also a perfect art form for a souvenir industry. As canal cargo-carrying was supplanted by canal pleasure-boating, the traditional decoration without any 'quality control' by working boatmen has degenerated sadly, and items are seen and sold as individual knick-knacks instead of as pieces of everyday working equipment. There are good collections in museums, however, and some dedicated enthusiasts still maintain the high standards of the working boatmen on their own private craft for us to admire and learn from.

Isaiah Atkins painting a castle scene on the top of a cabin stool in the style that was the painted trademark of the Lees and Atkins boatyard at Polesworth, near Tamworth in Staffordshire. The boatyard closed in the 1950s as the carrying trade declined, and Mr Atkins had to go into other work, but he took up the brushes again when he retired. He died in 1989. This photograph of him at work in 1975 is by Harry Arnold.

Amongst these subjects architecture and the landscape-with-ruin stood high, especially after the introduction of mother-of-pearl decoration. Thin slivers of shell were stuck onto the object to be decorated during the varnishing process, and decorative paintwork was carried out with semi-transparent colours over the shellwork, resulting in an attractive shimmering translucence. This was felt to be very suitable for the effects of silvery moonlight on gothic ruins, cathedrals and castles, and such scenes were very popular throughout the nineteenth century both on furniture and as pictures. At the cheapest end of this market were little prints that were transferred to the backs of squares of glass, mother-of-pearled behind the building, and then painted right across with a dusky blue night sky. With their dull velvet frames, they seemed to suit the maudlin public sentiment of Victoria's long widowhood very well.

Some time in the 1770s a new subdivision of the japanning trade had come into being in Birmingham: the production of white dials for longcase clocks. Prior to this the great majority of grandfather clock dials had been made of brass, with engraved numerals and decoration – sometimes the engravings were by the clockmaker himself – perhaps with some cast ornaments fixed in the spandrel corners outside the circular hour ring. They were polished, lacquered or silvered, and many were very beautiful, but they were likely to tarnish with age and were not easy to read. In addition they demanded that the clockmaker should be a visual decorative artist in addition to being a master

The landscape-with-castle theme of the canal narrow boat pictures was occasionally varied by other subject-matter, as in this cabin-block picture of a cockerel by Frank Nurser of Braunston, near Rugby. The block is a simple piece of wood used to prop up a gangplank on the cabin roof, but the mass of painted decoration enriches even this most utilitarian bit of equipment and turns it into an artwork (photograph by Harry Arnold).

mechanical craftsman, and some were not. The new easy-to-read non-tarnishing white dials that were offered direct from the makers, ready-painted and decorated, were an immediate success.

In the following twenty years the majority of clockmakers throughout the country availed themselves of this new business, and ordered dials from the Midlands. Brian Loomes' delightful book *White Dial Clocks* describes this development in great detail. It was only a short time before the corners, and the semicircular arched shape above the dial proper, were being decorated with tiny paintings and, as we should expect, all the usual themes were on offer: the flowers, birds, ships and, of course, the ubiquitous landscape-with-ruin. One of the commonest treatments of the spandrels was to paint a set of four matching pictures of rustic cottage with ruins, with the composition reversed on either side to suit the opposite corner shape, and nearly all the moon dials in the arch pair a tiny landscape-with-building to a seascape-with-ship for the spaces between the two full moons.

Little is known about the individuals who followed this trade, although the japanning industry is slightly better documented, and some names have come down to us. By the quantity of examples still existing we can be sure there were several hundred skilled tradesmen working in the Black Country in the first half of the nineteenth century, and quite possibly the same men, or perhaps women, were also employed to decorate pottery. The skills needed were similar, and the imagery used followed the same fashionable trends. The range of artistic ability was wide, and whilst much of the dial painting and japan decoration was of a very high artistic standard the other end of the range featured designs that were gaudy and slapdash, with all the slackness of attention brought about by boring repetitive work. Perhaps there was a great deal more of this work, but the poorer craftsmanship and the harder life led by these cheaper domestic objects has left us only the better, more cherished examples. The longcase clock dial, however, still offers us a window onto the taste and standards of the respectable working class in the nineteenth century, for these clocks were sold to middle-class villa and workman's cottage alike and, protected by glass, many are nearly as good as the day they were bought.

By 1800 the Black Country was also the centre of the network of canals which was home to the floating population of the **NARROW BOATS**, with their peculiar style of decorative paintwork. Amongst a colourful confusion of patterns and designs was the tradition of painting showy bunches of flowers and little landscapes on every available surface of the cabin, a tradition that survived well into the twentieth century and became known as the 'roses and castles'. Its origins are still pleasantly mysterious, but the canals' close association with Midlands industry suggests that the boat population would be very familiar with the common commercial decoration of the time.

Written references to the paintwork of the canal boats are very rare in the earlier days, which may mean it did not exist, but may equally mean that it was so normal as not to be noteworthy, just part of a common decorative fashion. In 1873 H. R. Robertson writes about the 'two or four landscapes (usually river-scenes) which are often painted on the cabin-sides', and a journalist in 1875 remarks on 'highly illuminated panels [and] a gay pictorial pail embellished with outrageous roses and sunflowers'. But the firmest evidence so far for a Midlands connection occurs in an 1858 magazine article by John Hollingshead, where he talks of a newly painted watercan sporting 'six dazzling and fanciful composition landscapes, several gaudy wreaths of flowers . . .' as well as the name of the owner. The sides of the cabin were painted with landscapes 'in which there is a lake, a castle, a sailing boat and a range of mountains, painted after the style of the great teaboard school of art'. Here is a perfect stylistic connection to the mainstay of the japanning industry, but the landscape ingredients are also exactly

Modern canal boat painters concentrate on executing simple roses with a few slick brushstrokes, but these two old cans from Northampton Museum's collection both employ a wide range of flowers in the decoration, with a continuous landscape picture around one culminating in the jolly sailing boat on the lake.

those of the cheap glass painting referred to earlier. It would not be surprising to find that they too originated close to the canals in the heart of industrial England.

One significant image which is often part of the standard picturesque landscape is the archway, a gothic arch since Byron and Scott, or a Roman arch in the classical garden ornaments of the eighteenth century. In either case the curving span, whether window, door or bridge, is an important element. When baby first stacks her bricks on top of one another she's on the first steps of architecture. When two separate piles are bridged with a long block a significant stage is reached, for the pile has become a structure, space has been enclosed, and a gateway created. This structure is visually comprehensible, even by the infant; what she is doing is counteracting gravity upwards with the piles of blocks and using gravity downwards to keep the cross-piece in place. The infant has been studying gravity in her legs ever since she tried to stand up. If the cross-piece lintel is strong the bricks can continue to be piled on top. Neaten up the piles, or replace them with upright logs and you have pillars; make a line of them and add a pitched roof and you have the Parthenon. The result is sublimely beautiful but the principle is simple.

But you cannot arrive at an arch by accident, by putting one block on another. The builder has to understand gravity and friction, and has to have the craftsmanship to shape blocks to a tapered fit. The idea must exist first, in order to create the shaped support on which the blocks will rest until the final keystone makes the structure self-supporting. The first archways must indeed have been magical structures. This elemental magic, overlaid with all our later historical and architectural associations, means that the arch, and particularly an arched doorway or gateway, still has considerable symbolic power.

We say, in a generalised simplistic way, that the Greeks invented the pillar and lintel and that the Romans invented the arch. Whether they did or not is less important here than the general acceptance of this notion, for the symbolic uses to which their architecture was later put reflect the attributes which later generations assumed the earlier ones to have had. Thus a Greek temple format was felt to be very suitable for government buildings which espoused the cause of democracy, whilst those of a more obvious Roman stamp reflect the power of empire and republic. Certainly each classic period brought each invention up to a peak of beauty and perfection which provides a touchstone for their successors, with the Parthenon providing the most obvious example from the Greeks, and the Colosseum, the arched remains of aqueducts and basilica churches as testimony to the Romans. (*To p. 136*)

One of the sites of antiquity recommended and illustrated in Rambles in Rome *by Frederick Fairholt in 1873 is the Arch of Trajan, one of the imperial inspirations behind the fashion for triumphal arches, both permanent and temporary, in Britain.*

The Arch of Trajan.

BANNERS

THE IMAGE of a procession carrying colourful silk banners through the streets has become linked in the minds of most people in the second half of this century with trade unions and their confrontations with authority. As unions adjust to a smaller membership and the changed state of modern labour relationships, those 'traditional' banners now appear less often. They are rather dated in spirit, and are getting older and more fragile, and modern marchers prefer to wave placards that demand immediate remedies for specific problems instead of the more stately statements of socialist intent and historical continuity that the old banners used to make. In this way the present banners are closer to their earliest ancestors, the protest flags of the Luddites and Chartists or the blood-stained shirt of revolution.

Warrington Walking Day in 1988 and the faithful begin to gather outside the town hall before the annual walk of witness, a traditional and still amazing display of marching bands and banners and a procession of holy images that entirely closes the town centre for the day.

But between these two there was a hundred years of banner-carrying of a different sort, by unions, by working men's clubs and friendly societies, and by the churches and Sunday schools. These were proud statements of faith rather than a call to arms. 'Defence not defiance' to quote one old saltworkers' union banner. They still survive in considerable numbers, some mouldering in damp lofts but many more, particularly the union ones, carefully preserved as fine memorials to a glorious past. A very few get a regular airing on a special local occasion, like the amazing display of church banners on Warrington Walking Day; Warrington is one of the few towns to continue the old north-western tradition of an annual town holiday and a 'walk of witness'. Many thousands of these painted banners came into existence during the Victorian period, and a small number of their descendants still perform their public job today.

Banners were not a new idea, of course, but they had been firmly associated with military pageantry and opposing armies. What were emerging at the beginning of the nineteenth century were the new armies of the poor, of industrial workers demanding change, and of religious dissenters. In all cases their banners became a way of stating their faith in public, especially after the repeal of the 1799 Combination Act in 1825 when membership of a trade union became legal again. The banner became the weapon, a symbolic statement of intent and, as its history grew longer, a record of achievement and an object of veneration. By the end of the century a parade of banners in aid of the local hospital funds contained portraits, coats of arms, landscape paintings of a church or a mine, emblematic characters of empire and trade, pious pictures of Jesus and the Good Samaritan, and some very obscure symbolism indeed on the banners of the Freemasons and the friendly societies.

These eighteenth-century brothers of the trade unions had a great liking for esoteric symbolism, partly as a way of teaching themselves a set of moral precepts, as visual aids for philosophy, and partly as – one suspects – a means of self-aggrandisement, establishing that they were an exclusive club. Their aims were mutual aid and general charity but obviously they also satisfied a need amongst their members for some theatrical mysticism, for they had all the trappings of secret societies, guarded by sworn oaths and complex initiation rituals. Freemasonry continues as privately and powerfully as ever, but most of the other societies have faded as National Insurance has taken over the job of distributing sick pay and burying the dead. However, during the nineteenth century they were very popular groups and their banners were out on the streets on public occasions and on the day of their anniversary walk.

Having formulated a mysterious code of symbolism it seems perverse to flaunt these secrets on banners, but a society that relies on regular financial contributions to maintain its benevolent and fraternal ideas needs a constant supply of young healthy members. A high-class banner was a high-quality advertisement for the nature of the group, and the symbolism was a temptation towards the mysteries to which the newcomer would be admitted.

The standard layout and design is remarkably consistent regardless of the organisation concerned, religious or secular. The central picture or symbol is presented like the shield in a full achievement of arms and many banners borrowed proper heraldic charges from older organisations. The Victorian love of elaboration usually fills the background with entwined renaissance scrollwork, with the lettering signwritten on a painted ribbon that echoes the material and movement of the banner itself. Pictures are painted in the style of acceptable if uninspired academic art, as befits respectable supporters of Culture, and some of the imagery leans that way as well. Stern gentlemen hold books and inventions whilst lightly clad ladies pose as allegories of Industry, Truth or Justice. The painters were often better craftsmen than artists, however, and the figure paintings often lack the skill that truly naturalistic painting requires; some of their charm for later generations is an element of touching naivety. The favourite subjects for Sunday school banners were Jesus as a

A Sunday school banner last used in Runcorn's Whit Monday Walking Day procession of 1975, but made redundant when the old chapel was demolished and the congregation was absorbed elsewhere. A strong piece of competent commercial paintwork in all departments: picture, scrolls and gilded lettering.

shepherd, and the 'Suffer the little children to come unto me' theme. Some of these are complicated compositions borrowed or adapted from the work of major easel painters of the nineteenth century, like Henri Le Jeune. There seems to have been little morality in terms of the designs, for paintings were copied or altered with no acknowledgement of the original artist, even in the banner catalogues.

Several professional companies came into being to satisfy the demand for banners and regalia, but one firm stands pre-eminent in this business, that of George Tutill of London. It began in 1837, and he is reputed to have started work as a fairground painter. Certainly what became the standard banner treatment was very similar to that of the show cloths of the travelling fairground, with central paintings surrounded by masses of rococo gilt scrollwork. He was apparently immensely and immediately successful, for in 1859 the business moved to new, spacious, custom-built premises in the City Road, where it remained until bombed

(Far left) *A Runcorn, Cheshire, banner delivered from Tutill's soon after the Second World War, although the design is a copy of its predecessor. The looms for weaving the background renaissance scroll patterns into the silk itself were bombed during the war, so it is elaborated with painted and gilded scrollwork, a mixture of fairground opulence and heraldic mantling (photograph by Ross Williams).*

out in the Second World War. The influence of this firm was considerable, and John Gorman in his masterwork on trade union banners *Banner Bright* estimates that three-quarters of all the union banners in this period came from the Tutill workshops. We can presume from the catalogues that a large proportion of all church and friendly society banners also originated there.

The highspot of banner-carrying and production was the period from the 1880s to the First World War, a confident period in which a majority of the population knew Britain was great and making progress, whatever the internal arguments. Union confidence was shaken by the failure of the 1926 national strike and many old banners were furled for the last time as the strike collapsed at its end. Church and Sunday school membership has been falling gently but steadily since the Second World War and public street parades have become less common in an age of faster cars and busier roads, so it seems unlikely that there will be a resurgence of banner-carrying on the Victorian scale. But both church and union continue to use them, and new ones are being designed and made in modern styles and materials. Many are beautiful strong statements, and fine pieces of public art, but what has gone is the extraordinary continuity of taste expressed by the old traditional-style banners. The 1890 Tutill catalogue was offering designs for Sunday school banners which were still being ordered and paid for in the 1950s. The design could have been older and the banners were still in proud use in the 1970s. That is surely popular art of a high order.

(Above) *A Cheshire friendly society banner, now in the care of the Salt Museum, Northwich. Made by George Tutill's company in London, it is in a very fragile condition but is still a good example of the complicated emblematic imagery that appealed to these working-class self-help organisations. Every item has a meaning, right down to the serpent carved on a pearl shell hanging round the Ancient Briton's neck: '. . . an emblem of universality . . . recalling the fall of man for disobedience to the Omnipotent . . . as a scourge to the Egyptians . . . the Druids' symbol of the Deluge'. The full explanation takes several pages, especially in worthy Victorian wordiness.*

Classical architecture as garden ornament on the grand scale, modelled on the ancient Arch of Hadrian. It was started by Admiral Anson at Shugborough Hall in Staffordshire in 1761 but he died before it was finished, so his brother completed it as an Anson memorial.

But the Romans also had a high regard for the Greeks, and their finest architecture blended the old with their new – pillars with arches, horizontal lintels with domes – and created rectangular-patterned buildings with semicircular holes in them. The architectural satisfaction of this blend of straight line and circle is very apparent in the surviving triumphal arch which the Romans built as memorials to great men and great deeds. The triumphal arches provided much inspiration for architects, both civic and private, in the eighteenth and nineteenth centuries.

The idea which appealed so much was the creation of a conspicuous symbol of veneration. In the Victorian period temporary arches were built to honour a person for just one moment; the moment when the queen, or whoever was being fêted, passed through it (with, one hoped, an admiring glance). They may have meant a lot to the town, business or organisation which commissioned or built them but they were essentially a stage set for a one-off event, whereas the Roman originators had something much more enduring in mind. Theirs were to be permanent monuments, not only to the man and his achievements, but also to the might of the empire which supported him and which they had no reason to suppose was not going to last for ever. As far as the arches went they were not far wrong, for three ancient ones survive in Rome and several more are scattered around the Mediterranean. However, these are only a small remnant of the large number which scholars know did exist.

In essence these structures are two massive blocks spanned by an arch with another 'storey' of masonry above, carved with figures, inscriptions and supporting sculptures recording the victorious hero and his deeds. Some have three archways, the large central 'roadway' arch flanked by a 'footway' passage on either side. This format suited the later designers of temporary versions very well in that it helped to keep the traffic moving, but it should be stressed that the ancient ones were not designed as gateways, as holes in walls, but as entirely free-standing structures – more like a massive sculpture than a building to be inhabited or used. They were built, however, like architecture, and were built within the architectural canons of the time exhibiting the full classic orders of plinth, pillar and pediment interrelated with the newer Roman arch. Massively built to be themselves, and therefore giving no one much reason to pull them down except to reuse the stone, the survivors provide a full three-dimensional treatise on classical architecture and wonderful examples to study and copy. They had a considerable influence on British architecture during the Renaissance and on all its later classical fads and phases.

In the eighteenth century some were built as garden ornaments, as part of the improvements of the landscape gardeners. Although built mainly to improve the view from the house, the triumphal arch format could also double-up as awe-inspiring park gates, incorporating the gatekeeper's lodge as well, and many still survive to do all three jobs. Most beautiful and poetic, however, are those which stand in graceful isolation in the park or crumble away in ivy-entwined romantic decay in the woods, engendering thoughtful melancholy on the brightest summer's day. Many, indeed, were designed to do so in the first place but now the lichen-covered stonework is a memorial to the eccentricities of the eighteenth century as well as the triumphs of the ancients. These extravagances and architectural follies may be fun now, but they cannot be regarded as part of the popular art of the majority of the population. However, they became part of everyone's visual experience, symbols of wealth and education, and added a new layer to the feelings naturally felt towards a doorway or gateway, with all its other historical and emotional attributes.

We go through doors to get out of the cold and into the warm, or out of an enclosed space into the open, from the dark into the light. Each journey is a transition, with possibilities yet to be explored, from the house to the open road, or from loneliness to company, but these transitions happen so often that familiarity leads us to undervalue the power of the doorway 'concept' today. If we can think back to a time with less central heating, and a more superstitious time when the house door held out the cold that could kill, the wild animals that could kill, and the unimaginable horrors of the dark, the magic fetishes and talismans associated with the threshold instantly become more understandable and one immediately feels more like going and nailing a horseshoe over the door – just for luck of course.

Iron implements and animal skulls were buried under the threshold and new wives were carried over it, and folklore has many ceremonies associated with doorways to keep out witches and the evil eye. Outside, the doorway may grow a porch, an essentially friendly idea that extends the house's protection outwards to the visitor and tradesman. On larger houses it was probably envisaged by the architect from the beginning and built with the main structure, but on smaller cottages and homes it is quite likely to be an afterthought, an improvement by the occupiers, and quite possibly their own work. Porches vary enormously in grace, clumsiness and delight but they form a fascinating subdivision of vernacular architecture. Some become so encrusted with gnomes, shells, or plant-pots that they become another part of the eccentric folly tradition, but most are more reserved than that.

Barbara Jones, in her book *The Unsophisticated Arts*, recorded the amazing rustic porches of John Hicks in Dorset in the last years of the nineteenth century, works that incorporated the natural curves and twists of timber in the round, which was carefully cut, jointed and entwined to create a beautiful set of thatched porches in Canford Magna. There are few workers of his calibre now, and even fewer landowner-patrons prepared to supply his needs of time and timber, but rustic trelliswork to support climbing roses around the door is still common in country gardens. In thatching areas the porch will be thatched, and slates are used where slates are common or easily acquired; in harbour towns old boats with the bottom cut out are mounted around the door of the house as a porch. The bow points skyward, and the lines of the planks reach up to make a pointed archway over the door like a miniature gothic arcade.

It's an accident of semantics, but this boat takes us back to the Romans again, to *navis*, the Latin for a ship, and thence to the nave of a church; the Church of Christ was often likened to a symbolic ship, the Ark of the Covenant, and the roof structure of the nave even has a resemblance to the interior of a ship upside-down. But it is the archway between the nave and the chancel which really establishes another thread of connection between the Ancient Romans and a more modern idea of an archway.

The earliest Christian churches were converted Roman buildings, or were built to the Roman basilica pattern. This is an oblong building with two rows of pillars inside to support the roof, resulting in a central space flanked by two aisles, and has a semicircular extension or apse built on one end. This space, the natural place for the holy altar, was entered through an arched hole in the end wall, which thus framed the altar as the visitor entered the church from the opposite end and was the main architectural visual feature of the basilican church.

As Christianity and church building developed through the centuries the apse was extended outwards and became the chancel, a space separate from the main nave of the church and entered through the chancel arch. Few did so, however, for this sacred space became sacrosanct to the priesthood and choir and was fenced off from the general congregation by a screen, above which was the 'Rood', a Saxon word for a representation of the crucifixion. This could be a free-standing carving above the screen, within the archway, or it could be painted on the wall above it, perhaps incorporated into the mass of instructional mural paintings that covered the walls of the medieval church. The expanse of wall above and around the chancel arch was the prime site for a depiction of the Last Judgement, the Doom. Here was painted Christ in majesty amongst his angels, the weighing of souls, the saved and the damned, and heaven and hell; as pardoned sinners knelt below to take the sacrament, the chancel arch must have seemed a very significant crossing-point.

Gateways usually have gates that can be locked to keep people out or in, and the device to unlock those gates, the 'key' in whatever form it takes, is an important secondary symbol. A key presupposes a locked door, or it would have no value. Jesus' remark to Peter that '. . . I will give unto thee the keys of the kingdom of heaven . . .' is seen as very significant and gave Peter a symbol which became synonymous with the first pope. A pair of keys, one gold and one silver, crossed in 'saltaire' like the St Andrew's cross, became and remains the heraldic charge of the papacy. It appears in many ecclesiastical or municipal arms that can claim any connection to St Peter, perhaps with a church or cathedral dedicated to him, Catholic or not. Historical, geographical and religious allegiances all account for the common use of the 'Cross Keys' as a **PUB SIGN** from the very earliest days, and its first use may simply have signified a religious house where some Christian charity and hospitality could be expected.

Keys as symbols of direct power are clearly understandable, unlocking the prison or the treasury, but a key is frequently used as a more mystical symbol of knowledge as well. It is used to represent the education or the secrets that will unlock life's mysteries and lead to the bliss of being enlightened, or the joy and personal power of being one of the initiates of the inner circle. But the meanings given to the key in these cases are rather esoteric – the precise meaning has to be explained to the participants before the symbolism is clear, and the symbol itself is thus some way from being an instantly understood archetype. The key of knowledge may mean democratic education for all, or it may represent the mysteries of an exclusive priesthood. Is it letting everyone in, or keeping everyone else out?

Medieval city gates were definitely designed to keep people out, but as more peaceful centuries went by and towns and cities outgrew their walled boundaries the old defensive gateways became anachronistic and largely symbolic. They also tended to block the traffic and most were removed in the first half of the nineteenth century, although not without antiquarian protest. As industrialisation and urban growth swept on, so an idealised image of the Middle Ages gained ground in the romantic imagination as a time of individual craftsmen working to high guild standards in independent, almost self-governing, secure city states. The town gate was the perfect symbol of those ideals, and being made a freeman of the city and handed the key to the gate became and remains a high symbolic honour.

Although most of the real gates have gone, the concept of a clear city boundary, with some proud fortification in baronial style to defy the neighbours, still appeals to the municipal mind. Major civic celebrations will still occasionally commission a temporary city gate, but the cost and the chaos of modern road traffic means we are unlikely ever to return to the mania for temporary gates and triumphal arches which marked the reign of Queen Victoria.

The population greeted the new young queen with some relief. Traditional patriotic loyalty to the British throne must have been strained to the limit in the first part of the century by the selection of old kings – weak, profligate or totally mad – that the people had inherited, and they were ready for a change. As a figurehead for the ship of state a young woman, soon to be joined by a handsome prince and a

A service was held at St Paul's in February 1872 to give thanks for the recovery of the Prince of Wales from serious illness. As it involved the whole royal family the event became a huge thanksgiving parade for the whole of central London, and the route was lined with flags, flowers, bunting and masts, with special grandstands and temporary structures which included a floral pavilion and two triumphal arches. This one near Oxford Circus was '. . . of an elegant and tasteful design. The . . . arches were covered with laurels and other greenery and flowers . . . across the top of the arch was the motto "The Nation's and the Mother's Heart are one" in large white letters . . .'. The Illustrated London News *devoted three weekly issues to this outburst of public loyalty. This picture is from the 9 March issue.*

string of children, was a popular symbol of much that became enshrined in the ideals of the Empire, the morals and values of a matriarchal family, even if it was largely run by men. She and her husband made it their business to travel the country a great deal, and the country responded by ever more lavish civic welcomes and triumphal arches in her honour.

Permanent ones in the proper Roman style were already in fashion to some degree in the capital, for both Marble Arch and the Hyde Park Corner Arch had been designed in 1828, and the idea was given a competitive edge by the Arc de Triomphe in Paris in 1836. Temporary triumphal arches were not a new idea either, for occasional ones had appeared ever since the Restoration, but young Queen Victoria and her increasingly popular consort were greeted by a plethora of welcoming archways wherever they went. Foliage, flowers and flags were the favourite ingredients, as befitted a young female monarch, but 'masonry' arches made of painted wood and canvas in all the accepted architectural styles, classical or medieval, also appeared regularly. This fashion that their state visits started, both at home and abroad, survived Albert's death and expanded throughout the century to honour any royal visit or special civic occasion.

Archways grew in size and elaboration as authorities vied with each other, and a number of professional companies came into existence as pageant masters and processional engineers. Most exciting of all, however, were those archways which reflected local interests and industry, and competitive ingenuity created some very bizarre structures indeed. Some seem to rank as a sort of civic folk art.

In 1866 an archway built entirely of coal from a local mine was constructed at Wolverhampton for the queen's visit, and another was

An arch built of salt blocks over the main street in Northwich, part of the civic celebration to mark the opening of the new Verdin Technical School in 1897 (photograph supplied by Cheshire Museums).

built at Dowlais in South Wales in 1912. There is a nice logic to the creation of a piece of architecture with the raw material of the local industry, especially when that material is a natural mineral. In Northwich, the centre of the Cheshire saltmining district, they made a salt arch to celebrate the opening of a new technical school. Although the lower courses were built of roughly dressed blocks of rock salt, which is hard and fairly permanent (at least for a few weeks), the archway and towers were constructed of the pure white, crystalline blocks of salt which were made by the brine pumping process. These are far more friable and hygroscopic, and collapse as they absorb moisture. Their use shows the Victorians' considerable faith in their ability to control the weather as well as materials. To welcome Sir John Brunner back from Parliament after the success of some local legislation, Northwich built an arch of salt barrels to support the message and the flags, whilst just north of the Mersey in Widnes the locals built a 50ft (15m) obelisk of soap boxes, for soap was the mainstay of the local chemical industry.

In her jubilee year of 1887 Queen Victoria visited Birmingham where a metalworker's arch was constructed of 20 tons (20.3 tonnes) of brass, copper and iron tubes, with a portrait of the queen and the Birmingham city arms made entirely of steel pens. Preston holds its guild celebrations every twenty years, and in 1902 one of the many street archways was made of bales of cotton to underline the city's connection with the Lancashire cotton trade. Local fire brigades were very proud of their extending ladders and there are several references to triumphal arches made with ladders and buckets, suitably adorned with flags and flowers. In 1900 Hastings Fire Brigade made one 35ft (10.6m) high to welcome Lord Brassey back from Australia, using 'four fire escapes, two on each side, lashed together at the top . . . supporting the word "Welcome" in red letters on a white ground fringed with roses'. They too must have had faith that there would not be a disaster on this auspicious day.

Lord Brassey had been an extremely popular Liberal MP for Hastings for nineteen years before being knighted and spending five years as governor of Victoria, an honour that the townspeople also felt quite keenly. When he returned the whole town celebrated, and the processional route was decorated and spanned by lots of archways. He had been particularly interested in helping the fishing industry, and the fishermen made a special effort to welcome him back in style. The illustrated supplement to the *Hastings and St Leonards Observer* of 11 August 1900 provides a consummate description:

> As a work of thorough originality, the Fishermen's Triumphal Arch was a decided success. It was situated opposite the Railway Booking Office, and was constructed from a design by Councillor W. H. Gallop, after one at Boulogne. The main erection was composed of fish salesmen's barrels, arranged tier upon tier. The whole arch was intended to represent the fishing industry. Upon it were various implements used by the fishermen,

including mackerel net, herring net, sprat net, trawl net, masthead lights, life belts, 'dans', shrimp nets, crab pots, lobster pots, whelk pots, buoys and anchors. There were flags and crossed oars at each end of the top of the arch, and in the centre a row boat decorated with bunting. Along the top also ran the words, 'Fishermen's Hearty Welcome', in black lettering on a white ground. The nets were draped curtain-wise, and coloured ships' lanterns were placed in various positions. At the two feet of the structure were four blocks of ice, in two of which were frozen ivy twining through the centre, and scarlet flowers. The other two had reeds encased within them. They were supplied by the Ice and Cold Storage Company, Rock-a-Nore, and were really beautiful specimens of work. 'Billy' Welch's two seals, caught off Hastings some time ago, rested on these ice blocks, and proved of great interest to the crowd. The fishermen have

The Fisherman's Triumphal Arch, 'a work of thorough originality' as the special illustrated supplement to the Hastings and St Leonards Observer *deemed it on 11 August 1900. This picture is copied from the supplement.*

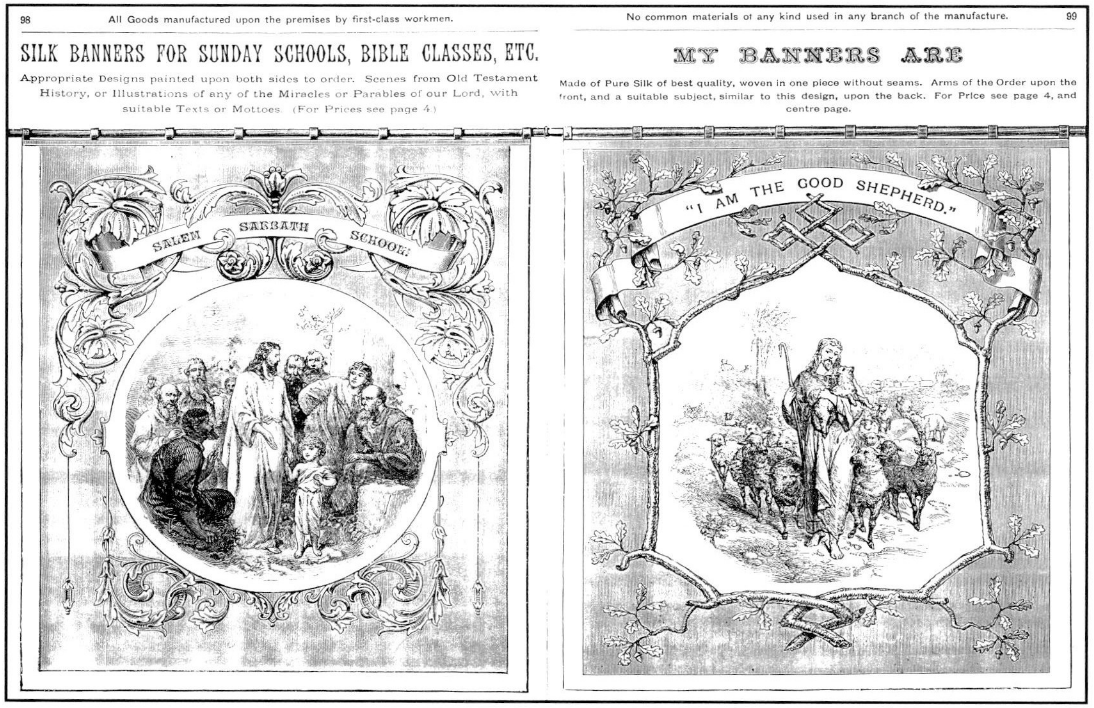
98 All Goods manufactured upon the premises by first-class workmen.

SILK BANNERS FOR SUNDAY SCHOOLS, BIBLE CLASSES, ETC.

Appropriate Designs painted upon both sides to order. Scenes from Old Testament History, or Illustrations of any of the Miracles or Parables of our Lord, with suitable Texts or Mottoes. (For Prices see page 4.)

No common materials of any kind used in any branch of the manufacture. 99

MY BANNERS ARE

Made of Pure Silk of best quality, woven in one piece without seams. Arms of the Order upon the front, and a suitable subject, similar to this design, upon the back. For Price see page 4, and centre page.

Two pages from the 1890 Tutill catalogue with depictions of centre paintings that were still being used forty years later (diagram by courtesy of John Gorman).

An odd but attractive emblem, painted in oils on canvas, now in the Museum of English Naive Art at Bath. There was obviously a very clear message at the time, but it is a puzzle today.

The truncated pillar in a churchyard usually symbolises a man cut down in his prime . . . but the arch with a keystone of friendship is secure enough. The motto says 'We grow in harmony'.

> every reason to be proud of their tribute to Lord Brassey, for no other arch in the town surpassed it in attractiveness . . .

Few even tried to compete!

One significant line in that description is 'the whole arch was intended to represent the fishing industry', for this was a three dimensional version of an idea that had become very common on the membership certificates and emblems of many friendly societies and trade unions. Most of these designs started fairly humbly in the eighteenth century from heraldic origins, and many of the early 'tramping' membership cards featured the arms of the old trades guilds, with a few suitable embellishments and new supporters, reproduced by black and white engravings. But as the groups expanded their numbers and aspirations towards the middle of the nineteenth century, the membership demanded something more substantial and more 'emblematic', where every element of the design must be symbolic of their hopes and intentions. Coloured lithography supplied the means, and allegorical figures of Justice, Peace, and Industry soon rubbed lightly clad shoulders with Faith, Hope and Charity, or some neatly dressed union officials; individual pictures of the trade or benefits of membership, were interwoven with tools of the trade and the society's title.

The underlying structure of the design is nearly always, however, a triumphal arch. It is built up on a massive plinth of marble or granite, inscribed with the membership information in chiselled letters as befits the foundation block of a reliable rock-steady institution, and supporting a towering structure of pillars and attic storey. Pictures appear in the arches or on inset panels on the piers, and the allegorical figures stand proudly in niches or on the entablature in the classical style. Above all is the all-seeing Eye of God looking down proudly on these mighty edifices of working-class power, these multicoloured printed representations of their trade and their political hopes.

As the century progresses the designs become more involved and less graphically architectural, but the main design features of lower inscribed plinth, side pillars and arched top can be discerned on certificates, BANNERS and advertisements well into the 1900s. The formal, comforting rigidity and grace of the Roman triumphal arch in new disguises probably still has a few hundred years to run.

GRAFFITI – VANDALISM OR INVENTION?

WRITING on walls used to be rewarded with a smacked bottom. It was childish and inconsiderate, and you were expected to grow out of it. If you didn't you were a hooligan, a vandal, or perhaps a political activist. And yet despite all this continuous disapproval the practice has continued and spread and now covers every public space with a rash of signatures and obscenities. Modern technology replaced chalk with far more effective marker-pens and spraycans, and increased the scale and the permanence with which graffiti can be done, and few bus shelters, parks or railway stations are now unaffected. Most is mindless scribble, a tangle of overlapping names, dates and messages, but they do occasionally become an accidental calligraphic design of abstract interest.

Cartier Bresson photographed chalked graffiti in the 1950s in France, and by framing it with a camera and exhibiting his results in an art gallery he created a new awareness in the gallery-goer of the art of the street wall. He would be overwhelmed today. At about the same period Jackson Pollock was making intricate textures of marks that recorded his actions as well as creating a mood, and he too would surely have been excited and delighted by the action paintings of the modern felt-pen scribblers. But this is all 'accidental' art, the *object trouvé* of an artist's eye or camera, whereas there are many examples of graffiti today which aim to be 'Art' of a much more considered and intentional sort, and which must be considered as a popular art of the 1990s.

Two cultural extremes of the late twentieth century, ephemeral spraycan art on the concrete permanence of the Westway flyover in London. Get it while you can, for it is an art without records and without dealers and it can vanish tomorrow, either removed by the council or covered by a new signature and symbol – like this one, unceremoniously sprayed straight over its predecessor.

Two things changed a bad habit into a new art. The first was the availability of the small pressurised spraycan, a portable painting system that could deliver intense colours onto almost any surface immediately and attractively. The second was the coming-of-age of an immigrant population, the emergence of a whole generation of black and coloured children born and brought up in Britain but lacking a culture that they could truly call their own. Cut off from their parents' countries by distance and from traditional British culture by prejudice and discrimination, this rebellious and largely unemployed group was especially hungry for some sort of aggressive or creative outlet.

Quite suddenly a complete vehicle combining both factors was offered by a new fashion from New York. There, a few young people from Brooklyn and the Bronx developed the daring habit of creeping into the railway sidings at night to spray their names or 'tags' on the sides of the subway cars. Bravado and competition made the lettering ever larger, more complex and colourful, and in the 1970s this fashion changed scribbling on walls into huge, full-colour travelling murals. News of this New York subway art found an immediate sympathetic response in inner-city London. Here was a ready-made means of colourful visual expression, a personal statement of identity which claimed membership of a group whilst simultaneously kicking against the buildings and property of the wider society. No wonder it spread rapidly throughout the country, jumping out of its ethnic racial origins to be colonised by the youth of every big city.

It has been fostered by the establishment to some degree, for it found some valuable advocates amongst professional community artists. Here at last was an urban art that owed nothing to old-fashioned rural folk art or established values, done with uncompromisingly modern materials and which made a significant alteration to the local environment. Trains are largely unaffected in Britain, but the factory walls and fences alongside the railway have become the main illicit graffiti art gallery, and officially encouraged work enlivens derelict sites and adventure playgrounds in town. In its most finished state it is a complete mural technique that is certainly an exciting addition to the urban scene, even if there is argument about whether it is an improvement or not. Painters were brought over from America to give seminars and workshops, and some local councils even supplied money for the paint. Graffiti quickly achieved a recognisable style as well as its own slang language, and considerable literature and documentation. It has also gained some bitter opponents.

It is not difficult to create a design in the spraycan graffiti tradition, which is of course part of the reason for its popularity. Techniques can be learnt, and provided the painters follow a few rules they will certainly achieve a result that is attractive enough to be good for their self-confidence. Natural artistic talent will eventually create the very best work, but a practised technique will save the less talented from disaster or embarrassment. Designs usually start with a short nickname written in a chunky ornamental style, with the lettering overlapped or entwined to make an expressive linear tangle which is elaborated until it becomes quite difficult to read. Graffiti tries to break all the rules of normal lettering, as befits a visual protest, mixing capitals and lower case, and introducing serifs and 'swash' flourishes at random. Little matters but the creation of an original, self-contained, personal logo, and most spraycan graffiti remains at this level, repeated – apparently mindlessly – for miles.

A place to practise skateboarding and writing your name on the wall; under the flyover near Royal Oak station in London.

Colour, comic-book characters and a remarkable variety of inventive letter styles enliven the back walls of these industrial premises alongside the Metro railway line near Wallsend, Tyneside, and provide the passengers with a fleeting gallery that changes month by month. Is it worse than what was there before?

The results are as variable as the practitioners, from tangles of spaghetti calligraphy to letters like misshapen lumps of putty. A larger, more involved 'piece' (a modest abbreviation of 'masterpiece') will be worked out on paper first, as in any other large-scale artwork, to envisage the complete job and allow the design to be marked out to scale. All the trickeries and shadows of blocking out are employed to make the lettering stand out in three dimensions, cracked like ancient concrete or dripping from the wall like melted plastic. The letterface and background are painted with a riot of blended colours and designs, outlined and sparkling with highlights and shines. Actual pictures are fairly rare, and the images that do appear are usually stolen cartoon-book characters or a pastiche of the horror-comic technique. Originality is expressed in the treatment of the name – it is not what you say but the way you say it that impresses your peers – the form is the content.

Two elements of graffiti art depend on constant practice: the confident manipulation of the spray-can which records the unhesitating grace of the arm movement, and the individual stylisation that results from constant repetition – the same process that alters the act of writing one's name into writing a personal signature. One of the public problems is that, in order to reach this standard, the painter has to practise; and unlike the violinist, whose practice notes evaporate into the air, the marks of the graffiti writer's exercises remain behind. There is no way to become good at writing on walls without writing on walls.

Graffiti has little respect for architecture and its bitterest opponents are those who hate to see the crisp lines and bland colours of the architect's designs blurred by unconsidered additions. When those additions break all the rules, change the colour, the neatness, and the mood by shouting an entirely unrelated message, the architect and public have good reason to complain. But they must look and listen too. The spaces most commonly chosen are the factory walls, bridge abutments and hoardings alongside the railway, and the backsides of industrial premises, all designed to keep people out as cheaply as possible, regardless of appearance. This is not architecture but industrial expediency, and with such an uncaring attitude to people expressed by brutalist buildings it is not too surprising that the graffiti response spreads over everything within reach, regardless of historic value or aesthetics. Everybody has had to pay a high visual price for losing the interest and respect of a large number of the younger generation. On the positive side, railway journeys through London, Leeds or Newcastle now reveal occasional gems of huge colourful design that demand admiration, and provide an optimistic relief after miles of rubbish-strewn embankments.

Layer upon layer of sprayed colour and names has turned this plain concrete bridge foundation pillar into an explosive block of expressive patternmaking. Westbourne Park, London.

BIBLIOGRAPHY

Because the subject-matter of this book is so disparate this bibliography has been arranged in a similar sequence to the text, under chapter and subject headings. Titles which are particularly relevant to each chapter are grouped with the specialist titles which refer to the subjects discussed in the separate essays within that chapter. All books were published in London unless otherwise stated.

Introduction and General Bibliography

AYRES, JAMES. *British Folk Art* (Barrie and Jenkins, 1977)
AYRES, JAMES. *English Naive Painting 1750–1900* (Thames and Hudson, 1980)
BREARS, PETER. *North Country Folk Art* (Edinburgh, John Donald, 1989)
CARRINGTON, NOEL AND HUTTON, CLARKE. *Popular English Art* (King Penguin, 1945)
CHAMBERS, R. (ed) *The Book of Days* (W. and R. Chambers, 1864)
DURR, ANDY. *Popular Art, The Emblems of the Voluntary Associations* (Brighton Polytechnic, 1991)
FLETCHER, GEOFFREY S. *Popular Art in England* (George G. Harrap, 1962)
HALL, JAMES. *Dictionary of Subjects and Symbols in Art* (John Murray, 1974)
HONE, WILLIAM. (ed) *The Everyday Book* (three volumes, 1837)
JONES, BARBARA. *The Unsophisticated Arts* (Architectural Press, 1951)
JONES, BARBARA AND HOWELL, BILL. *Popular Arts of the First World War* (Studio Vista, 1972)
LAMBERT, M. AND MARX, ENID. *English Popular Art* (B. T. Batsford, 1951)
MARX, ENID AND LAMBERT, MARGARET. *English Popular and Traditional Art* (Collins, 1946)
PACEY, PHILIP. *Family Art* (Oxford, Polity Press, 1989)

CHAPTER 1. *Shop Signs and Trading Symbols; Gypsy Caravan; and The Fabulous Fairground*

BROWN, FRANCES. *Fairfield Folk* (Upton upon Severn, Malvern Publishing Co, 1988)
DELDERFIELD, ERIC R. *British Inn Signs* (Newton Abbot, David & Charles, 1965)
EVANS, BILL AND LAWSON, ANDREW. *A Nation of Shopkeepers* (Plexus, 1981)
HARVEY, DENIS E. *The Gypsies, Waggon-time and After* (Batsford, 1979)
HEAL, SIR AMBROSE. *The Signboards of Old London Shops* (Batsford, 1947)
LARWOOD, JACOB AND HOTTEN, JOHN CAMDEN. *The History of Signboards* (Chatto and Windus, 1866)
A revised and modernised version is published as *English Inn Signs* (Exeter, Blaketon Hall, 1985)
RAYNER, JOHN. *Wood Engravings by Thomas Berwick* (King Penguin, 1947)
WARD-JACKSON, C.H. AND HARVEY, DENIS E. *The English Gypsy Caravan* (Newton Abbot, David & Charles, 1972)
WEEDON, GEOFF AND WARD, RICHARD. *Fairground Art* (White Mouse Editions, 1981)
WHITLOCK, RALPH. *Bulls Through the Ages* (Guildford, Lutterworth Press, 1977)

CHAPTER 2. *Pub Signs; Mummers and Morris Men; and Political Murals, Northern Ireland*

ALFORD, VIOLET. *Sword Dance and Drama* (Merlin Press, 1962)
AVELING, S. T. *Heraldry: Ancient and Modern, including Boutell's Heraldry* (Frederick Warne and Co, 1873)
BAKER, MARGARET. *Folklore and Customs of Rural England* (Newton Abbot, David & Charles, 1974)
CHRISTIAN, ROY. *Old English Customs* (Newton Abbot, David & Charles, 1966)
GAILEY, ALAN. *Irish Folk Drama* (Cork, Eire, Mercier Press, 1969)
HELM, ALEX. *Eight Mummer's Plays* (Ginn, 1971)
LEESON, R. A. *United We Stand* (Bath, Adams and Dart, 1971)

SHESGREEN, SEAN. (ed) *Engravings by Hogarth* (New York, Dover, 1973)

WHITBREAD AND CO. *Inn-Signia* (Whitbread and Co, 1948)

CHAPTER 3. *Staffordshire Pottery Figures; Ship Portraits and Pierhead Painters; Scrimshaw, the Art of the Whaling Trade; and Soldier and Sailor Woolwork Pictures*

BEDFORD, JOHN. *Staffordshire Pottery Figures* (Cassel, 1964)

BYROM, MICHAEL. *Punch and Judy, Its Origin and Evolution* (Perpetua Press, 1978)

FINCH, ROGER. *The Ship Painters* (Lavenham, Suffolk, Terence Dalton Ltd, 1975)

FRAZER, SIR JAMES. *The Golden Bough* (Macmillan, 1922)

FRERE-COOK, GERVIS. (ed) *The Decorative Arts of the Mariner* (Cassel, 1966)

GRETTON, THOMAS. *Murders and Moralities. English Catchpenny Prints 1800–1860* (British Museum, 1980)

LEWIS, CHARLES. *Pierhead Paintings (Ship Portraits from East Anglia)* (Norfolk Museums Service, 1982)

MELVILLE, HERMAN. *Moby Dick or The Whale* (First published 1851. Oxford, Oxford University Press, 1920)

MORLEY, JOHN. *Death, Heaven and the Victorians* (Studio Vista, 1971)

WILLS, GEOFFREY. *English Pottery and Porcelain* (Guinness Signatures, 1969)

CHAPTER 4. *Ships' Figureheads; Gravestones; and Well-dressing*

BARTRAM, ALAN. *Tombstone Lettering in the British Isles* (Lund Humphries, 1978)

CHRISTIAN, ROY. *Well-Dressing in Derbyshire* (Derby, Derbyshire Countryside Ltd, 1983)

HANSEN, HANS JURGEN. (ed) *Art and the Seafarer* (Faber and Faber, 1968)

JONES, BARBARA. *Design for Death* (André Deutsch, 1967)

LINDLEY, KENNETH. *Of Graves and Epitaphs* (Hutchinson, 1965)

NORTON, PETER. *Figureheads* (National Maritime Musuem, 1972)

PORTEOUS, CRICHTON. *The Well-Dressing Guide* (Derby, Derbyshire Countryside Ltd, 1978)

QUARLES, FRANCIS. *Emblems Divine and Moral* (First edition 1723, republished 1823)

RIPA, CESARE. *Iconologia, or Moral Emblems* (P. Tempest, 1709). Reprinted Augsberg, south Germany, J. G. Hertel, 1750s; republished in facsimile New York, Dover Publications, 1971)

STAMMERS, M. K. *Ships' Figureheads* (Aylesbury, Bucks, Shire Publications, 1983)

WARNER, MARINA. *Monuments and Maidens, the Allegory of the Female Form* (Weidenfeld and Nicolson, 1985)

WHITNEY, G. *Choice of Emblems* (the first emblem book in English, 1586. Facsimile published in 1866)

WHITTOCK, NATHANIEL. *The Decorative Painter and Glaziers Guide* (G. Virtue, 1827)

CHAPTER 5. *Signwriting; Made in Wood, Made in Britain; and British Coastal Fishing Boats*

BREARS, PETER C. D. *Horse Brasses* (Country Life Books, 1981)

EMERALDA LTD. *The Story of the Lovespoon* (Cardiff, Emeralda (Welsh Mills) Ltd, 1973)

GERAINT JENKINS, J. *The English Farm Wagon* (Reading, Oakwood Press, 1961. Newton Abbot, David & Charles, 1972)

HEARN, B. *The Art of Signwriting* (B. T. Batsford, 1953)

JARRETT, DEREK. *The Ingenious Mr Hogarth* (Michael Joseph, 1976)

LEACH, JOAN. *The History of Knutsford Royal May Day* (Knutsford, 1987)

LEWERY, A. J. *Signwritten Art* (Newton Abbot, David & Charles, 1989)

LONGMAN, E. D. AND LOCH, S. *Pins and Pincushions* (Longmans, Green and Co, 1911)

PINTO, EDWARD. *Treen* (Batsford, 1949)

PINTO, EDWARD. *Treen and Other Wooden Bygones* (Bell, 1969)

SUTHERLAND, WILLIAM AND SUTHERLAND, W. G. *The Sign Writer and Glass Embosser* (Manchester, Decorative Arts Journal Co, 1898)

SUTHERLAND, W. D. (ed) *The Modern Signwriter* (Manchester, Decorative Arts Journal Co, 1923)

TEBBUTT, C. F. 'Some Cart and Wagon Decorations of the British Isles and Eire' *Man* (August 1955, Vol LV. Journal of the Royal Anthropological Institute)

CHAPTER 6. *Tattooing; Narrow Boats; Banners; and Graffiti*

CHALFANT, HENRY, AND PRIGOFF, JAMES. *Spraycan Art* (Thames and Hudson, 1987)
CLARK, KENNETH. *The Gothic Revival* (Constable, 1928)
CLARK, KENNETH. *Landscape Into Art* (1949. Murray, 1976.)
COOPER, MARTHA, AND CHALFANT, HENRY. *Subway Art* (Thames and Hudson, 1984)
DeVOE, SHIRLEY SPAULDING. *English Papier Maché of the Georgian and Victorian Periods* (Barrie and Jenkins, 1971)
EBENSTEN, HANNS. *Pierced Hearts and True Love, the History of Tattooing* (Derek Verschoyle Ltd, 1953)
FLICK, PAULINE. 'Triumphant For A Day' *Country Life* (26 November 1987)
GORMAN, JOHN. *Banner Bright* (Allan Lane, 1973)
GORMAN, JOHN. *Images of Labour* (Scorpion Publishing Ltd, 1985)
JONES, BARBARA. *Follies and Grottoes* (Constable 1953, revised/enlarged 1974)
LEWERY, A. J. *Narrow Boat Painting* (Newton Abbot, David & Charles, 1974)
LICHTEN, FRANCES. *Decorative Art of Victoria's Era* (New York, Bonanza Books, 1950)
LOOMES, BRIAN. *White Dial Clocks* (Newton Abbot, David & Charles, 1981)
MANWARING, ELIZABETH WHEELER. *Italian Landscape in Eighteenth Century England* (Frank Cass and Co, 1965)
WILSON, ROBERT J. *Roses and Castles* (Northampton, Waterways Museum Stoke Bruerne, 1976)

Stately Roman-style lettering, although of a very personalised variety, on a shopfront fasciaboard in Ulverston, Cumbria. This is one of the instantly recognisable styles of the local signwriter, the late Billy Gilpin. The shop is a handsome survivor as well, with fine acanthus leaves and volutes on the console brackets of this Victorian commercial version of classical architecture.

INDEX

Page numbers in **bold type** are references to illustrations on that page.